TO CHINA AND BACK

TO CHINA AND BACK

JAN BREDSDORFF

———

Translated from the Danish by Alice Roughton

 Pantheon Books, New York

Library of Congress Cataloging in Publication Data
Bredsdorff, Jan.
To China and back.
Translation of Revolution tur/retur.
1. China—Description and travel—1949-1975.
2. China—Description and travel—1976-
3. Bredsdorff, Jan. I. Title.
DS711.B73513 951.05 79-1875
ISBN 0-394-50706-1

Manufactured in the United States of America

First American Edition

Contents

Note: *The spelling system Pinyin is used throughout for the transliteration of Chinese names.*

TO CHINA AND BACK

The following illustrations were taken by Stine Heger, the author's wife: 1, 2, 4, 7, 10, 12, 13, 15, 17 and 18. The remaining illustrations were taken by the author.

Introduction

This book is the product of the total of three years I have spent working and living in China during the period 1965–76, and as such it has a dual character: it is partly a book about China, partly a book about myself in China. After re-reading it, and prior to its publication abroad, it occurs to me that this introduction is called for. Domestic and international events have taken place regarding China since I completed the book, and questions and comments from readers have led me to realize that I ought to clarify my own position and background on certain points.

To proceed chronologically, and with the most frequently asked question: how did I happen to find myself in China in the first place, at a time when China was all but shut to foreigners? How did an unqualified twenty-two-year-old Dane manage to get a job as a teacher of English at a southern Chinese middle school?

The answer may be given as an anecdote, an absurd chain of events, but I find many elements of this account so characteristic of Chinese procedure—and possibly of my own attitude—that it stands as a prominent first example of much of what was to come: the uncertainties, the haphazard developments, the enthusiasm and, primarily, the opportunity for me to learn, to receive a political education.

Some time in late 1964, with the background of being a foreigner who had lived in England for a period of years since the age of five, I heard through the jungle drums that the office of the Chinese *chargé d'affaires* in London (diplomatic relations between the two countries were established, but had not yet been elevated to full ambassadorial level), was interested in applications from people willing to come to China to work in teaching, foreign language publishing or in the foreign section of Radio Peking.

At the time I was in many senses rather down and out, a newly emerged novelist with two recent books to my name, critical successes but financial failures, managing a meagre day-to-day existence as a punch-card operator on night duty in a market research firm, generally bewildered by and fed up with whatever surrounded me. They were not, therefore, political motives that led me to apply for an interview with the Chinese mission. In fact, I must in retrospect acknowledge that at the time I was a disinterested political blank, which, when I arrived for my interview with the Chinese diplomats, caused me to fear for its outcome. In the room, sparsely furnished and with the curtains drawn shut, there was a large map of Vietnam. Although public opinion in the West about the war had not then escalated to the heights of later years, I felt that I ought to have known more about it than I in fact did. I feared that I might be questioned about my political views and asked to declare myself about the US–Vietnam conflict, which to me was more than geographically remote.

But the interview, held in this eerie semi-darkness and punctuated by mugs of tea and Chinese cigarettes, turned out to be a very informal affair—compared to the standards to which I had been accustomed by endless unsuccessful applications for work in London. I found it right, however, from the outset to make it clear that I was formally unqualified for much, having dropped out of school at the age of fourteen. With relief I heard that Western exams and diplomas meant little to them, that the essential thing was that I had mastered English sufficiently well to be able to use it in the job I might be assigned. This led me to say that I was perfectly willing to try my hand at any job they might offer me with the exception of teaching. Fear and sheer lack of knowledge would, I stated, prevent me from standing before a class of students. We never got round to the 'interrogation' on my political views that I had foreseen, but however encouraging I had felt the interview to be, it ended on a somewhat negative note, their cordial farewell being supplemented by the not unheard 'Don't call us, we'll call you.' And with that remark ringing in my ears I left the mission, more or less forgetting about my application and the possibility of going to China—the China about which I knew so little, and which therefore was so attractive to me.

Almost seven months later to the day, I was to receive a small note by afternoon delivery, stating in very few words that I had been given a job in China and would I come to the office the following day to collect my visa and a single ticket, and then depart the following week. By this late stage nothing was further from my mind than the prospect of going to China. With the help of close friends I was to some extent able to overcome my fears of the unknown, and went to the *chargé d'affaires* to ask where I was to be stationed, what my job was to be and the general conditions of my employment there. All three questions remained unanswered, with the statement heard so often later: 'It hasn't been decided yet'—a curiously vague, occasionally Kafkaesque statement referring to unknown authority and a substitute for such specifics as 'we don't know', 'we don't want to tell you' or other face-losers. All I was told was that there would be a two-year contract ready for my signature on arrival in Peking, that the details of this contract naturally 'hadn't been decided yet', and that I would be given a single ticket from London to Moscow. A man would meet me in Moscow to give me a ticket for the last part of the journey.

Thus, with my own lack of knowledge enhanced by the apparent lack of information between Peking and diplomatic offices abroad, I found myself at Peking international airport, received by representatives of a school and someone from the Ministry of Education—the presence of the latter led me to realize with horror that my categoric refusal to teach had never reached Peking. And here began my many years of preoccupation with China—from the mild and bewildering days of acclimatizing to this unknown, with which I had no common points of reference, through many of the disturbing, yet stimulating manifestations of the Cultural Revolution in the late sixties, up to the present; from my own relatively uncritical enthusiasm for what I saw, and especially for what was to come, to my present concern, indeed dejection, that the promises held by the China that was have not been fulfilled.

I was stationed in the southern city of Canton, and it turned out that it was lucky that my refusal to teach had not been registered. For of the few types of work available to foreigners it soon became obvious to me that here was my only possibility of getting into fairly close contact with daily life, with Chinese colleagues and students.

In the present book it has been of great importance to me to distinguish between my own development through the years and that of China, although naturally this is not totally possible since so much of my own development is a direct product of my years spent in China and many other years spent, at a distance, concerned with China.

The question of my own political position has, understandably, often been raised: how I felt I fitted into the often drastically varying patterns of political change that China has been through, and into which political category my friends and colleagues, students and authorities have placed me. In describing my own political stance I must try to avoid meaningless labels. I do not know what a 'Maoist' is, although at home I have often been described as one or asked to identify myself as such. I believe that I approach a truer description of myself by stating that I have been able to use the valuable political education I have received during my years in China. Not, as one might think, through studies of the works of Chairman Mao (although I have taken part in these studies together with Chinese friends) but through being a witness to the practice of socialism, Chinese style. The visible evidence of lives morally, materially and emotionally improved through the introduction of common ownership has impressed me far more than any amount of learning through theoretical study might have. I therefore soon came to identify myself by the somewhat sweeping label of a 'socialist'.

The question as to how my Chinese colleagues viewed me is far more complicated for me to answer. They have never 'formally identified' me in any way, although I have reason to believe that many have considered me a 'progressive'. In the Chinese context, these labels—vague to the point of meaninglessness to us—are highly specific. One does not bandy about these descriptions; a 'friendly element', a 'progressive', a 'socialist' and a 'communist' each having its very sharply defined meaning and place as far as protocol is concerned. Only rarely is a foreigner awarded the highest accolade of socialist or communist: it is my experience that if one supports the Chinese political cause fairly enthusiastically, even to the point of working for it, one is a progressive, whereas the interested but critical guest seldom reaches higher than the somewhat cool description, a 'friendly personage'.

But progressive as I might be in the strict Chinese sense, I was and remained a foreigner. And this appears to be a real hindrance to any true political definition. At times the category 'foreign' appears in itself to be a political identification. On occasion I have been addressed as 'comrade' by students or colleagues, usually resulting in embarrassed outbursts of giggling from others present—as though the very idea of a foreigner being a comrade were an absurd *faux pas*, a ridiculous contradiction in terms.

And yet I was made an honorary member of the Revolutionary Red Rebels of the Chinese Union of Writers; ceremoniously given a Red Guard arm-band at the height of the Cultural Revolution, specifically for my efforts in 'defending the correct line of Chairman Mao' in book form; and 'decorated' with a special badge of Chairman

Mao, restricted to the fighters and commanders of the People's Liberation Army. I have been, and to some extent still am, doubtful as to what extent these very significant gestures of acceptance, even 'ennoblement', were genuine and sincere, or how much they were intended to flatter a young man considered to be politically naïve—and vulnerable to flattery.

My first two-year term, interrupted by the onset of the Cultural Revolution and the subsequent closure of schools and universities, lasted from 1965 to 1967. For a long period of that time I was the only foreigner in Canton, apart from a Polish consul and some shipping people; and in spite of this city being only a few hours' train ride from Hong Kong, the 'ultimate West', I felt totally immersed in China, attempting in every way to put distance between my present self and the capitalist West, working successfully at breaking down my other self, the inevitable luggage of prejudices and established standards against which to measure and compare everything new. And I was naturally restricted and frustrated by the absence of common ground with the people among whom I worked.

One thing that is seldom touched upon in literature on China is the remarkable apparent absence of sexuality in society. During my original two-year stay (when I was single) I noted it but, strangely, did not miss it. This, of course, is probably connected with the fact that there is also a total absence of the sexual stimuli to which the Westerner is accustomed—posters, films, newspapers, fashion and habits of dress—but the very impossibility of striking up sexual relationships, combined with the (by our standards) harsh puritanism of society, somehow made celibacy a natural element of life, rather than a forced denial of opportunity. Years later, when I returned to live in China with my wife, she approached our clinic in Peking in order to get a prescription for contraceptive pills. She was questioned about her marital status, a prescription was written when she had replied satisfactorily but was then torn up again when she happened to inform the doctor that she was to embark on a three-week journey round China, without her husband. This at least indicates that there are no double standards in the treatment of Chinese and foreigners as far as sexuality is concerned.

On one occasion, when I questioned a colleague about the eradication of prostitution in post-revolutionary China, I was told that 'we have no prostitutes any more. There are some women who "do it for money", but no prostitutes.' I had little success in trying to establish the subtle distinction between doing it for money and being a prostitute, and my informant couldn't or wouldn't clarify. Possibly he was trying to draw a line between professional full-time prostitution and semi-professionalism.

My second visit came unexpectedly in the summer of 1974, and was by invitation, accompanied by my wife and two other Danish authors. It was very much a VIP tour, with lavish Chinese hospitality and a status far removed from what I had been used to. I managed to arrange a meeting with some of my former students, then in their mid-teens, now smart young army men and women. The meeting was cordial, but far more formal than I had envisaged—I was not merely their former teacher, but an honoured guest. Once more protocol did for me what I did not wish, elevating me out of reach from the people I had been fairly close to once.

My third and final visit came in the summer of 1976, after the Chinese embassy in Copenhagen asked me whether I would take up a teaching post once more. The terms, I was told, would be unchanged from my first contract, and we were to be stationed in the city of Xian. It was with some hesitation that we decided to accept the offer. Our hesitation was not politically founded—I still found reason to believe that China (after the somewhat erratic course of the Cultural Revolution) was headed in the right direction, that the experiment was still under way to create a new form of society. Our fears were more concerned with ourselves. We realized that we would be very isolated in Xian, there would be no possibility for Stine, my wife, to work or study. We asked whether she might possibly be able to get an ordinary job at our institute, and were politely told that this would be out of the question. This didn't really surprise us—it would have been a gross breach of protocol to allow a person with the status of 'foreign expert's wife' to take up a menial job.

But our return to China was more complicated than we had foreseen. Some would claim that the disappointment in returning to China would be best described as disillusion, but that presupposes an earlier *illusion* and a sudden realization that I had been manipulated, or had manipulated myself, into a false picture of China before. But that is not the case. I still largely stand by my previous books on China, which describe the period before and during the Cultural Revolution and which were written with great enthusiasm. The critical attitude of the present book does not, therefore, constitute a total revision of my views on China. It is a description of the tragic change in the course of China, as I have witnessed it, after the death of Mao Tse-tung and the *coup d'état* that brought to power the present leadership. The totalitarian state has always held the danger that the people lose (or never gain) power, and this also holds true for China. But it is my experience that the dictatorship of the proletariat has now suffered a setback and is in the process of becoming the reverse: the proletariat of the dictatorship.

It was a confusing and to some extent depressing year that my wife and I spent with our child in China, and our premature departure was very much connected with the political events that took place during the year. There seemed to develop a growing political antagonism between myself and the leadership of the institute in which I taught—they, of course, merely mirroring the official party line. But in this mirror I saw what had not been evident in the China I knew before: a catastrophic creeping gangrene of untruth and hypocrisy, both in China's relations with other nations and, worse, towards her own people. The old academic system, which had been denounced and demolished during the Cultural Revolution, in fact offered a greater degree of knowledge about affairs Chinese and foreign. And whereas the old system was under attack for cultivating bookishness and 'bourgeois specialists', the present system outdoes the old in producing academics with a high degree of specialization and very little general knowledge. I eventually came to the conclusion that the system does not wish general knowledge to be imparted to its students.

My wife's situation was clearly different from my own. As far as our hosts were concerned, there was an element of conflict in that she was finally allowed to study Chinese, which gave her low 'foreign student' status, but at the same time she carried relatively higher status as 'wife of expert'. Looking back, it appears that many of the problems that arose between us stemmed from the fact that we were so differently placed, with different functions in society. While she with much energy and enthusiasm devoted her time to studying Chinese and taking part in the occasional stints of manual labour obligatory to foreign students, I found myself working in and for a system in which I had less and less faith. Not, as I have said, because I was changing my outlook, but because Chinese policy was changing with great speed, and refusing to admit it.

Whereas my students in 1965 were children of 12–14, selected at a very early age to become language specialists, my students in Peking eleven years later were in their early or mid-twenties. Thus I had the opportunity of teaching the very same group that I had left during the Cultural Revolution, although naturally not the same individuals. But this gave me the unique opportunity of comparing then and now, of trying to determine just what effect the Cultural Revolution has had on this group of people.

I have hesitated a great deal in writing this book. My main concern has been whether it might not be used as fuel for the right wing: 'There, you see, socialism does not work. . . .'; but I realize that this fear has been groundless. Events in the past years have shown that China herself has delivered more than enough fuel for that point of view: her amazing admiration for and cultivation of so many of the vilest elements of Western capitalism; her drive to reach Western standards with little apparent thought of whether we are in fact worth emulating; the uncritical admiration of politicians of the extreme right—West Germany's Strauss, England's Thatcher, Nixon of the United States and the former Shah of Iran, to name but a few. And a form of paralysis seems to have set in where the Chinese people are concerned—a paralysis that was unthinkable during the Cultural Revolution, but which might reasonably be seen as a product of it. I think that ten years of revolution—(in which mainly the younger generation were active participants), a struggle for power that now appears to have been concluded—have exhausted and defeated the people who carried out this revolution. And the very man whom they denounced, and who denounced himself, as a 'vile capitalist', Deng Xiaoping, is now back in absolute power.

In this book I concern myself only with the China I knew during the two periods when I was present as a witness and participant. When I left, in the late summer of 1977, it was by a mutual face-saving agreement, a fiction that my contract had not been terminated or broken by either side, but that it had expired 'according to plan, a year early'. In my experience China is not a country where one declares oneself openly—I had experienced a slow murder of my enthusiasm for working there, an increasingly impenetrable façade to cover up the reality that was emerging; and that is now becoming evident to anyone.

And it is odd to experience, after having written this book, attacks for 'slandering China' by the very same right-wing groups that had previously, before China's recent change, attacked me for 'uncritical propaganda'.

Yet I feel very close to China. A major part of my life and development has taken place there, and if I am to give any thanks it will be to the hundreds of students I have had, the scores of colleagues and the very few, close friends. They have been my eyes and ears in China, and it is them, after all, that it is all about.

JAN BREDSDORFF
Copenhagen, Denmark
April 1979

At Another Time

The days lie before me like a wash-board, ripple after shiny ripple. I have had this experience before, have once before moved about in this uncertainty, this hall of mirrors which is China, where one now and then catches a glimpse of oneself as one is trying to decide where the limits are, what is unending reflection and what reality.

In time and place my angle of entry is different. I do not see it as a return to the China I lived in ten years ago. Since that time there has been the Cultural Revolution, leaders have fallen, others taken their place, conditions have become unsettled, and in the last few weeks there has been the earthquake in Tangshan, not far from Peking, where current guesses put the dead at half a million. But, overshadowing the consequences of the earthquake, and even more important than its half-million dead, is the death of one man. Mao is dead.

We sink into the impossibly deep sofas in the cathedral-like silence of the waiting-room at the border station of Shumchun. The train lies behind us, littered with Coke cans and Cadbury's wrappers, and so too do the platform pedlars who have followed us all the way from Hong Kong's inferno and who now see their customers slipping through their fingers. We cross the little footbridge, past the Red Army border guards with black crêpe bands on their arms, into the oppressive silence and tropical heat on this side of the bridge.

It cannot be pressure of work which is the reason for the waiting time being so long at this point of entry into China. Besides ourselves, that is myself, my wife Stine and Lulu, our two-year-old daughter, there are only a couple of couriers, their diplomatic bags chained to their wrists and clutching with the other hand an even bigger bag full of State Express 555—which for some reason have special associations with China. They appear to be the favourite cigarette of most of Peking's diplomatic corps, and in a picture of Mao, taken many years ago, it is just possible to see a packet lying on the table in front of him. This gave rise to the rumour that he had access to a private source of supply of British luxury cigarettes.

We eat in silence in the cool waiting-room on the first floor, seated under a portrait of Mao framed in black. The white-coated girls with their black mourning bands who wait on us ask the standard questions of this unusual restaurant: 'Where do you come from?' (although in a miraculous way they always seem to know who comes from where); then, 'Are you Muslims?' so they will know which menu to give us.

The station is surrounded by fields where loudspeakers bombard the silence with endless monotonous dirges. Meanwhile, we know that beneath us, in the belly of this enormous building, thousands of Chinese are going through a lengthy, gruelling and sweaty entrance procedure. We travelled up to the border with them, or at least on the same train as they, pulled by the same diesel engine. Chinese apartheid in reverse begins in Hong Kong. There is a special waiting-room for the non-Chinese taking the border train, where cool refreshing drinks are served, and luggage is looked after by uniformed porters who accompany the train to the frontier, over the bridge and as far as the Chinese passport control, where they touch their caps politely and smile goodbye. But the Chinese who are going to visit friends or relations in Canton have to stew together in the long string of ordinary carriages hitched behind our first-class ones.

Mao is dead. We are not witnesses of that grief and despair we saw on TV a week ago. We have arrived in the aftermath, in a vacuum, a standstill. Four weeks of national mourning have been declared, and we have come to a land of silence, decked with white paper flowers and black crêpe.

Even a completely unexpected meeting with colleagues and friends from long ago falls flat. When the train creeps into Canton's brand new station, there, at the spot marked on the platform as being the place where the 'foreign carriages' will stop, stands a little group of people. Two middle-aged men and a woman stand before us. Quietly and in exactly the right place. Well-trained Chinese delegations of welcome have an uncanny ability of knowing exactly where their guests will be. Hence one does not have to fight one's way towards them, worry in case one is late or gets out by the wrong door. I have never been able to understand how they do it. How could they know, for instance, that we would not get out of the door at the other end of the carriage?

'Are you the Bredsdorffs from Denmark?' asks the slender little man with the clear eyes and the filigree face. And then I recognize him, and he apparently me. It was he who, eleven years ago, was standing with a bunch of flowers in his hand at the foot of the gangway in Peking's red-hot airport. On that occasion he had introduced himself as Director Li, explaining that he was a representative from the school I was going to in Canton, and that he had been sent to meet me. A train journey of a few thousand kilometres but, he said, that was nothing compared with the thousands of miles I had journeyed, crossing rivers and mountains, in order to come and work in friendship with the Chinese people.

And now, here I am facing that same Li, whom I have not seen for ten years. He has aged, but so must I have done. The slight uncertainty in his eyes as he asked my name and looked at me is a mirror showing that I am perhaps as much marked by the intervening ten years as he is.

As soon as I have confirmed who I am, the other two members of the group come forward with outstretched hands. There is a confused shaking of sweaty hands while we identify one another. Meanwhile our luggage disappears, without our even noticing it, from the little pile which has been accumulating behind us. This does not bother us. We have gradually got used to the fact that one's luggage is always there when one wants it and tends to disappear when it gets heavy.

'You must need a rest!' This is one of the things I have got most used to hearing during my sojourns in China. We sit down with our little reception committee in the deep armchairs draped in antimacassars and are served with tea and juice, while the fourth member of the committee, a middle-aged woman, remains discreetly in the background. She can immediately be identified as the organizer, the practical person who is always about on these occasions, the one who sees to it that the guest does not have to go personally to the passport control, customs, ticket office, public health authorities, luggage depot, get a taxi, or deal with any of the other endless formalities which have to be gone through.

There we sit—Director Li, Headmaster Li, and she whom I have had difficulty in recognizing, but suddenly do. It's Xiao Pang, 'Little Pang', one of my colleagues of ten years ago, who had the classroom next to mine on the open gallery among the bamboos' greenest leaves, there where the ground begins to rise to become the distant White Cloud Mountain. The last time I saw her was that spring day in 1966 when she came to give me a cool friendly handshake and explain that she was leaving school as she had been selected to take part in manual work in a people's commune a long way off. She had a brand new straw hat hanging by a thick cotton cord from her shoulder, and hanging from her back, crammed with clothes, soap, a tin mug and other small items, a round enamel basin with a pair of straw sandals tied to it.

She and Director Li were in the first group to be sent away during the first weeks of the Cultural Revolution, the extent and consequences of which no one could foresee. I asked them how long they were likely to be away and they said they did not know. Perhaps only a month or two, perhaps six months or even a year or more. 'It hasn't been decided yet,' they said, with that characteristic reference to a faceless and unknown decision-making body.

I ask them now how long they did, in fact, spend in the country doing manual work. They look at one another and laugh, that special laugh which may be concealing embarrassment, amusement or uncertainty; one never knows.

'I was away for several years,' says Director Li, somewhat evasively. I have learned that these general answers indicate that the matter had better not be pursued.

'I am not Xiao Pang any more,' says Pang. 'Since we last met I have got married and I have a little girl just like yours.'

'The Great Proletarian Cultural Revolution has changed many things,' says Headmaster Li, nodding solemnly. One of those remarks which is supposed to help a conversation along, but usually has the effect of bringing it to a standstill.

'We would have liked to have given you a proper welcome,' goes on Headmaster Li, 'but, as you know, our great leader Chairman Mao has passed away. Our hearts are heavy with sorrow and we cannot celebrate, not even a reunion with an old friend. It is many years since you were with us but we remember it very well and we are glad to see you back in China. But at the moment it is difficult for us to express pleasure.'

At this first reference to Mao's death and the mourning which had stolen in upon us at the frontier, there is silence round the little glass table at which we are sitting. Stine and I must be about the only people in the country who are not wearing mourning bands, but so far no one has offered us one. And even though we knew, before we left home, that such bands would be on every arm in the country, we had not been able to bring ourselves to buy them so that we would have them as we crossed the footbridge at the frontier.

I ask after other colleagues and pupils, and am told that they are all all right. They still remember individual students who were mine, mention some by name and tell me what they are doing now.

'We are in contact with them all the time,' they say. I try to imagine those twelve-year-olds, as they were then, as teachers, interpreters or soldiers, as they nearly all are now. They tell me that there is only one who dropped out. She was one of my best pupils but, they say, she gave up school and higher education during the Cultural Revolution. She is now with a touring ballet company. 'She always loved dancing,' they say, and when I ask if China is not more in need of academics than dancers I am told, 'It was her own choice, she loved dancing and she was very good at it.'

With this the subject is dropped, but I would have liked to know more. Whether one goes on with or leaves training is seldom one's own choice, and I would like to know how it came about that she left the tightly knit group which was her class, and her school, and that during the Cultural Revolution, when so much emphasis was placed on putting the community first, and not giving way to one's personal needs and wishes. But Li and Li and Pang are obviously not prepared to say any more, and I realize that perhaps this is not the time to ask them how they themselves fared during the Cultural Revolution either.

In those days, the 1960s, I myself quickly became isolated from what was going on in my school, the Foreign Languages School of Canton. But I did know that the first clashes there were pretty tough, not to say bizarre. The students took over from the leaders of the school, the headmaster and the director, who are presently sitting opposite me, and subjected both the school leaders and the administrators to public criticism on the school parade ground. Verbal criticism was rapidly followed by physical attack and some were stoned and beaten up. But at the same time, all were told, as I was, that although for the time being they were suspended, they were to hold themselves in readiness and that their salaries would be paid every month as usual.

Criticism of and attacks on Headmaster Li had been particularly intense. I was not given details, but it seemed that he was considered a bourgeois reactionary, behaving in an arrogant manner and considering himself superior to the people. He was therefore unsuitable to be headmaster of a school in socialist China.

As far as some points of criticism were concerned, I had tended to agree with his critics. It was he, and he alone, who selected the

children who were to enjoy the privilege of attending our school.
His method of selection was simple: he made all the children, who
had been selected by their units in different parts of the country,
parade through his office; each had to stop in front of his desk and
he would say a few words in English. Those who, in his opinion,
were best able to reproduce what he had said were accepted.

When I heard about this I decided to make an investigation
among my pupils, in order to find out how the different social
classes were represented. I came to the conclusion, with the willing
help of the pupils, that the peasants, who make up more than 80 per
cent of the population of China, were grossly under-represented in
our school. They made up only 6 per cent of the pupils, the remainder
coming from the families of party functionaries, academics, high-
ranking officials, doctors, scientists, artists and people from the press
and theatre.

'We are the over-privileged children of the coming bourgeoisie,'
one of my pupils once said to me, 'and our school is to blame. That
is why we have to fight against our school, its methods, and everyone
who supports them.'

Old Headmaster Li had naturally been seen as one who clearly
supported the 'careerist hothouse', as one of my pupils who had
enough linguistic ability to do so, once described the school to me.

Now he is sitting here, my host for a short time, ten years later.
He has lost weight and he is a little stooped, but there are other
changes too, things I notice even during this short meeting. Some of
that arrogance of which he was accused has been replaced by
friendliness and an unassuming courtesy. In the past he never spoke
to me in English, always in Chinese through an interpreter, as
became a man in his position—in spite of the fact that his English
was nearly perfect.

He is back in his old post with his old title and rank, but I don't
like to ask him whether it is because he has changed and atoned for
his former misdeeds, or whether things have turned full circle and
the crimes of which he was accused in the past are no longer considered crimes. There were certainly others at the time who held the
same views. I recall one teacher responding to my research into my
pupils' background with the remark, 'The reason there are not more
children from peasants and workers is quite simple: they are less
intelligent.' I often wondered if there were many among the teachers,
including the headmaster, who were in full agreement with that
sentiment.

Avoiding sensitive questions about such things as the success of rehabilitation and re-education, I enquire if everything is the same. Not quite, I am told; the school, which was formerly an independent institution, has been amalgamated with Canton's School for Foreign Languages, a place of further education for adult students. Starting children specializing from the age of seven, which had seemed promising at the time, has now been discontinued. As far as they know there is only one such school left in the country and that is under the direct supervision of the Ministry of Education, as an on-going experiment.

All the staff, bar one, have moved with the school. Old Hou, who was my closest colleague, has been transferred to another institute at the other end of town. Without my being told specifically why, it was hinted that he had been considered one of the most politically tainted of the whole staff. Common politeness dictated that this could not be said to me directly, but it seems that one of the charges brought against him was that of being too friendly with foreigners: that is, with me.

We had seen a good deal of one another apart from things to do with work. But always with the formalities in order, never without the permission of the appropriate authority. He was among the few whose private house I visited, for meals and late-night chats, while he came just as openly to visit me at my flat in the centre of Canton. He was a colleague who was also a friend, and he was an interested critic of the articles I sent to newspapers in the West about the situation in China. He belonged to that circle of colleagues and pupils who helped to open the massive doors which stand between the foreigner and the real China.

He had been a cobbler in northern India, but had come to his native country, in which he had not even been born, during the time in the fifties when so many Chinese living overseas returned to help with the reconstruction of China.

At one point during the Cultural Revolution I had asked the group who had been selected by the pupils to look after me whether I could possibly see Hou. The school was closed; I had not seen him for nearly a year and was generally missing the contact with my colleagues and pupils. The group was, I felt, a little put out by my request, and I was told that as far as they were concerned of course I could see him, but the decision did not rest with them. They would have to bring it before the pupils' revolutionary committee. And some days later, as expected, I was told that the pupils regretted, but they had decided to refuse. There must be no contact between us.

In the meantime, the practical lady, having finished running round and arranging things, comes to tell us that three cars are waiting to take us and our baggage to the airport. On the square outside the station, where agoraphobia begins to grip us, my old colleagues insist on accompanying us to the plane, and we then begin the ritual: insisting, refusing, insisting and refusing again, followed by resignation to the fact that here a plan cannot be changed at the last minute. I know how far outside the town the airport is, and that they will have to take the bus to get home late in the evening. In a little cortège of pale grey cars we drive through the streets of Canton, where I spent the better part of two years so long ago. I would have liked to have paid a brief visit to my old school and that part of town where I lived. My hosts understand this but regret that there is not time.

Again a rest, this time in the airport, the same big waiting-room where I sat one night ten years ago. I had finished my two-year contract and had been asked to prolong it for a further year, but everything indicated that it might be a long time, possibly several years, before the schools reopened. International traffic at that time was very limited, there was only one flight a week between Canton and Karachi.

There were different arm-bands that night. Broad red bands with characters in shrill yellow printed on them. The Red Guard. I sat there with two colleagues who, during the two years, had become good friends of mine. We were about to take leave of one another. The huge lounge was almost empty apart from ourselves; the plane several hours late. We were tired, restless with the tension which a prolonged leave-taking engenders. We just sat there looking at one another and round the half-dark hall. Everything which should be said at parting had been said.

Finally a signal from the tropical darkness outside, indicating that the plane was about to come in; and the fluorescent lights flickered into life. We sat up, as one tends to do when light suddenly follows darkness, and the hitherto invisible airport staff began to appear from their holes and corners, putting on their jackets with the Mao emblems, and their Red Guard arm-bands.

A little group of them came over to us while the others formed a circle round the few other passengers sitting there. These others, diplomats and foreign businessmen, were soon left to themselves and the young customs officials, passport officers, students and workers enquired of my companions who I was.

'You are a friend of China,' said their spokesman when they had finished their interrogation. 'You have travelled thousands of miles over rivers and mountains, through great difficulties, in order to work with the great Chinese people, to work for our common cause, socialism and the great Cultural Revolution. We are representatives of the revolutionary youth and workers in the airport and we will fight to the death for the carrying out of the correct revolutionary line of our great Leader, Helmsman and Teacher, Chairman Mao. We will fight against the line advocated by The Top Party Person Taking the Capitalist Road. People all over the world are watching the Great Proletarian Cultural Revolution, which we are carrying out at this moment, with amazement and hope, and when you have left us it will be your duty to spread the knowledge of our great movement, and to fight in your own country for revolution and socialism. Your country is far away but a thousand seas cannot separate revolutionary friends from one another. There is still some time before your plane leaves and we would like to spend that time with you to strengthen our revolutionary friendship. We will sing together. Do you know "The East is Red" and "Sailing on the Sea Depends upon the Helmsman"? We will sing them together.'

'I am very bad at singing,' I said. 'I am almost tone deaf and I find it very embarrassing.'

'If one can speak then one can sing and we have just heard you speaking. We will take it line by line and your revolutionary colleagues can translate it as you learn.'

I realized that it would be pointless to tell them that I knew every word of the text. For more than a year we had been singing those songs at our morning and evening meetings, heard them from dawn to dusk over loudspeakers in the town, in the fields, on the radio, at the big meetings called for public criticism, at demonstrations, on marches, in the train, on planes and in hotel rooms all over the country. I gave in and we sang. First line by line, then both songs in unison—customs men, workers, my colleagues and myself in the echoing hall. And finally, as the machine outside was searching out the runway with fingers of light, I had to sing them solo. A couple of the passengers at the far end of the lounge sniggered, and the diplomats from the West pretended not to notice this 'compatriot' making a fool of himself.

And now, here we are again. The same hall, the same furnishings.

But outside, in the quivering heat, stands a whole fleet of brand new Tridents and Boeings, which have replaced the old Ilyushins and Antonovs, which, we were told, were not safe because they were made in the Soviet Union.

Today there is no singing; the sending-off procedure is politely efficient. Our conversation while we wait is about books: if we have any good ones with us, and how difficult it unfortunately still is to get foreign books in China—but of course that is due to the currency restrictions, they say.

We are told that it will be late before we reach our destination, that there is no service on the plane and so we had better go to the restaurant upstairs and have a proper meal. We invite Li, Li and Pang to come with us, but they decline. It is not quite convenient, they say. They will eat when they get back to the institute, and they are sure we would prefer to be alone. The truth is probably that this is a restaurant for visiting foreigners and that the plans for our reception did not include sharing a meal.

'You must come again when you have more time. We would very much like to have you at the institute; time has been too short today,' Headmaster Li says when we are finally called for the plane.

I ask him to remember me to old pupils and colleagues, and say that if any of them should come to Xian they must look me up. But I know that I can neither expect anything to come of their invitation to us nor of ours to them. The ten years that have passed and the Cultural Revolution, which in so many ways has been a tremendous strain, have come between us and prevent any contact other than polite exchanges.

Our departure today is marked by neither songs nor exhortations. Broad smiles and energetic waving from Li and Pang follow us right out to the plane, while Headmaster Li waves discreetly, the palm of his hand raised to shoulder height, with only a hint of a smile. He has always given the impression that he felt there was someone standing just behind him, someone he must beware of.

Friendship Again

There were the baggy dark-blue trousers and the jackets a little too short at the waist, but apart from that, and the lack of make-up, there was not much difference between the Chinese air hostesses and their opposite numbers in the planes of other countries. They dealt out the usual sweets before take-off and I wondered whether the management of the sweet factory in Shanghai which produced the cellophane-wrapped acid drops had any idea of the associations Mickey Mouse, who appeared on the wrappers, has for foreigners; whether Walt Disney meant anything to them. To the ordinary sugar-boilers surely he meant nothing.

But, in the days of the Cultural Revolution, as soon as we were airborne and the plane had attained sufficient altitude to fly straight and level, a dramatic change in the air hostesses took place. They disappeared into a little cabin at the end of the plane, shortly to reappear with carmine lips, pencilled eyebrows and brightly rouged cheeks, wearing long clinging silk dresses. In this attire they went to the microphone, but not in order to announce: 'In a minute we shall have the pleasure of serving you refreshments, and on behalf of the captain and crew we wish you a comfortable flight.' No, what they announced, their voices particularly penetrating, as voices are coming from a microphone, was that they represented the Red Guard, and it was their revolutionary duty to fight for the spreading of Chairman Mao's revolutionary ideas. They would now do so by singing and dancing for us. And for the rest of the flight they danced up and down the aisle, waving red flags and weaving intricate patterns in the air with their long silken sleeves as they did so. In a series of little sketches they showed, with the aid of gestures borrowed from the traditional Peking opera, how the invisible enemy, writhing on the floor, would be annihilated by the elegant fingers pointing at him like guns. And the white glint of fury in their eyes, accentuated by the dramatic make-up, shot like bullets through the narrow cabin.

It was theatre played sideways on, as they rushed past our shoulders, political theatre which one could not have got up and left had one wished to. They had all the props—sheaves of corn, sickles and little red books—but it was demonstrations, rifles, popular risings and crushing defeat of the ideological enemy which thundered up and down the aisle.

And then, as landing time drew near, the great public parades, crowds of clenched fists raised in unison and endless torchlight processions, slipped silently away to the changing room at the back, from which a few minutes later ordinary unmade-up Chinese girls emerged with short cropped hair and baggy trousers, and began to distribute our Mickey Mouse sweets to us. As if the little four-fingered mouse could stem the floods of adrenalin pouring out in the wake of the revolution we had just been in the middle of.

Today it is different. The plane climbs to a higher altitude, flying time is halved, we are seated in Boeing's blue upholstered seats and are presented with little cartons of Zhong Hua cigarettes, with the compliments of CAAC, China's national airline. Lulu is asleep across a row of seats, one of the young hostesses softly stroking her neck, while Stine and I sit and try to catch a glimpse of the vast expanse of China which is beginning to grow dark beneath us. We are on the way to Peking, where, we have been told, we will be met by a man with the tickets for the plane to Xian, many hundreds of miles to the south-west of Peking. Our route is such that we have almost flown over Xian and will have to go back on our tracks in order to get there.

We will be there for two years, and find it impossible to visualize. We have been told that we will be the only foreigners in the town's language institute, but apart from that we know nothing. When we were offered a job we accepted it on condition that it was not in Peking. I know the city well, Stine has been there, and we had decided that it must be somewhere new to us both. So it suited us very well to be invited to Xian.

There are three men waiting for us at the bottom of the gangway. 'We have come to meet you. You must be tired and in need of a good rest.' And once more our luggage unostentatiously disappears. Lulu is still sleeping, hanging open-mouthed over a tired shoulder, and does not notice the cautious Chinese finger which gently follows the contour of her jaw. Once again the waiting-hall, the armchairs, which here in the north are harder, more upright, than the up-holstered caverns of the south. We are sitting in the very same

waiting-hall as that in which Director Li met me eleven years
ago, facing the three men who have come to give us our tickets for
the last part of our journey. We have not arrived yet; the real
landing in Xian will be some hours later.

One of the three, a fairly young man sitting right on the edge of
his chair, appears rather nervous. Perhaps this is his first job as an
interpreter. The two others, older men, sit relaxed, their hands
hanging over the arms of their chairs. They smile distantly, nodding
encouragingly from time to time to the young man, who is having
trouble with his maiden speech. He presents the group in order of
seniority and translates the polite introductory questions as to
whether we have had a comfortable journey, aren't we very tired,
and so on.

'You have no doubt been under the impression that you were
going on to Xian tonight,' he translates, 'but we are very glad to
welcome you here. We represent an institute in Peking, and we have
had the privilege of having you assigned to us. We would very much
have liked to welcome you with a small banquet but, as you know,
the Chinese people are in mourning for our great leader, Chairman
Mao, and for the time being we cannot celebrate.'

Peking! All our hopes of arriving at a new town dashed. I know
immediately what this means. In Russia it is called Druzhba, and in
Chinese Youyi Bin Guan: Friendship Guesthouse, the big area of
dwellings and pavilions in the very north of Peking, where I used to
stay when I visited during the Cultural Revolution. An enormous
area, in which a few of the compounds are reserved for those who,
like us, have come to the country as 'foreign experts'. From that
time in the sixties, I remember it as a gilded ghetto, a mini-Europe
full of intrigue, political bruising, hysterical back-stabbing. A
collection of adventurers; progressive foreigners still weighed down
by the white man's burden; of those known as the 300 percenters,
whose revolutionary fervour, knowledge and attitude put the Chinese
in the shade; and lastly, a small group of thoughtful people who had
come to China hoping to do a job of work and had become stuck in
the hopeless conditions in Youyi, divided as it is, by brainless
arrogance and insensitivity, into 'territories'.

An hour later we are halted by the Liberation Army guard at
Youyi's gate. The queue of cars stops. Our young interpreter gets out
to show our passes. A soldier with a submachine gun looks into each
car to make sure that the number of people stated on the pass is
correct, and waves us on. Past the main building with its impressive

curving ramp and its traditional style roof, round to the back where
a narrow passage runs between the two windowless ends of the four-
storey blocks. On our way, along the fifteen-kilometre avenue which
leads from the airport, I have done my best to avert the anti-climax
of having to remain in Peking. I have explained to the oldest and
most responsible of our hosts that we had explicitly stated that we
did *not* want to be in Peking, and given him our reasons for this.

'The decision is not ours,' he replies. 'We were only told a few
hours ago that we were to fetch you. It must have been decided after
you left Canton, during the flight. We are not responsible—but we
are happy to have you working with us.'

I try to make it clear that of course it is through no dislike of
Peking, nor of Peking's institute or schools, and he says again that
he does not know what has happened, but that he is glad to see us.
It would of course be more polite to reply that we are glad to be
here, instead of grumbling and complaining—but we *are* disappointed.

Apart from getting on a high horse and talking about breach of
contract, being taken here under false pretences and so on, I can see
only one possibility. I ask the older responsible man, who is the dean
of the English department at the institute, if we could not be given
quarters in the institute itself. I know, I say, that this is a request
which must be made by most newly arrived foreigners, but we do
want to avoid Youyi if possible.

He smiles a tired smile, deplores the situation we are in through
no fault of our own, but says that the institute, unfortunately, suffers
from terrible shortage of space; there is hardly room enough for
their own staff. For the time being, he says, we must try and make
the best of it here.

The number 8733 is painted in tarnished bronze on the dark
brown door: eighth compound, seventh staircase, third flat on the
third floor. The door opens into a narrow entrance hall, there are
two small rooms, kitchen and bathroom. An unshaded 40-watt bulb
hanging from the ceiling illuminates the few bits of furniture with its
pale yellow light—two armchairs, modern Peking style, a bookcase
and two glass-topped desks, three kitchen chairs and a small round
coffee-table. We ask our hosts to sit down, and they do so.

They don't stay long. Peking does not go in for night-life, as we
know from previous visits. It is late and the working day is long.
They stay only long enough to write the English translation of their
names on a piece of paper, together with the telephone number of
the institute, and to hand us an envelope containing money. 'A

small advance on your salary, so that you won't have financial problems.' They tell us that an interpreter will come the following afternoon to take us downtown in case there is anything we need, and that they will contact us in a few days. And then the inevitable admonition to have a good rest and take care of ourselves.

On our way to the flat we had noticed faces peeping out of door-ways; Occidental faces, stealing furtive glances at the new arrivals. Some of the faces we saw looked confused and bewildered, but perhaps it was because we were so tired that we felt as though we had come to a madhouse.

There we sit. Disappointment, desperation fill the room like the smell of an old cigar butt. The light shines in our eyes and the paint is peeling from the walls. Later we lie on the big iron beds, which we have pulled into the middle of the room so that they are side by side, and tell one another that we really are a couple of selfish bastards to complain, that we must not let the situation get us down. There was a time when one was urged to seek out difficulties, take on the most unrewarding tasks—something which some are able to achieve and others have thrust upon them.

We tell ourselves that it has nothing to do with the standard of our accommodation, which we know to be considerably higher than that of most Chinese. We have both wooden floors and central heating, while most people have only concrete or clay floors and a small charcoal stove. We have our own kitchen and bathroom, luxuries rarely found in Chinese flats. We have a large bakelite telephone—but no one to ring up. It is not so much our physical environment which is depressing, it is our emotional state. We simply do not want to spend two years in this concentrate of the rest of the world, this mini-Europe of friends of China. This is no good, we think, but neither dares say it to the other. The house is completely silent. Peking has switched off for the night. It is ten o'clock.

In the night I am wakened by Lulu's crying. I get her to sleep again and then cannot sleep myself. I sit out on the little balcony in the sultry night looking out over the feeble lights, between the trees in our compound, which illuminate the place I first knew ten years ago. There was that Englishman who had been in the Foreign Service. As a promising young diplomat he had been stationed in the British Embassy in one of Her Majesty's former colonies, where he had looked after her interests and dealt with the local population on her behalf. There had been some unrest in the town, which eventually found a target in the British Embassy, and one afternoon he found himself sitting at his desk, covered in splintered glass, and a brick on the papers he had been working on. His first reaction had been annoyance, he said, and he had got up to look out of the broken window at the demonstrators who had ruined the polish on his desk. He had never taken any interest in politics, but now it suddenly dawned on him, with the speed of splintering glass, that he was in the wrong job. He went to his ambassador and handed in his resignation. 'Those people had every *right* to throw bricks through my window,' he said in his resignation. He then applied for a job as a language teacher in China. 'Instant socialism,' he had called it. 'Just add the bricks.'

I sit wondering what it is that has brought us here now, and why it is that our disappointment over being lodged in Peking and not in Xian is as great as—no, greater than—our excitement at being here at all. Perhaps it is because we are tired, perhaps because of the unexpected truncating of the last part of our journey. Inside, in the big iron bed, my wife is sleeping. In Chinese she would be called my 'beloved person'.

Things always look different by daylight, and in the early morning summer sun I go out into our compound to buy food for the family. I remember from my earlier visits that Youyi has shops, restaurants, a swimming-pool, clinic and gymnasium, but I cannot remember the whereabouts of any of them, not even the restaurants. Although no new buildings appear to have been built since I was last here, the physiognomy of the place has changed. Everywhere, between the buildings and on every bit of open ground, large or small, there are huts and khaki-coloured military tents, earthquake shelters, whose stays seem everywhere, enveloping the whole area like a giant spider's web. I wander round between the empty tents, whose sides are rolled up to keep them from getting damp, with the feeling that I am on a battlefield where the soldiers have got tired of fighting and have wandered away.

Chinese are not usually very big, but this one is. He is standing in front of me, big as an ox, bald as a coot and with an enormous belly which stretches his white jacket to its limits. He lays his huge hand on my shoulder and leads me through a door.

'Breakfast,' he shouts in English. He must have read it in my face. A wandering foreigner, early morning, unknown face, searching look. He leads me into his canteen; I can see that the kitchen is closed and I mumble something about not wanting to be a nuisance, that it's too late or too early or something, and that I have had difficulty in finding my way.

'Never mind,' he shouts, slapping me on the back several times, 'never mind!' And then I recognize him. It's him, the big waiter in the experts' restaurant, who appeared to have set himself the task of learning the names of all the foods, drinks, furniture, tools, sums of money, and anything else relevant to his work. And now I am getting the lot. He cannot put together a sentence such as, 'What will you have?' But he can look questioningly at me as he runs through all the possibilities of his kitchen: eggs, bread, coffee, tea, ham, pancakes, milk, bacon, porridge, noodle soup, rice broth, jam, marmalade, juice, plates, cups, knives, spoons, glasses and bill. I order extravagantly and he goes into the kitchen. Soon things begin to pile up on the counter between us.

He cuts bread with his big supple fist, piles a tray with cutlery and food, shouting incessantly, 'Never mind, never mind.' Finally he takes me over to a table where he writes down the times of the meals on a paper mat for me. And the world's best waiter, who did his job to perfection eleven years ago, escorts me to the door with my tray, which I carry home through the confusion of trees and tents to the family I had left an hour before and who by now must be beginning to wonder where on earth I have got to and whether they will ever see me again.

It has always been the lot of a new arrival anywhere to be stared at. It is the same in Youyi, where there is perhaps good reason to stare at the newcomer with whom one is going to have to work, be a neighbour to, and so on. It is important to find out as soon as possible whether so and so are impossible shits, racists in reverse, or whether they will be agreeable neighbours. For we have a tendency to sit in each other's laps here. Most things are communal. Work, transport, the dining-room, free time, facilities, staircases, problems: all are in common.

In Youyi the parade ground for the 'new ones' is the long dining-room adjoining the theatre—an arena which, over the years, has arranged itself so cleverly that the unoccupied tables are always at the far end. Most of the inhabitants of Youyi are nice people, like ourselves, and do not stare straight at you, rudely and uninhibited. Nor does the sound of chopsticks and cutlery stop, and conversation at the little round tables continues. But glances are stolen over the rims of rice bowls and teacups, through the bottom of a raised glass, between crossed chopsticks, and out of the corners of eyes. And as one runs the gauntlet of all these discreet glances to the little round table standing empty at the far end, one may, under cover of a yawn, steal a sideways glance oneself at all the different faces in this canteen which caters for the whole world.

African frizzy hair, fair northern Europeans, moustachioed Latin Americans, veiled Arabs, sweeping gestures from the northern coast of the Mediterranean, a sniff of Gauloises (must be a new arrival, or someone who has got them from the Embassy). The smell lingers in the nostrils, while the eye takes in a silent straight-backed family from one of the countries in South-East Asia which has just gained independence. And over in the corner a silent grey being, sitting and sucking her soup from a spoon, a fart which has drifted out from between the snow-covered buttocks of the Alps. And at a large conference table, a group of West German political heavies who have entrenched themselves behind a barricade of rigid backs and stiff necks.

Youyi lies on the edge of the countryside in the northern part of Peking. Our surroundings are an extraordinary mixture of fields and shops, factories and ministries, schools and universities, small houses and big blocks of flats. Mostly fields. If we go out of the main gate and cross the road, which is solid with horse-drawn vehicles, lorries, carrier cycles and handcarts, we come to a little cluster of shops, the people's commune co-operative. There is a bank and a barber's shop, a family photographer and an open-air greengrocer, stove pipes in season, and a tailor, a china shop and a bicycle repair shop. And finally, a very small department store where you can get bicycles (though, for some reason, ladies' are very rare), ironmongery, painting materials and enamel jugs, babies' clothes and cloth by the yard, toys and medicines. The last includes marijuana, which is on sale legally and without prescription and is taken mainly for insomnia. The literal translation of the Chinese name for marijuana is 'heavenly grass'. Most chemists in the city have instructions not to sell to foreigners, because they are notorious for not knowing how to use it and are liable to get into trouble.

We are looked after well in every respect. Immediately on arrival we were sent to have our photographs taken by the friendly little perfectionist installed in a basement with an old-fashioned box camera. He took a whole sea of photographs for use in our various passes. They arrive a few days later; cards of various shapes, sizes and colours, some in plastic covers, others in canvas wallets. There is a card which gives admission to our guarded living quarters, an identity card for whoever might wish to see it, a work permit giving entry to our place of work, a doctor's card which entitles us to free treatment, not only at the clinic in Youyi, but also at the old American hospital in the middle of town. In addition there is a health card which gives admission to the swimming pool, and a cyclist's card for whoever of us is going to bicycle, and finally, a kind of internal passport to prove that we have a valid permit of residence, and which has to be produced if we go more than twenty to twenty-five miles from the centre of the city, or to other places in the country.

In one of the blocks in our enclave a military platoon is stationed. They do guard duty at the gate and along the high iron fence which surrounds the whole area. They move about silently in small columns, inaudible in their brown plimsolls, are blank and unapproachable in manner, neither hostile nor friendly. It is as if we didn't exist. They pay no attention to us foreigners when we walk, bicycle or drive in and out of the main gate, but any Chinese who has business inside is brusquely stopped and asked for his pass.

We are told that this is for security reasons. It is never made clear what security, or whose. We are hardly a group at political risk, and it is questionable whether it can have anything to do with our physical security. Perhaps it has to do with the political security of the Chinese. Perhaps the authorities do not wish to run the risk of more political contamination than they think they can control. We are isolated to such an extent that we even have our own local epidemics and are seldom affected by those which from time to time break out round us in Peking.

Inverted apartheid, a seclusion which depends on the exclusion of others, a seclusion chock-full of material privileges—this is one's experience of life as a foreigner working here.

'The Friendship Palace' it has been dubbed by local residents.

1/60,000 of China's History

If China's history dates back 5,000 years, the first month of my diary covers 1/60,000 of it; but the events of that month possibly overshadow much of what happened in the years before, throwing into relief the developments of the last ten years, and suggest a change of course on a scale unthinkable till now.

25.9.76. Everything seems better today. The sun is scorching hot and some of the travel weariness has left our systems. The flat looks more welcoming than it did late last night. Stine has already been out and bought hectic-coloured tissue paper to hang on the rather grotty walls. Our neighbour's son, who is from the Sudan and is the same age as Lulu, loves our walls. He has been standing there all morning with his face glued to the rough surface, licking it in long pink stripes. His parents come to apologize, explaining that it is due to the lack of calcium in Peking's soil and water. Egg shells, it seems, are fragile for the same reason. He has already licked the walls of their flat bare up to a metre from the floor.

In the late morning an energetic lady of about forty, her hair in a tight bun at the nape of her neck, turns up. She says that her name is Bai Li, that she represents the Experts Bureau, the authority which has direct responsibility for us, and has come to invite us to a meeting with the directors of the Bureau. The meeting is just the usual small talk. What was the climate like in our country, what a long journey we had had, had we got used to Chinese food yet—we only arrived yesterday!—ending up with assurances that we would find everyone open to suggestions and criticism. Bai Li acts as interpreter. As we sit there discussing matters of no importance, I suddenly recognize the man who appears to be in charge. He had been one of the reception committee which met me at Peking airport eleven years ago. He was the practical chap in those days, and it was he who acted as interpreter for his superiors. Now he is sitting back

with a half-smile and that air of slight boredom which seems to be
the hallmark of those big shots who have to be frequently on
reception committees for foreigners. Is it a reflection on us, this
putting on of a mask, or an expression of that arrogance which
seems to go with positions of responsibility here?

I tell him that I think I recognize him from some years back, and
his reply clearly indicates what he thinks about the propriety of
referring to former contacts. 'We were aware that you had worked
for us on a previous occasion some years ago. I myself have worked
for the Experts Bureau for a number of years and have met many
foreign friends. Time passes and we are always glad to meet old
friends. We hope you will get on well here.'

Eleven years ago the tone was different. He was my guide, interpreter, companion on walks round the city; he ate sandwiches with me
in the shadow of the Great Wall, called me in the morning and generally looked after me.

I have been told that there is an Englishman whose job I am to
take over. We go over to the canteen for lunch earlier than usual
today and sit watching the people come in. Neither he nor his wife
has been described to us, but we manage to pick them out all
the same. We introduce ourselves and have lunch together. They
will be going home in a week or two, having completed the standard
two-year contract. In the evening we join them at the restaurant,
together with another English couple who arrived yesterday and a
French couple who have been evacuated to Peking from somewhere
near Tangshan.

If one looks beyond the outward expressions of mourning, it is the
earthquake, more than Mao's death, which sets its seal on daily life
here. The tents standing in Youyi's compounds are an ever-present
reminder and it is not long since all the experts here were evacuated to
them. They lived in them for three weeks in the pouring rain, and
there were rumours that the Experts Bureau was going to move
everyone to a safer town. While we are eating there is a slight
tremor. Those who, at that moment, were off their stools reaching
to the dishes in the middle of the table did not notice it, but for those
of us who were sitting it felt as if the chair legs were concertinaing
under us. My heart rate doubled, and I wondered how much longer
we would have to live with this. I had not thought at all about the
physical dangers before now.

30.9.76. Yesterday there was a phone call from the dean of my institute, Zou Bowen, asking me to take a car over to the institute this morning. I meet Hugh, whose place I am taking, on the small square where, every morning, stand long rows of the little light grey Shanghai sedans and a couple of Zises, Soviet limousines from the Stalin era. Zou and Zhang Zai, the nervous young interpreter who met us at the airport, are at the institute waiting for us in such pouring rain as can only be imagined in a country of China's dimensions.

In blinding rain, equipped with Wellington boots and umbrellas, we struggle round the enormous area which surrounds Peking's Foreign Trade Institute. My companions keep on repeating their regrets that it was not possible to give us a proper welcome before the period of national mourning is over, a month after Mao's death.

The institute is a mixture of old—that is, dating from the time when friendship and co-operation existed between China and the Soviet Union—and brand new; of plan and chaos, superficial maintenance and traumatic dilapidation. A big group of buildings, which were the studios of Peking Films and now make up the institute, stands domed and broad-shouldered under the leaden sky. They were left empty some years ago when Peking Films had to move to another site. It was not that they were no longer fit for studios, I learn, but that the Ministry of Rail had suddenly laid some new goods tracks immediately behind the biggest studio, which made film-making quite impossible.

A five-storey tower, constructed entirely of glass, rears its head in the middle of the long low administration buildings. The glass, they tell me, is of a special kind made only in the Soviet Union. It allowed the studio's actors to lie comfortably indoors and still get sun-tanned. The heroes in Chinese films are workers and peasants, who in real life have a natural tan which actors have to acquire in other ways than working outside. Half the glass is now broken and there is no means of replacing it.

The studios stand empty. At the moment no one dares use them on account of the earthquake danger, although they were used regularly before for mass meetings of teachers, students and staff.

Teaching takes place in a completely new building: a long five-storey box which accommodates 1,000 students and 600–700 teachers, administrators and staff. The building has cracks from top to bottom as a result of the earthquakes, first the big one and then the lesser one. I am told that English, French, German, Spanish, Italian, Japanese,

Korean, Vietnamese, Arabic and Kampuchean are all taught here. English is much the most in demand, with more than 600 students learning it. Some of the other languages listed have no students at all. This is a phenomenon I have encountered before—one is told such and such a thing goes on here, but on further enquiry what appears to be meant is: 'according to plan such and such should be going on here, but when it will actually happen we don't know.'

Zou, the dean, has an excellent grasp of the English language, a knowledge and articulation which make one wish he were a teacher and not an administrator. He is a former diplomat, but why he was transferred from the foreign service to education I have not discovered.

Zhang Zai, Hugh's secretary/interpreter/organizer/provider and contact with higher authority, and who will now be mine, is quite young. His English is halting and he constantly apologizes for it— not making the usual excuse: 'I am not a very good socialist, I have not worked hard at my studies,' but the much more engaging one that: 'I am bone idle and am liable to sit and daydream or fall asleep when I should be working at my English.'

The institute has a language laboratory, a small room for tape-recording and several classrooms equipped with overhead projectors. There are facilities for printing texts, two halls where films can be shown, and a miserable library.

Through the pouring rain, one can see a factory chimney between the main building and the big building with living accommodation. The students work in the factory producing endless rolls of PVC. At the time of the big earthquake, the chimney suffered a whiplash which displaced the top half so that it ended precariously balanced on the bottom half. As a result of the little quake a few days ago it moved almost back into place again. 'We may well pull it down,' they say.

1.10.76. National Day, even if we are hardly aware of it. We have not been told what is likely to happen this year, on this day which, since liberation, has been the most important celebration of the year. Normally the vast square in front of the Gate of Heavenly Peace is filled with people, long parades filing by for hours, but—and this is perhaps characteristic of modern China—never military parades. Columns of technical groups, lorries laden with flowers, cogwheels, oversized sheaves of corn, and calligraphic pens (representing the workers in the fields of art and culture) the size of rockets. Whole battalions of colourful minority groups and, at the last National Day parade I attended, in the middle of this crowd of half a million people, a group of six saffron-robed Buddhist monks, each with a faded flower in his hand.

But this year it is quiet on Tien An Men. Quiet but crowded, because everyone wants to be there just in case something happens. There are one or two things which mark the twenty-seventh year of the founding of the People's Republic. There are red flags flying from the corners of the big buildings which form the long sides of the square, the Museum of the Revolution on the one side and the Great Hall of the People on the other. The big portrait of Chairman Mao, which has for years hung on the deep red wall of the old imperial buildings, has today reappeared in colour, having been replaced by a black-and-white version after his death.

And then we notice that there are many who are not wearing their black arm-bands and others who, observing this, take theirs off and slip them in their pockets. The Chinese are very symbol-conscious. How does one deal with this odd mixture of joy and sorrow, of mourning and rejoicing? How can one do the one without offending the other?

2.10.76. Everyone who yesterday took off their mourning bands has put them on again today. A one-day interruption of mourning without its exactly being rejoicing. Mourning is resumed because regulations must be observed. Perhaps also because the grief is real. A portrait of Mao hangs in my office, the official mourning portrait, and Zhang Zai has written the official slogan in coloured chalk all over the blackboard: 'Turn grief into strength.' A very rational proposal.

But we are talking about this strange mixture of ignoring and celebrating this particular National Day. One of the distinctive things about National Day used to be that the leaders of the country appeared under the great red lanterns which hang under the eaves of the imperial yellow-glazed roof of the Tien An Men building. But who are China's leaders now?

Were I to ask Zhang or Zou or one of the 'responsible comrades' at the Experts Bureau, 'Has China any leaders now?', I would put them on the horns of a dilemma. They can only answer yes or no. In the first case they would be expected to say who the leaders were, and that is something no one knows until it has been officially announced. But if they answer in the negative they would be admitting that their country, which has laid so much stress on the importance of strong central leadership must, without leaders, be in a state of crisis.

It is this kind of thing which makes it all too easy to ask impossible questions in this country, and it is, I suppose, as a consequence of this also that so many Chinese have acquired the ability to answer, in the politest possible way, a question other than that which has been put to them.

4.10.76. Work begins today. I have been given a very large office in the institute, with a desk which really should boost morale. I have a telephone, so at least Stine and I can ring each other up. Against the walls are a long sofa, a low coffee-table with a glass top and a couple of armchairs. Under the blackboard and Mao's portrait there is a small stand with an enamel basin for washing which Zhang Zai fills with water every morning. There are soap and a clean towel. And, in a little glass cupboard there are a tin of tea, cups and a teapot. My desk is empty; the drawers sound hollow. I just sit at it, looking at Zhang, who has a smaller desk at the other end of the room. I have been told that I will be informed in due course what I am to do. In the meantime I should just get going on things. What things?

The office is on the first floor and below my south-facing window a pompous drive leads from the main building to a large gate. The entire institute is surrounded by a twelve-foot wall and there are some students doing something down by the gate; they are assembling stones, big tubs of mortar and bamboo poles bound together with cord.

During the course of the day, the first day, people pay courtesy calls. Other teachers, a few nervous students, and some representatives of the leadership. The teachers, I discover, are divided into three groups: the young, the middle-aged, and the veterans. On my asking to which group I belong there is a period of embarrassment, smiles and looking out of the window, before I am informed that I belong to the middle-aged. This might, I suppose, be considered rather offensive to someone in his early thirties if it were not for the fact that a few years ago the average life expectancy in China was only fifty.

A young teacher comes in to ask if I would like to sit in on one of his classes. Some veterans who are sitting with me at the time nod approvingly at this suggestion. They come with us and we enter a classroom where about twenty young men and women are standing to attention. 'Comrades!' commands the teacher. 'I suggest that we welcome Expert Jan with a big hand!'

The students break out into rhythmic clapping which makes me wince. I know it is a gesture of politeness, of course, but it is foreign to my nature. I don't like it and have always had problems in knowing what to do about it. Politeness demands that one claps in unison, but I have never been able to bring myself to do that. On the other hand, I feel I am being snooty if I don't do it. And I don't like being addressed or referred to by that pompous title, 'Expert Jan', either. Political apartheid comes through here, the usual form of address being 'comrade', and by that difference alone one is separated from a company of which one would rather be a part.

It is also disappointing to find that what at first sight had appeared to be a spontaneous invitation turns out to have been carefully planned in advance. He is the best teacher in the institute and therefore, presumably, has the best class. It was a polite gesture, but at the same time showing off. And if I am going to work with them, teach and help to plan teaching, it is not showing off that I need. In other circumstances it would be understandable to show visitors the best you have. When one visits communes, factories, nurseries, schools and clinics, it is always the best which are shown. But here, I feel, the situation is a little different.

Following the part of the lesson which I was intended to sit in on, there is another round of clapping, a short speech and the usual request for comments, criticism and suggestions. But the discreet movements of my older colleagues, without their actually getting up and moving towards the door, indicates to me that this is not the moment to make comments.

However, a few minutes later, back in my office, the veteran teachers who had been present in the classroom ask me what I thought. The young teacher had remained behind; I would have preferred to discuss things with him rather than with his superiors.

A text in which Lenin has a conversation with a Russian kulak had been used. The lesson had for the most part consisted of the teacher explaining parts of the well-known text, and then asking simple questions such as: 'And what did Lenin reply to that?' There was not much room for imagination or interpretation and the students obviously knew it all by heart.

It happened to have been an exercise in fluency, and I suppose as such it was not bad. But I had a reservation. The teacher had made a pupil repeat more or less word for word a passage about why Lenin was right in not trusting the kulaks. The pupil, standing to attention, had rattled off the passage with great concentration, after which the teacher answered, 'Thank you comrade, your opinion is quite correct, we must never trust class enemies.' My objection concerned the last point, and I indicated that while I agreed with the sentiment surely it was language rather than opinions we were meant to be teaching here; and although his opinions may well have been correct, his language was, to say the least, pretty poor.

This produced the usual laughter, always hard to interpret. But one of the veteran teachers took up my point.

'I agree that we teach parrot fashion too much and do not spend enough time teaching how to use the language,' he said. 'It is one of our major problems.'

I am glad to find that it is possible to penetrate the system to some extent, but I wonder how many would really prefer to go on teaching by rote and how many would welcome a change.

10.10.76. The rumours of the last few days have been confirmed today, and in the canteen this morning we were aware that something has happened. Our service comrades are gathered together in a corner of the hall, crowded round a table with an open newspaper on it and the wireless on. This has never happened before. We foreigners, none of whom speak Chinese, discuss the possibilities: is it the announcement of a new party chairman or a new form of collective leadership? Or is it, as has so often been the case in recent years, something none of us would ever have thought of?

Many, supporting the last, have let fantasy run riot and have come up with some pretty absurd ideas: the country is to be divided up into autonomous regions to stop a power struggle in the central government; a measure of private enterprise will be introduced in order to boost production; or China has resumed friendly relations with the Soviet Union. These and other theories which, in these empty, leaderless days, reflect the hopes, fears or prejudices of those who propound them are tossed out all round.

The truth did indeed turn out to be something that none of us had thought of. The big news of the day, one month after Mao's death and coinciding with the end of the official mourning period, is a decision by the Central Committee to build a mausoleum. That is all; it is difficult to see how it can fill the front page of the *People's Daily*. The decision has been made that such a building shall be built, but not a word about where, what it will look like, or when it is likely to be begun or completed.

There is also an announcement that it has been decided to bring out volume five of Mao's selected works, and at a later date a complete edition of all his works. The latter seems rather unlikely. It is well known that, in his younger days, Mao wrote a number of articles which he later withdrew and which are no longer available. But of course it is possible that 'complete' means those of his works which were agreeable to him and to the editor involved in publishing them. There is another, and in the long term more exciting rumour, which is that the Central Committee is about to appoint a new party chairman. He is a man about whom none of the rumour-mongers know anything other than that he was formerly Minister of Security. His name is Hua Guofeng.

11.10.76. Lulu has Peking tummy, something which is bound to happen sooner or later. A few days ago I asked Zou to enrol Stine for a course in Chinese at the language institute. Today he asked for a written application. This I take as a positive sign. At least they— whoever they may be—have decided to let the decision-making machine roll.

12.10.76. In the afternoon the bomb exploded. The one which has been spluttering for several days without anyone's having been able to locate it exactly. Someone has heard that Mao's widow, Jiang Qing, and three important members of the Central Committee have been arrested in a bloody coup.

One of the odd things about this country is that there always seems to be something in the air which tickles one's antennae before, during, or sometimes after something happens. It is not a case of being wise after the event to say that we all had a feeling that there was more in store than the building of a mausoleum. But we cannot discuss our forebodings with anyone, and often they are not sufficiently concrete even to constitute a rumour, but are just vague feelings that something is in the wind.

None of us had expected this. It is still only a rumour, but there is much about it which makes it credible to all but the most bigoted Marxist–Leninist foreigners, heavyweights for whom the immutability of everything Chinese is pacemaker and iron lung in one. They are convinced that it is all lies; that Jiang Qing and the three others are guarantors of the continuation of Mao's line and that the rumour is bourgeois propaganda.

Apart from the fact that the four are named and that Hua's appointment is now official, there are concrete accusations against the four—of attempting a coup and of falsifying documents left by Mao, or drawn up by the Central Committee. If there is any substance to these rumours, who is now who? Who represents the right wing, who the opposite? Is there a struggle going on between the two wings, or is it just a split within the one?

At our various places of work and round the town it is obvious that most Chinese, apart from the high-ups perhaps, do not know anything more than we think we know.

Another question presents itself. Have the persistent rumours about the imminence of fresh earthquakes, which have been circulating widely lately, been intended to distract attention from what was going on? It has been particularly noticeable during the last week that the building of huts has been intensified. Peking is plastered with huts, and if the entire population is working so hard building, how can they get involved in a power struggle between the party's highest leaders, and aren't the best conditions for potential coup-makers created by fomenting anxiety and uncertainty about something else?

Official mourning is over. I have just been told that our welcoming dinner will be tomorrow. Peking duck at the exclusive little restaurant in the inner city. The leaders of my institute, whom I have not yet met, will be our hosts. Can we ask them what is going on? Of course we can, but as long as nothing has been announced officially we cannot expect an answer. Miserable foreigners like us are told nothing before it is officially announced. And why should we be, seeing that China's own people are told nothing either?

This leads to the question of how these rumours reach us in the first place. I had the experience several times during the Cultural Revolution that we foreigners knew, or thought we knew, something which, from all appearances, had not even reached the rumour stage as far as the Chinese were concerned. Sometimes one gets the feeling that there is an unofficial but calculated leakage to certain foreigners whose channels of further communication are regarded as being acceptable. At the moment the Japanese seem to have the best antennae.

Lulu has recovered, but has got into the habit of wanting to be carried everywhere. In a few days' time she will begin full-time at the institute's nursery school. She has already spent one or two mornings there together with Stine in order to get used to it. On the first day she fell in love with a two-year-old naval man from the Liberation Navy, and he with her. He stood with his willy hanging out of his open pants stroking her hair, their respective noses dripping. Emotion, or only forecasting a change in the weather?

We have been instructed as to what she must have when she goes full-time: two towels, one for use as a nappy during the mid-day rest, an enamel cup and a bottle, sheets and a quilt. It is not possible to buy ready-made quilts so we have been out and bought sheets of cotton, and Stine is lying on the floor at home trying to follow a Chinese pattern for quilt-making.

13.10.76. This morning the rumour spreads that another thirty or forty members of the Central Committee have been arrested. One foreigner assures us that he has had some kind of confirmation that *something* has definitely happened, but without names, time, place, or even *what* has happened. One small pointer, which is actually visible, is the increased numbers of military vehicles on the streets. A certain number of jeeps and lorries drive about all the time, but one has the strong impression that there are significantly more about than usual.

This evening we are picked up by Zhang Zai and taken to the inevitable banquet. It follows the usual pattern: small talk about the weather and one's home country. A direct question is not appreciated. I try wrapping my questions up. I ask if it is true that there has recently been an earthquake of a slightly different kind. This is greeted with deadpan faces. There are so many kinds of earthquake, was the reply, some big, some small. But of course the worst are those which destroy towns. However, Chinese scientists, in collaboration with the workers, are getting very good at predicting earthquakes. But, of course, it is very difficult to prevent them.

That's how it goes. When one thinks one has disguised a question neatly and elegantly, one gets an even neater and more elegantly disguised answer.

Our hosts are the president of the institute, two vice-presidents, and representatives of the local party, the students and the workers respectively. The student representative seems to me very smooth, sophisticated and not entirely trustworthy in appearance.

Apart from a little initial nervousness, probably made worse by the presence of the high-ups, Zhang Zai shows himself to be an unusual specimen. Sweat dripping from his upper lip, he keeps on breaking off his translation to apologize for his bad English. But once the speeches are over he seems able to relax. 'If I make mistakes you really must correct me,' he says. 'We must never be afraid of having our mistakes corrected.'

A little later, when I am momentarily confused about some of the new names surrounding us, Zhang describes one of those present as 'the elderly man with less than the usual amount of hair on his head'. Thinking to help him and perhaps tell him a word he has not come across before, I say, 'We would say the *bald* man.' He nods gravely. 'I know the word but I wouldn't like to use it about one of our leaders.'

Afterwards he sits, still a little nervous, and entertains the company with an account of how impossible he finds it to get out of bed in the morning, how he never makes his bed and is completely unable to make up his mind about anything. 'But now, fortunately, I have found a very strong-minded girlfriend—if only she will marry me.' I have the feeling the others regard him as an amusing and harmless buffoon. They themselves are all very formal and protocol-minded. In spite of the fact that most of them speak English and that we will be working together in that language, they only speak to me or Stine through Zhang Zai—the same ritual which was such an irritation to me years ago with Headmaster Li.

There is a new expert from Egypt with us, who has just arrived. He has left his family behind in Cairo and is supposed to stay here for five years.

15.10.76. Rumours are still circulating, but one feels frustrated in that they are the same old rumours, and they are neither confirmed nor denied.

There is an odd character wandering around Youyi. He looks like a mixture of Ivan the Terrible and Lenin ten years after his death. It seems that none of the Europeans have ever spoken to him although he is said to be French. He will not have anything to do with anyone except the Chinese and people from the Third World.

The only thing he has been heard to say is that when his time in China is up 'there are scores of other countries expecting me'. Some of the Palestinians are convinced that he is an Israeli spy and avoid him like the plague.

During the course of the afternoon I have a long talk with Zhang Zai. He belongs to the same age group as the pupils I had ten years ago. We discuss the way in which character changes, whether it can be done deliberately, whether it is possible or desirable to change human nature. I also remark that it is now forty years since Mao put forward the idea of 'fewer troops and simpler administration'. I do not feel that this had been achieved, while Zhang thinks it has been. I then point to concrete instances of over-administration and overstaffing. 'There is no overstaffing and no unemployment,' I am told. 'And in administration lies leadership. Leaders are necessary.'

I would like to be able to make contact with some of my former pupils, who would now be the same age as Zhang. That would give me a point of reference. Perhaps it is for this very reason I have not been offered a job in Canton, or even been allowed to visit the institute there where some of them might still be studying. To what extent is Zhang symptomatic of his generation? Had he the same sorts of ideas ten years ago as they did? His is a generation which, during five years of the Cultural Revolution and perhaps more, had to fight innumerable ideological and sometimes physical battles. They sang, marched and made pilgrimages all over the country. They criticized, were themselves criticized at mass meetings and in small groups. They interrupted the process of education over the years in order to do such things as write wall newspapers attacking national and local leaders. How typical is Zhang of the country's students, of those who have just completed their studies? How typical of the worker/peasant class from which, following the Cultural Revolution, all young academics were to have been recruited?

17.10.76. Great piles of maize lie drying in the sun outside the Ming tombs to the north of Peking, where the institute has invited us to a picnic with Tsingtao beer and a packed lunch, under the trees, just beginning to turn scarlet, on the slopes of the Western Hills. Ssü, the institute's vice-president, is with us; he is a tall, smooth character, who talks fast and much. This not being an official occasion he does not use an interpreter. Zhang is playing with Lulu.

Ssü is a former diplomat and was a member of the first delegation to the USA when China took her seat in the United Nations.

I try pressing him a little about Stine's application to attend the language school and am met with a disarming smile. 'They have not yet decided,' he says. This is the usual reply, which tells one never to expect so much as a hint about the possible outcome of anything. When the time is considered ripe one will be told. I have never heard anyone say something like: 'We don't really know yet, but without making any promises I think I can say the decision will probably be so and so.'

20.10.76. Yesterday, large posters were being put up on the security wall opposite my office window. The only characters I could decipher were those for 'four' and 'person', followed by rows of exclamation marks. I asked various colleagues what had happened and was told that they didn't know yet. One of them did go so far as to say that I may have heard some totally unconfirmed rumours about which he could not, of course, make any comment. But he would not be surprised if I had some idea of what was going on.

It reminded me of an endless conversation I had during the first year of the Cultural Revolution. Criticism of leaders actually mentioned by name crept higher and higher up the ladder, until the last rung when the object of criticism suddenly became 'the top party person who follows the capitalist line'. I found this a long-winded substitute for a name and one day I asked a friend if we couldn't shorten it a bit.

'The person in question must have a name,' I said.

'Of course he has. Everybody has,' I was told.

'Can't I persuade you to tell me his name?' I asked.

'I am sure you know who it is,' was the reply.

'Why won't you tell me?'

'You know who it is and I know who it is. We all know who this person is, so there is no need to mention names yet.'

Weeks later the name was revealed: Liu Shaoqi, the then president of China.

But why this caution, this secrecy about something which is no secret? Is it because of the faint possibility that in spite of everything, things might not go according to plan, and one does not wish to compromise oneself by criticizing someone by name who in the end turns out to be a winner? But in this particular case it would have been pretty well the entire population which had compromised itself. And how does one know when it is all right to stand up and spell things out?

The posters the students are pasting up will tell us that something has happened, but not before the glue is dry. We foreigners are in the curious situation of being among the first to know about things via rumours and feelings, and the last to be told anything officially. During the last few days there has been a big attendance at the daily, very bad, tape-recorded news bulletins of Voice of America from Manila, and from some of the words which Zhang and others ask me to explain, I can guess what the news is about.

What was a gate in the wall is now covered in posters. The students who some time ago brought stones and other things have walled up the gate so that the only means of access to the campus is the small side gate at the northern end of the wall. I ask why the main gate has been put out of action and am told that it is because the peasants from the commune round us had got into the habit of using our campus as a short cut. That is why the wall was necessary in the first place, I am told. 'People can't just come and go as they please here. One must have good reason.'

One of the reasons why schools and universities were closed at the time of the Cultural Revolution was their exclusiveness, their snobbishness and superior attitude towards ordinary working people. The money spent on building schools and universities had been earned by workers and peasants and therefore, it was reasoned, they should not be for the exclusive use of the superior classes.

And later, at the beginning of the seventies, when teaching began again, it was on condition that schools and universities should open their doors to workers and peasants. Entrance requirements were changed, so that class background, ideology and industry became more important than academic qualifications.

And here I am watching the students blocking up the main gate to the biggest language institute in the country, so that the local peasants shall not ruin our dusty grass with their carts, taking a short cut from the fields to the threshing ground.

21.10.76. At dawn we hear the first distant sounds. The metallic singing of cymbals and the deep pulsating throb of drums come to us through the open verandah windows. A ring of percussion instruments of all kinds from the outlying districts of Peking is converging on the centre. We live on one of the main roads into town, and through the still, leafy tree-tops we catch glimpses of big clusters of red banners, queues of lorries full of people, all moving in an endless stream towards the city. All traffic is one way today. Crowds of people carrying little paper flags wind their way among the teeming vehicles. Unit after unit, brigade after brigade, carrying the newly issued truth, are marching to the heart of Peking, the heart of China. There has been a fence of rumours around Peking, too high to jump and with too few knotholes through which to see. That fence is now no more.

Here, society, unlike the individual, has the right to keep secrets. Perhaps the individual has learned to do without this right.

A portrait of Mao pasted on cardboard and attached to a long stick marks the beginning and end of each column. Here and there we catch a glimpse of the new chairman, Hua Guofeng. Everything has happened so rapidly that in spite of the almost reverent attitude the Chinese have for pictures, it is remarkable that although throughout the mourning period Mao's portrait was in black and white and is now in full colour, that of Hua is in grey. Decisions must have been overtaken by the speed of events, since the organization was not able to produce colour pictures of Hua in time.

At my institute irresolute groups of students are standing about attempting to form columns on the big parade ground. They have not yet been issued with banners or slogans, have not yet had their marching orders. It is said that the pilgrimage to Tien An Men will go on for three days so that the entire population of the city, six to seven million altogether, will all be able to get there. That is the plan.

When the first group is finally given word to leave I am asked whether I would like to join. We will march the six to eight kilometres to the centre, and it will be splendid, I am told.

'Who is the demonstration supporting and who is it against?' I ask because now it is official. They have been dubbed the 'Gang of Four' and consist of Wang Hongwen, Zhang Chungiao, Jiang Qing and Yao Wenyuan. It is typical of China that although they have been denounced, damned and discarded, they are still referred to in the order of precedence they had in the Central Committee. Protocol must be observed, so Jiang Qing is number three, even though many seem to think she is the worst offender.

'I can't join in when I don't know who is responsible for what. I can't go and cheer Hua Guofeng if I don't know who he is or what he represents. It is important for me to know what I am doing.'

They assure me that he is Chairman Mao's only rightful heir, that he has warded off a villainous and treacherous attack on the security of the party, the people and the nation by exposing the 'Four'.

But later on the decision is made for us. Buses are suddenly organized and we are driven, by back streets so as not to get stuck in the crowds, to the Imperial Palace, where seats have been reserved for us directly under the rostrum where the 'top people'—whoever they may be—are; we cannot see their faces.

There are elements of the National Days of the past. The square, which can hold a million, is teeming with people, flags, music; security guards, unarmed and wearing white gloves, separating the crowds on the square from the rostrum. Sounds bubbling from the loudspeakers drown in one another's echoes.

But the atmosphere is different. It is subdued compared with then; the slogans fall a bit flat, as if there had not been enough time to practise them. Four unknown speakers represent and express the anger of the peasants, workers, soldiers and students respectively.

But in today's half-hearted chaos, in the very un-Chinese disorganization, I feel that perhaps here are the beginnings of a new China. Today may ultimately prove to be as important a day as that day in October 1949 when Mao proclaimed the liberation of China with the words: 'The Chinese people have stood up.'

Turning

It is far too early for us to see any clear change in the political
climate yet. There is too much uncertainty, people are too non-
committal for us to be able to get any idea of the nature of the times
we are about to enter. The echoes of that hypnotic droning, the
exorcizing of evil under the late summer skies above the red and gold
Imperial Palace, are still ringing in our ears. Wang Hongwen, Zhang
Chunqiao, Jiang Qing, Yao Wenyuan repeated with cabalistic monotony in every fresh speech. Wang, Zhang, Jiang, Yao—this string of
words lacks nothing in intensity as it pours out of the loudspeakers
in every classroom I pass. Wang, Zhang, Jiang, Yao, recited in
melodious tones on every floor of the building, vanishing as a
shadowy echo across the scorched grass of our deserted campus, to
be tossed back to us over the high white wall from the fields round
us, from the engineering works beyond the railway lines behind us.
Wang, Zhang, Jiang, Yao repeated so often that in the end they are
no longer names but just sounds; sounds like the metallic clatter of
a train going over the points. Wang Zhang Jiang Yao.

There is no one who can give any good reason why the 'Four' are
always enumerated in what was their order of precedence in the
Central Committee. One student finds it quite natural that, 'Until
they have been officially dismissed from their posts in the party, we
must, of course, name them in the correct order. And the Central
Committee has not yet officially dismissed them.'

In these early days, detailed accusations have not yet reached the
public. So far the charges are rather ill-defined, such as having
attempted to seize leadership of the party, of having misrepresented
Mao's words and directives, of having practised divisive politics
and, on his widow's part, of having plagued the Chairman as he
lay dying.

The first caricatures are appearing—caustic, clever and only thinly
disguised—horned devils, the dowager empress, Chiang Kai-shek,

and a Chinese version of Hitler. Lack of concrete accusations means
that the drawings show no action, only figures. The artists do not
yet know in what compromising situations to depict them. On many
of the drawings they are shown kneeling in terror with hands held up
in supplication to the superman who, with clenched fists, is on his
way down from the top left-hand corner of the picture.

I am standing looking at an exhibition of these drawings on the
wall outside my office. The group of students who have done them
are in the process of putting them up and decorating them. In the
bookshops in the town one can buy booklets giving the basic
principles of decorative borders, using sheaves of corn, cogwheels,
pennants on poles, tractors and a half-risen sun. One of the figures
in the collection is wearing a characteristic Chinese military uniform
but has a little square black moustache right under his nose, a lock
of hair hanging over his forehead, and an arm-band with a swastika.

'Who is that?' I ask the artist.

'One of the "Gang of Four",' he says.

'Yes, but who is he supposed to look like?'

'Hitler of course.'

'Who was Hitler?' I ask.

There is a short discussion among the students.

'He was Minister of Defence in Mussolini's Germany,' is the reply.

A veteran teacher standing near turns to me: 'Don't be too
depressed by that. At least he is aware that there were people called
Hitler and Mussolini.'

As I have said, there are as yet very few concrete allegations
against the 'Four', but there is a general feeling that some people,
somewhere, are working at high pressure to unearth ammunition
against them. And in the expectant atmosphere one can detect a
kind of euphoria. It is not openly expressed because as long as we
do not know what the accusations are, it is not possible to know in
which direction things are likely to go.

There is a pile of newly written texts lying on my desk. It is part
of my job to go through such a pile every day, correct the English
and assess them as teaching material before they are printed. The
texts are compiled by groups of veteran teachers and have had
political approval before they reach me. The local party office goes
through them all so I know that they must reflect the official party
line. Here I have a chance, from little changes in style, new topics
and other hints to make guesses at which way the political wind is
blowing. I can, of course, overestimate the importance of a detail

and attach to it a significance which it may not possess. But then again it may.

One of the questions which now, at the end of 1976, is hovering on the fringe of consciousness without coming into the open, is the question of Deng Xiaoping. Twice he has been at the top and twice he has been denounced and dismissed, the last time only a year ago. On both occasions the campaigns against him have appeared to be as intense, violent and spontaneous as has been the homage paid him when he has been in power. We are still using texts accusing him of being the foremost spokesman for and supporter of capitalism in today's China. He is accused of being a traitor, scab, and enemy of the people. His name has reverberated through the corridors outside my office with the same intensity as those of Wang, Zhang, Jiang and Yao do now, but recently, of course, there has been no room for any names but theirs.

I have just been looking at a text written for the second-year students and at our daily meeting go through my corrections with the author. There are linguistic details of varying importance we agree on. The text in question is in itself as neutral and as lacking in content as any text intended only for swotting can be. But there is one thing in it which intrigues me. Among the many short sentences there is one which could be of significance in the China of today. It reads: 'I have a red pencil and a blue pencil. The one writes just as well as the other.'

With Deng in mind, this trivial sentence in a duplicated text assumes importance. One of the accusations made against him was that he put efficiency above ideology and he expressed this attitude in a much-quoted saying: 'It doesn't matter if the cat is black or white as long as it catches mice.' On this he was nailed, and it was not mild names like 'pragmatist' he was called.

'Take this sentence,' I say, pointing to it. 'What about it?'

The old man bends over the text. He is a kind, friendly man and a perfectionist in even the smallest matters. He holds his folded glasses in front of his eyes and reads it half aloud several times.

'As far as I can see it is quite correct,' he says finally. ' "I have a red pencil and a blue pencil. The one writes just as well as the other." The grammar and language are correct, the students know all the words.'

Well, I think, it seems I have over-interpreted. Things begin to dance before one's eyes if one spends too much time looking for clues everywhere. It is just a boring sentence of the kind we use so much in teaching.

'There is nothing new in it for the students,' he continues. 'We have just agreed that it would be a good thing for them to learn to use constructions like "just as . . . as".'

'It reminds me of something,' I say awkwardly, still not quite able to give up the idea that it might be a pointer in some direction or other.

'I see, I see,' he says softly, and I hope he will go on to say that he sees the same thing I do. 'I agree it is not a very inspiring sentence,' he continues in a different tone of voice, 'and I know we have often discussed trying to get away from these meaningless texts: the "this is my sister, that is my brother, I have a book, you have a bag" style. It is a bit difficult to introduce more meaningful content, but we do our best.'

I do not know whether I am being given cryptic messages or not, I drop the subject and go on to discuss the next exercise. A little later, when we have finished the work and are sitting chatting, he says: 'By the way, I have heard that a unit in Peking has decided that from now on Deng Xiaoping will be referred to as "Comrade" Deng. That is very interesting, although, of course, it is perfectly correct, because even though he was dismissed from all his posts inside and outside the party he was allowed to retain his party membership. And as a party member he is entitled to be referred to and addressed as Comrade Deng.'

'That is something I have never been able to understand,' I say. 'How can he be allowed to keep his party membership and at the same time be accused of being the arch enemy, the capitalist supporter *par excellence*? By so doing they are allowing a declared traitor to be a member of the party.'

'It gives the impression of a conflict, yes; it must certainly look like a conflict. We must be more energetic in campaigning against him to the uttermost.'

'You mean that he won't appear so much in our texts?'

'At the moment it is important that we bring to light and analyse the crimes committed by the "Gang of Four" over the years. It is very important to carry out the criticism thoroughly.'

'Forgetting about Deng Xiaoping for the time being?'

'We must have a united and broad popular front against all enemies of the party, state and people.'

'What is your personal opinion; do you think that Deng might come back one day?'

'At the moment I have no personal opinion. Everything depends on what happens. So much can happen. We have seen so much. It is difficult for old people like myself to keep up with it all.'

It is the same reticence, the same caution one experienced in the early days of the Cultural Revolution. Friends and enemies were seldom mentioned by name before, in one way or another, the green light had been given. And those who were a step ahead of the green light in stating their position were rewarded with the status of leaders and pioneers or, if they had backed the wrong horse, with loss of status, criticism and condemnation.

'Of course, it was no surprise to us to hear that the "Four" were a lot of bandits,' says one of the young teachers. 'We have thought so all along.'

'Did you ever discuss it among yourselves?'

'But we couldn't! Well of course we could discuss it with our very close friends or our families. But none of us would have dared to say openly what we all felt. We are greatly relieved now. We can speak freely about all the things which have bothered us for many years.'

'What about the new party leaders?'

'We are all delighted that China is on the right course again now that our beloved—respected chairman, Hua Guofeng, has got rid of the "Four".'

That is a slip of the tongue one often hears nowadays. For decades people have been accustomed to putting the word 'beloved' in front of the word chairman and constantly forget that the new chairman has not yet achieved that status. The word 'respected' must be used. As far as I can make out, there has been no official decree; it has just become established practice. Perhaps it is intended to indicate that no one is on the same plane as Mao: and perhaps no one is. According to André Malraux, who had several talks with Mao, the latter is supposed to have said: 'De Gaulle and I have one thing in common, we have no successor.' But the French maintain that Malraux was well known for his preoccupation with myths.

'So there is no criticism of any of China's new leaders?'

He looks at me in astonishment. 'Why should there be? They have rid China and every one of us of a scourge. We can now speak freely about things we have never been able to talk about before.'

'Like the Cultural Revolution and its consequences?'

'That is a very difficult question. The Great Proletarian Cultural Revolution was a triumph for Chairman Mao, our beloved leader who has now passed away, for his line.'

There are many, mainly young people, who regard the linguistic/

political ritual as more important than syntax. We have had many discussions about the use of English with a Chinese flavour—that linguistic bastard known as 'Chinglish'.

'Why do you continue to use the expression "passed away"? We don't use it in modern English.'

'Because we wish to show our respect for Chairman Mao.'

'Why is it more respectful to use an old-fashioned expression, a euphemism? Why do you never speak of him as "dead" or as "having died"? You certainly don't pull your punches when it comes to criticizing the "Four".'

'That is a completely different matter. We use strong language to express our boundless hatred and contempt for those traitors who have corrupted China, sought to change its colour, and contributed to Chairman Mao's passing away. We show our respect and boundless affection when we use the expression "passed away" about Chairman Mao.'

'In English that just means that he is dead. There is nothing derogatory in that. It is a simple fact.'

'We cannot say that in Chinese.'

'Isn't there a word for "dead" in Chinese?'

'Of course. But you don't use it about everybody. A sorrowing father can say that his son is dead, but the son must use the expression "passed away" if he speaks of his father in the same context. That is why we use the expression when we refer to Chairman Mao.'

'That is not the case in English.'

'Well, it is in Chinese.'

'We are teaching English here. And it is not just words. We should also try to teach the students to use good modern English.'

'You can't make me use any other expression concerning the passing away of Chairman Mao. Possibly you are right, it is a Chinese habit I have carried over into English. But it is hard to change one's habits.'

Now that official mourning is over, I have been wondering what will happen in my office. Work has been going on normally, except that I have not been able to use my blackboard. As I said, Zhang Zai covered the whole thing with a picture of Mao, and the slogan enjoining us to 'convert grief into strength'. What I am wondering is how long the blackboard is likely to remain covered. I would like to use it for the small groups I have. On the other hand, I have a feeling that it would be highly improper for me to remove the picture and rub out the slogan just because I want to get some work done.

But this morning when I arrive at the office, two young men are quite unconcernedly clearing everything away. One is scratching off the adhesive paper with which Mao's picture had been fixed to the matt surface of the blackboard, and the other is in the middle of washing out the elegant calligraphy. When they have gone I sit and watch the wet board, like a slow motion film, getting less and less shiny as it dries. When it is quite dry I can still detect Zhang Zai's beautiful calligraphy, like a translucent echo of the chalk he pressed with such precision into the porous surface of the blackboard. On the part where the sticky paper was, my chalk won't bite. My blackboard has suffered little irreparable damage. It can be used, but what has happened to it will affect all the other words which are written on it in the future.

Now and then I receive visits from institute leaders of the middle grade. They are polite visits, which always begin with non-committal small talk, giving no indication of the reason for coming. I now know that these visits usually have a reason, but that we never plunge straight into the matter in hand.

Naturally it is most often things to do with work. Suggestions about new methods, new projects, requests to take part in discussions on how we can improve standards, requests for a report on a particular student or teacher. But occasionally they come to deliver a purely personal message.

Just as the country is divided up in a para-military way, just as the communes have their work-teams and brigades, their leaders at different levels, so the workers and intellectuals are also divided into groups. Everyone belongs to a unit which, for the most part, is their place of work. The unit is father and mother to us. It supervises, looks after us and knows us. It issues prohibitions, permissions and sanctions. Most people live in or near their unit.

In this respect I, being a foreigner, differ from my Chinese colleagues. For the Chinese, the unit has to give permission to buy more than a given amount of any one thing at a time. This serves both as a form of rationing and a built-in control over the spending of money which may have been unlawfully acquired. It is one's unit which issues the coupons for the few things which are subject to shortage. These are rice and flour, and sometimes cigarettes, cotton and vegetable oil. But all rations seem to be perfectly adequate. Bicycles are rationed, but only in Peking. This is not because there is any shortage of cycles: on the contrary. But they have become a traffic problem and so it has been decided that the number of cyclists must be controlled. Each unit is allotted an annual quota which it distributes within the unit.

My unit is father and mother to me too. It is true that I can spend my money as I like and have access to the special shop catering for foreigners, the Friendship Shop, if I wish. The only rationing which applies to us is cotton goods. Cigarettes are freely available at the moment, but the ones with filter tips are reserved for foreigners and those higher-ranking Chinese who have special permission. Among other things, one learns to observe what brand of cigarette people are smoking and whether it is tipped or not.

If I have a problem it is to my unit I must take it. Public authorities are not so public that one has immediate access to them. As a rule they hide behind names like 'relevant competent authority' and one never quite knows who this authority is, or where it is to be found. It is the unit which is the contact between us and them. Sometimes I get a funny feeling that the 'relevant competent authority' is, in fact, to be found here in the institute, and that the process of decision-making goes on within these very walls and never gets outside.

It is virtually impossible to speed up a decision and useless to press for an answer. We have been waiting for several weeks for the outcome of Stine's application to attend the Chinese course and when I try pressing my unit for an answer I am told that the matter is no longer in their hands. When I ask in whose hands it is, I am told 'the relevant competent authority'.

When the matter finally reached the stage of our being asked to submit a written application, I asked to whom it should be addressed. 'To the relevant competent authority,' I was told.

I have again been pressing for an answer. Term has begun and it is important for Stine not to have to begin with too great a handicap. I do not know if it is the result of weariness or what, but my unit suddenly tells me that it is no longer 'the relevant competent authority' to whom I must go, but the Experts Bureau, which is next in line in the bureaucratic bodies we must deal with. The Experts Bureau is an unusual body in that it seems to be fairly independent and is directly responsible to the State Council. It goes without saying that this gives it very high status, and that is perhaps one of the reasons we cannot go and see them. It is known that they have an office somewhere in Youyi but no foreigner has ever found out where.

'It is out of consideration for Youyi's leaders. They are responsible for the buildings and their maintenance and will therefore, unfortunately, not allow our offices to be open to foreign experts,' was the explanation we were given for their whereabouts being kept secret. However, we have a telephone number, so we can ring up and leave a message when we are in need of their assistance, and they do appear promptly. And occasionally they visit us unexpectedly and seem to have a remarkable flair for knowing when we are in need of their help.

So when Stine's application has apparently ground to a halt, and as my unit refuses to take any further responsibility for it, I go to the Experts Bureau. They disclaim all knowledge of and responsibility for it, and refer me back to my unit. As they have already also disclaimed all responsibility, and as neither party can or will tell me who the 'relevant competent authority' may be, we are completely stuck.

'It would not be unreasonable to say that perhaps we are burdened with rather a lot of bureaucracy,' says one of the responsible comrades of my unit, continuing after a pause with the universally heard comment of these days, 'but I think we can say that that is due to the evil influence of the "Gang of Four".' 'Well,' he hastens to add, 'perhaps one can't quite say that.'

The World Outside

The Bamboo Curtain was a concept of the late 1950s, the eastern equivalent of the Iron Curtain of the West, intended to draw attention to China's unapproachability and self-imposed isolation. That such a barrier did exist there can be no doubt, but there is equally no doubt that much of it was the product of outside thinking.

It is an historical fact that there have been periods in China's history when she has rejected all foreign culture, but during the first years after liberation there was a rich cultural life which flourished comparatively unrestricted. Foreign plays were performed in the theatres, and there was some access to foreign literature, either in the original, for those who were able to read it, or in Chinese translation.

Today, when China, to an increasing extent, is turning towards the outside world, there are very few Chinese who have had, or are likely to have, an opportunity to see that world. The few who do have such an opportunity know that it is a once-in-a-lifetime experience and not likely to be repeated. They are mostly public servants, businessmen, sportsmen and delegates to scientific and cultural congresses.

Selected students from my institute are sometimes sent abroad on an exchange basis. In this way they have an opportunity to make up for the facilities so sadly lacking here, and to study a language in the country in which it is spoken.

For many of these students being sent abroad is a disturbing experience. They write long letters home to those comrades and teachers they feel they can trust. In some of the letters one can detect uneasiness amounting almost to panic, complete bewilderment that life in foreign countries should be so different from that to which they are accustomed. One young woman devoted a whole letter to describing her feelings of outraged modesty when she had to study classical love poems at the university to which she had been sent.

She had to force herself to take part in discussions about the language used in the poems. But the friends to whom she wrote were so far away that it was difficult for them to understand what she was talking about and I had the impression that they automatically labelled it 'decadent Western culture' and felt sorry for her that she should have to put up with it.

The problem might not be so great if these students were in any way prepared for what they are likely to meet when they go abroad. Most of them have not the slightest idea, as I know from hours of discussion with them. It is true they are given a briefing; shortly before they leave they have an interview with an older teacher who has been abroad himself. They are given a general introduction to the country they are being sent to and are told a little about the local culture and conventions. But at the same time they are also given a powerful political harangue. They are being sent abroad not in order to see the world, but to work hard for their country. It is impressed on them that it is the Chinese workers and peasants who are paying for their having this chance, that it is not for their own advantage they are being sent, and so on. After this they receive any practical advice the teacher in question is in a position to give them. How much use that will be depends on how long it is since the teacher has been abroad himself. Students frequently set out with very old-fashioned ideas—in any case, if one is starting from scratch, a couple of hours of conversation is hardly enough. It is difficult enough anyway to find out what it really looks like, the world outside.

There are, in fact, many of my colleagues who recognize that the information given to students before they go is so minimal as to be virtually worthless. During my time in China I have been asked many questions by students, the answers to which they expect will help to give them a picture of the world. A selected question will show how little they know. 'Are the people in England black?' one wanted to know. But on the whole, questions tend to fall into two main groups: questions trying to establish some similarity between China and the outside world (some points of resemblance sufficiently close as to be comprehensible); and those which seek to establish that there are differences (but without any idea of the magnitude of those differences). In the first group belong such questions as whether the police and other authorities have the same wide-ranging power over the individual as they do in China, the position of the working classes (but seldom anything about trade unions), the revolutionary attitude of Western peasants, and so on. Questions about the peasants are, naturally, often put and the answers must often be disappointing to the questioner. In the group concerned with differences, I am often asked about things like the Church, the Royal Family, votes, energy crises and unemployment—phenomena which are known to exist, but about which they have no detailed knowledge. It is seldom that anyone asks about culture, history or social structure. These appear to be subjects which are either restricted by some form of taboo, or rejected as being of no practical value and therefore of no interest.

It is daily apparent to me that there has been a significant decline in the standard of general knowledge, not only about what is going on in the outside world, but also about what is going on in China itself. This seems to have happened since the Cultural Revolution stopped all formal education for a number of years. Many of the more realistically oriented educators admit this, particularly now that they can blame the 'Gang of Four' for the consequences of what has proved to be a faulty educational policy.

The students who are now enrolled are, on average, older than those who were studying at the same level before the Cultural Revolution. This is partly because of the new requirement that one must spend two or three years doing practical work before applying for higher education. But though contact with real life may have led to a better knowledge of social and political conditions than was the case before, it does seem to have had the effect of lowering the level of general knowledge. Chinese teachers frequently complain nowadays about the difficulty their students have in expressing themselves even when writing in their own language.

So the generation which has just completed its higher education is far worse equipped, academically speaking, than any generation before it. It has even come to the point where voices are being raised in favour of abandoning 'proletarian conscription' and bringing back 'professional students', students whose aim is to acquire as much knowledge about their particular subject as possible. It was this idea which Deng Xiaoping was supporting when he said: 'The Chinese Academy of Science is an academy of science not of cabbage soup.'

Seeing that most of the students here are destined for jobs as interpreters or trade delegates, most of them will in the future have a good deal of contact with foreigners, I think it is important not only that they should master the language but also be given an opportunity of studying its background. But many of the questions I am asked refer only to such things as the etiquette at the banqueting table, and which subjects one must avoid in polite conversation with a European. Apart from these simple introductions to the elementary rules of social behaviour and the odd political question, they seldom express any desire to know anything at all. It startles me to find that my students, to a growing extent, are unable to answer general questions reasonably adequately, let alone thoroughly, and that this applies to questions about China, too, and quite basic political questions at that.

This was brought home to me one day when one of the younger teachers asked me to come and sit in on his class and criticize it afterwards. His teaching lacked nothing. It was lively, imaginative and stimulating. He has a flair for language and is very good at illustrating things. At one point he asked the students: 'What would you call me if I began treating you very badly, beating you up and so on?'

A bright student answered promptly: 'A capitalist.' I expected a discussion to begin after this but the teacher just nodded approvingly and praised him for answering correctly.

Following this incident I asked some students I was talking to, 'By the way, what is capitalism?' I assumed that it would be easy for politically schooled 25-year-old students in China to define capitalism satisfactorily. I was wrong. Most of the answers were completely inadequate. Many simply said 'capitalism is evil' or 'a bad system', and if I asked for a more precise definition of its badness, I was told that it does bad things to people.

This made me ask one of the political teachers whether the students have ever had capitalism described and explained to them in terms of ownership and production. I was told that it had been explained to them, but possibly they had not been very attentive that day.

It may have something to do with the fact that the mere idea of private ownership is almost incomprehensible to the younger generation in this country, where agriculture is co-operative to such a high degree and all industrial production in the hands of the state. But one can also see this ignorance as being the result of oversimplification, a rather dangerous oversimplification, of things with which one does not agree; and also of things with which one does agree.

I go through most of the texts we use to check the language, whether they have been composed in the institute or have come from outside. The material coming from outside is from three sources: the Chinese newspapers and news bulletins published in English (which linguistically are of doubtful value); texts from other language institutes; and occasionally material taken from foreign sources. The last happens seldom because, naturally, the material has to be politically acceptable, and therefore can only be taken from a rather limited field. Whatever material does come from abroad can be divided into three parts: texts which deal with China's attitude *vis-à-vis* the Soviet Union, texts describing the conditions of the worker under the capitalist system and, finally, texts dealing with the absolute superiority of Chinese Socialism. Politically speaking, three very important subjects in China today.

The one essential is that the texts must have had political approval. They are not all of equal value, particularly from a teaching point of view. They also, as I have already mentioned, suffer from the over-simplification which pervades everything here. In China today one cannot split hairs or even ask for distinctions between good, less good, and bad in one system as opposed to another. But I do ask, and I have asked many times in long discussions with colleagues, that at least what we tell the students should be the truth. One of my arguments is that if one has to lie in order to make capitalism appear worse than it actually is, then basically one must be aware that it may not be so bad after all. And conversely, if one finds it necessary to embroider on the facts of socialism in order to make it attractive, then it must be because one is not entirely satisfied with it as it is. In any case, the students have a right to know that whatever we tell them is, to the best of our knowledge and belief, the truth.

On this point there are only a few of my colleagues who agree wholeheartedly. There is evidence of deliberate and calculated falsification in some of the teaching material. That it is deliberate can be deduced from the fact that it has not been corrected even when I have drawn attention to it before it was printed. This does not, of course, apply to all teaching material, but it does to a significant part of it.

One instance of this involved a couple of chapters from an American novel which had been duplicated and distributed to the students. I was asked to give a talk on how one tackles reading outside the classroom, without the help of the teacher. On the first page was the title, name of author and year of publication, which was given as 1960. This surprised me when I read the text because the style and content did not quite fit so recent a date. I looked up the author and found that he had died in 1911 and that he had written the novel in question five years before his death. I assumed there had been a printer's error and that it should have been 1906. I drew the attention of the teachers responsible to this, but was told that it was not important, only a minor detail and I shouldn't bother about it. There was no need, they said, to point it out to the students. I agree that the capitalism at the turn of the century in the USA is far easier to describe and comprehend than the sophisticated and complex version we are landed with today. But I object to deliberately letting the past play the present for the sake of convenience.

On another occasion, a group of students wanted to put on a play at the end of term. Their teacher found a piece for them on the theme of the exploitation of young people by capitalist employers in British coal-mines. The capitalist in the piece was a really objectionable character, and I made it my business to point out that coal-mines have not been privately owned since the fifties, when they were nationalized. I suggested that, if the students are going to put on the play, they should at least be made aware of the fact that it is not set in contemporary Britain, even if the conditions in the coal-mines may not be so very different from what they were in the days of private ownership. But my suggestion is rejected.

'It would be too difficult,' I am told, 'to begin explaining about nationalization. Some of the students might think it is the same as socialism. They might want to know the difference between state enterprises in a capitalist country and China. That would be too complicated to explain. It is much better to let them perform the play without all these explanations. They can recognize the capitalist of course, and he demonstrates the nature of the system very clearly.'

With that I had to agree, but still protested, in vain, that we were distorting reality.

It is seldom that those at the receiving end complain about the level of information they are given, but it does happen. A student came to visit me at my flat one day and said, with surprising candour: 'I know that much of what we students are told about conditions in the West is inaccurate, but I cannot find what the truth really is. Can you tell me about it?' Apart from the fact that this is rather a tall order, it puts me on a political tightrope. He is asking me to put him right on information he considers to have been misleading. But that is not my job, nor have I any interest in making excuses for the political systems of the West.

A sceptic might see his 'illegal' request as being a test, a test of my loyalty through a trustworthy student asking planted questions. I don't think that was the case. There was nothing in his question which suggested that it was *my* political temperature he was measuring and, as I said, I have no capitalist nest to feather. His question was genuine enough and, in the light of the teaching materials we use, quite understandable.

This sparseness of information about the outside world is reflected in the bookshelves and reading-rooms of the different libraries. In the literary part of the foreign section one does not find much more than the odd Shakespeare, Dickens and Shaw. My unit takes the *Christian Science Monitor*, London *Times* and *Financial Times*. The latter seems a sensible choice for an institute like ours, which is concerned with international trade and economics. We take two periodicals—*Newsweek* and the *Reader's Digest*.

The latter has been the cause of much discussion. I have often suggested that the subscription should be cancelled and something of better quality taken in its stead. But this does not happen. There are two reasons, I suspect. Firstly, the *Reader's Digest* is anti-Soviet, which automatically gives it quality in Chinese eyes. The fact that it is also anti-Chinese and, indeed, anti-everything, is of less importance. 'If it is against the Soviet Union it must be good,' is the tacit assumption. I point out its poor quality, not only politically but also in style and content, all to no purpose. I am told that 'the "relevant competent authority" which subscribes to the papers on behalf of the institute does not like cancellations or changes. We have signed a contract for it and it is binding. That is what they say, unfortunately. We do not know the reason.'

And when all is said and done, my intervention is pointless anyway. All foreign publications are locked in a reading-room to which only cadres have access. They are classified 'Nei bu': material inaccessible to students. The only room to which the students have access is the reference library, which is clinically free of everything except dictionaries and books of reference. And the staff in the cadres' room have, among other jobs, that of covering with a ball-point pen the navels of the bikini-clad models in the *Newsweek* advertisements.

It is understandable and, perhaps, reasonable that political taboos should exist. But it is neither understandable nor reasonable that young Chinese students should be so badly informed about global and national events which concern them.

One day I was teaching from a text about forms of energy and energy crises. Since nuclear power, an area which presupposes some common or general knowledge, had been mentioned, I asked the class to what extent nuclear power was being used in China. They looked at me in surprise and then at each other and no one answered. I explained that I did not mean military nuclear power, in case they were worried that I was trying to get secret information out of them.

'We don't know,' one of them said finally. 'Perhaps we have nuclear power, perhaps not. If we have it is an official secret, and nothing to do with us.'

If I have spent time describing some of the negative aspects of Chinese education, it is not because it is predominantly negative, but because these faults exist and ought to be taken into account in a general evaluation. In the field of popular education, on the other hand, by means of radio, printed matter and television, a tremendous amount of work is being done in disseminating information about technology, public health and agricultural matters.

Even if over the years China has pulled many twigs from the Bamboo Curtain, the structure stands there still, and its isolating effect has now begun to make itself felt within the country.

Foreign Devils—Foreign Friends

Statements are often made, or questions asked, about whether the Chinese have not a special attitude to foreigners and foreign things. The statements vary in tone from those which suggest that the Chinese are shy but friendly towards foreigners to those which make positive assertions that they reject outright everything which is not Chinese and socialist. Statements of this latter kind suggest deep-rooted and unpleasant racism.

The truth, as always in such matters, is not absolute. What certainly is true is that it is difficult, no—more than difficult—impossible for Westerners to fully integrate with the Chinese. Quite apart from the physical characteristics which distinguish one race from another, there are other factors which make integration next to impossible. There are probably few countries in the world where the adjective 'foreign' is used so often. In the old days and up to the middle of this century, the derogatory terms 'foreign devils' and 'big noses' were used to describe Western people and 'foreign devilry' their products and culture. And as up until that time the only foreign culture the Chinese had experienced had been various forms of imperialism, it is, I suppose, not surprising that it should be described as devilry.

Western culture has, in fact, had little impact on China. Among other things it is worth noting that even at the time when China was most subject to foreign domination, mainly in the form of English imperialism, the language was kept pure. Chinese has astonishingly few loan words. Many tales are told of the scorn and ridicule to which the Chinese of the past were subjected if they returned from abroad wearing foreign clothes, without a pigtail, or showing other signs of foreign influence.

In the China of today there is great use of the word 'internationalism', in striking contrast to the equally frequent use of the words 'foreign' and 'foreigners', though without the addition of the more derogatory words. Whereas the word internationalism should be seen in a political context and as a declaration of socialism, the other words have their roots in a strong sense of national pride.

It can be difficult and at times painful to have to accept the discrimination to which a foreigner is often subjected. The pain is not so much a case of personal pride as the realization that there is a barrier between us, an obstacle to the internationalism which is the theoretical goal. And if I use the word discrimination, it is not in its narrow racist sense, but in the sense that we are treated differently, be it in a positive or a negative way. In fact, this different treatment has the peculiarity of being both positive and negative at the same time. At the beginning of the Cultural Revolution there were, as opposed to previously, definitely no sacred cows. Prominent political personalities and hitherto unassailable leaders at the very top were suddenly subject to as violent attacks from the Red Guard as those below them. Nobody could hide behind a cloak of prestige, position or influence. During this time, when everyone else was a legitimate target for criticism, there was one group which by and large went unscathed, and that was the group of the few hundred or so foreign experts who were working in China at the time. When I say 'by and large', it is because there were a few who directly and actively involved themselves in the Cultural Revolution. Among these there were some who backed the wrong horse. A few were imprisoned, some unjustly. But for the most part we were not considered fair game.

It is true that on several occasions the Red Guard plastered the walls of the house I lived in with posters, and I knew from the many exclamation marks and the painfully good caricatures of myself that these posters were directed against me. But nothing more happened, and when I asked Chinese friends to translate the content for me their over-politeness to foreigners came out very strongly. Some of them managed to talk round the subject at great length, others excused themselves, saying that they had not got their glasses with them (the characters were two or three inches high!), or that there were one or two characters they did not know and therefore they could not translate anything at all. A few did give me a reluctant and certainly watered-down version of part of the contents, from which I gathered that some of the criticism was about the length of my hair and my jeans, which were considered too tight to be in accordance with good socialist thinking. I was told that I was more than welcome to take the matter up and they would willingly help me to write my reply in Chinese, which I could then put up. But I found this very difficult because I did not know exactly what was on the posters.

Some time in September 1966, when the Cultural Revolution had been going on for about six months, during which time we foreigners had been effectively isolated from events, there was an announcement. Mao had issued—in the terminology of the day—a 'supreme instruction' which read: 'We must treat foreign experts and their families in the same way as we treat Chinese. We must treat them as equals and as members of our family.'

Until this point in time, those of us who might have wished to exercise them, had had no political rights. We had been stopped from taking any part in the course of political events which, we were told, were an internal affair, a matter for the Chinese and nothing to do with us. A few demonstrations and some confused and confusing meetings concerned with day-to-day affairs were all that came our way.

But Mao's excellent instruction to break down the barriers between the Chinese and foreigners, an instruction directed at the Chinese people, was treated as a piece of political rhetoric, an empty phrase, which is certainly *not* what it was intended to be. Most responsible Chinese took it only as general permission for them to allow us to take part in more meetings without thereby overstepping their competence, which in those unstable days was all too easily done and could lead to serious consequences.

Most foreigners who are at all acquainted with the more recent history of China will have heard of the infamous notice at the entrance to the British colonial park in Shanghai—'No admission to dogs and Chinese'. That time is definitely over. The Chinese are undoubtedly their own masters now, and that particular example of racism and snobbery is in a museum. How then should one interpret the fact that in China today there are buildings, means of transport, shops, restaurants and waiting-rooms where, though there may be no notices prohibiting Chinese from entering, only foreigners are actually *permitted*?

In those circles in China where people have to deal with foreigners professionally, they are very protocol conscious. Foreigners are rated not so much by their country of origin—because we are still all foreigners—as by their standing in their own country, their political standpoint and relationship with China. Foreigners, broadly speaking, are divided into four grades which, if one begins with the lowest, are: 'foreign guest', 'friendly person', 'foreign friend', and finally, for the relevant political VIP, 'foreign comrade'. The nature and number of one's hosts grows with one's status, as does the nature and number of one's means of transport.

When one arrives in China for the first time—ignorant but with an open mind—to live and work here, one comes with expectations of being able to integrate to some extent, to make friends with colleagues and students; friends with whom one can exchange visits and so on. One's illusions are quickly shattered and one soon learns that it would be un-Chinese to be too friendly straight away. A polite distance between host and newly arrived guest is more characteristic. Each has to look the other over.

I have had friends and there have been people I could visit and who visited me, but that was in the China of the 1960s. Even at that time they had to get permission from their unit before visiting or receiving me in their homes; one did not just drop in. And some of these friends, I know, were criticized in the early days of the Cultural Revolution, criticized for having had too close contact with me, a foreigner. In this connection, it was my 'foreignness', not my assumed or real political views, which made it wrong to have close contact with me, and even though foreigners were not considered fair game for criticism there was still an aura of 'foreign devilry' about us which made it incriminating to visit us.

On 8 March 1973, Zhou Enlai made a speech to the foreign experts in the Great Hall of the People in Peking. It was an unofficial impromptu talk and therefore note-taking and the bringing in of tape recorders were forbidden. But someone was brave enough to take it down and, through a Chinese friend who, over the years, had shown himself to be much interested in the relationship of the Chinese with foreigners, I was able to get hold of a copy of the script.

In this speech Zhou Enlai said that the 'supreme instruction' issued by Mao concerning foreigners being treated on equal terms with the Chinese had been annulled by the Central Committee shortly after it was issued. This had been done because certain foreigners, those who later were imprisoned, had been getting involved in a very complicated and difficult political situation. He went on to say:

> More than five years have passed since that decision was made. During that time the political life of our foreign friends has been separated from that of the Chinese. On behalf of the Central Committee I offer apologies to all of you for this. But now we

are liberated. Take, for example, the comrade sitting here. Imagine if he had been released two years ago; would any of you Chinese have dared speak to him? No, you would not, for then if you had, you would have been accused of associating with a suspicious foreigner. There is a woman comrade here who can confirm this. It was through her that I heard about this case. You foreigners may say that you have not been through a difficult time, but you have. You have been excluded and cold-shouldered. We have all been through a process of tempering. Even though you have been excluded you also have been through that process. But at the time it was better for you foreign friends to be outside rather than in. But of course, you were not happy at being excluded; that is understandable.

Zhou Enlai then said how important it was to give foreigners the political and other rights which would put them on the same footing as the Chinese. But discrimination is not done away with by decrees or laws, and he commented on the faults in the attitude of the Chinese towards foreigners and foreign things. He said:

Chairman Mao said recently that we Chinese are often very conservative. We feel that there are so many of us that we prefer to stick together and are unwilling to make contact with foreign friends. Chinese men are unwilling to marry foreign women and Chinese women are even more unwilling to marry foreign men. They stick together. But how can we thus forward world revolution or practise proletarian internationalism? How can we make a real contribution to humanity? This criticism made by Chairman Mao is well grounded. Of course, say our friends, there are reasons for Chinese exclusiveness and hatred of foreigners. For hundreds of years we were subjected to foreign aggression and exploitation. But now, when foreign friends and comrades wish to make contact with us we must show ourselves willing to co-operate and to learn from one another. The Chinese as a race have a natural tendency to keep themselves to themselves. Overseas Chinese have, for decades, lived in Chinatowns, have spoken Chinese, eaten Chinese food, and when they died have sometimes even had their earthly remains sent back to China for burial. This must not continue.

The natural exclusiveness to which Zhou referred is evident within China's own borders, as far as visiting foreigners are concerned. In the sphere of human relations, we are still social outcasts, in reverse. We are treated with a politeness which is so studied as to be at times almost offensive.

There have been instances of foreigners, generally women, who have established a close enough relationship with a Chinese to contemplate marriage. In many of these cases it happens that when the couple go to the authorities to ask permission to marry, the Chinese involved suddenly disappears. He has usually been assigned work in some far distant place so that all contact between the couple is effectively broken off. This is not an expression of 'civil xenophobia', but of the official, if unstated, attitude of the government, in spite of Mao's and Zhou Enlai's well-known points of view and their instructions. Because their attitudes on this subject are well known, there is seldom a direct refusal of a request for a marriage permit. Just a bureaucratic decision which makes it impossible.

When I sit in splendid isolation in the spacious office which the institute has allocated for my exclusive use, when even the dean has to share a room half the size with three or four other people, and think how I am brought here every morning in a car 'class two', it makes me wonder what social contacts I am missing here—in my unit, round the town, in the country. And when I travel about the country in the four-berth compartment I often have to myself, even though there is usually a shortage of seats in the train, I could, from a superficial point of view, see myself as a highly privileged person, who is given every attention by his hosts. And when I visit a commune and people line up along the roadside to clap me, I could imagine that I was getting an insight into the Chinese way of life. That is, if I judged only by external appearances.

One soon gets quite used to being stared at. After a time, one scarcely notices that people are staring as one walks down the street. It is a stare which is neither hostile nor friendly, just a neutral registration of the fact that there goes one of *them*. But I cannot deny that I find it irritating when I am invited to a political meeting directed against Jiang Qing to find myself, as a foreigner, the real basis of the criticisms levelled against her. It is a little difficult to take part in a discussion about how she was a traitor to her country, a reactionary and a fascist when the reason given for these accusations is that she maintained 'illegal contacts' with foreigners, watched foreign films, read foreign books and bought foreign objects. I could take part in a criticism of her leading a life of such luxury as to be beyond the wildest dreams of most Chinese, but it is not her life of luxury which is under criticism, but the fact that her luxuries were mainly of foreign origin. I can sit there and look round at my students and the young teachers and ask myself what effect this constant bombardment against everything foreign is going to have on them in the long run. What effect will it have on their personal opinions, on their internationalism? The majority of them, at some time or another, have almost certainly been shaken vigorously by the arm by their father or mother—I see it happening still—in order to draw attention to a passing foreigner.

During the latter part of the Cultural Revolution it became a serious matter for anyone to have anything to do with a foreigner. Today, the outward manifestations have changed, but the political thinking about foreigners has not. True, I have come here to work, not to lead a social life, but looking back on the evenings and afternoons I have spent with my friends, colleagues and pupils at their houses or at mine, and comparing that time with the elegant play-acting which goes on now, I begin to feel cold shivers running down my spine.

When I eventually departed from the institute, the president, according to protocol, gave a banquet at which he made a farewell speech. Among other polite phrases Xiao Wang translated a particular passage as, 'During the time that you have been here we have had a good relationship with one another.' The president, who speaks excellent English himself, broke off to correct him: 'A good *working* relationship with one another,' he emphasized.

I have at hand a letter. It was written to me by colleagues and pupils shortly after my departure from China during the Cultural Revolution. It is a letter full of self-criticism to the effect that they blame themselves for having laid too much emphasis on my material welfare while I was in China. 'And,' they wrote, 'we neglected to think of you as a human being with social and political needs as well.' They wrote with great clarity about how in discussing our relationship after my departure they realized they had not, in fact, treated me as an equal and a friend, which they had always assured me I was.

But that letter is from another time, another China.

Fragments of Conversation

Heroes, or rather a variety of heroes and heroines, are a constantly recurring theme in education and propaganda, those two overlapping areas of daily life here. The modern Chinese hero differs from earlier political heroes and those in other countries in that less emphasis is placed on physical prowess and more on moral rectitude and disregard of self. It is not the size of their biceps but the purity of their morals which makes them an example to be followed. Over the years a small band of them have become particularly famous, a few on account of incredible valour in times of war or revolution, where an enemy had to be fought and defeated with very few and poor weapons. But the majority of these are famous for their behaviour in everyday situations of work, often very inglorious work, which thus acquires an aura of special importance.

One thing all these heroes have in common is that they are dead. Like saints, heroes are almost always only recognized posthumously, and so the hero is never there to give his account of what actually happened. This is not to say that they are fictitious paragons of virtue created by a wily propaganda department for edification and imitation. It is certain that these people whose names are known by everybody *did* exist and *did* do the things for which they became famous after their death. But one finds oneself asking, is it death which is the ultimate heroic deed, or is there a built-in reluctance to recognize people as heroes while they are still alive? Is it a socialist equivalent to promises of paradise, the promise of being on everyone's lips after death?

'Why has China no living heroes?'

'But we have. There is hardly a factory, a commune or a military unit where there is not one or more worker, peasant or soldier known for his unselfishness, his contributions, in various ways, to the social good. Here in this institute we have a board where people can commend comrades for good deeds.'

'Yes, I saw that today. There were two students named who had been observed cleaning a blocked lavatory by hand although no one had ordered them to do so. They were doing it voluntarily. It wasn't a duty.'

'But in a sense it was. It is everyone's duty to do everything. No one should have to order anyone to do such things. If it comes to it, I suppose no one wants to do an unpleasant job like that, but *someone* has to, and these two students did it. It is to everyone's advantage that they were able to overcome their aversion and do it without being told.'

'But it hardly falls into the category of an heroic deed.'

'In one sense everybody is a hero. At least anyone who so decides can be. But we can hardly put forward every individual who prevails upon himself to do that little bit more than his daily work requires. So we put forward the people. It is the people, the broad masses, who are the heroes in our society.'

'But you still do put forward individuals—both at local level, as in the case of these two students who have done an unpleasant job for the good of the community, and at national level. At the moment Lei Feng turns up everywhere, even in our texts. He was on everybody's lips ten or twelve years ago when I was teaching in Canton. We are using his life and deeds as teaching material again now. All those heroic deeds he is supposed to have carried out anonymously.'

'He *was* a hero, and we know a lot about him. It is possible, of course, that a little has been added to the picture here and there, that he has become, so to speak, a synthesis of many different people. But broadly speaking I believe the stories about him are quite authentic. He was an ordinary young man, a young soldier who, neither physically nor intellectually, was more endowed than others. But he always used such abilities as he had for the benefit of the community, never for himself. That is why his is an example worthy of imitation. And what he did is, after all, no more than anyone could do if they tried. He was no Stakhanov, physically better endowed than the majority. It is moral courage, purity of mind and love of the community which make a hero.'

'But one thing common to all these heroes, which comes up time and again in teaching and propaganda, is that they are dead. It seems that for the hero to have died is almost as important as for him to have done the heroic deeds he did during his lifetime.'

'Of course, that may sometimes be the case. In times of war, for example, where it may be a question of one or more sacrificing their lives in order to save the majority so that they can fight on.'

'But all these heroes we are talking about died not in war, but in everyday life, in peacetime. Zhang Zide, for example, about whom Chairman Mao wrote in 'Serve the People', did not die fighting against the Guomindang, although it was during the revolution, but when a charcoal furnace he was looking after fell on him. Is he really a prototype of the modern hero?'

'One could say that he is the first example. True, he was not known or decorated, he just did his ordinary job steadily and dutifully. But it was a necessary job. It is important that our young people understand that one job is not more "glorious" than another. The glory lies in making the best of what one has got. Looked at in this way, there is no difference between a swineherd and a field-marshal. The field-marshal plans his strategy to win with as little loss of life as possible, while the swineherd and the rice planter see to it that there are rations enough for the soldiers to be able to carry on fighting.'

'I would like to return to the question of death. It seems to me that, from a purely economic point of view, death is less valuable than life. And yet death often seems to be regarded as an essential part of the heroic act. Death is not seen as a tragic ending.'

'It is natural for people to be afraid of death. And it is important for people to learn not to be afraid of anything—not even death, as long as it is for the benefit of the community. No sacrifice is too great for the community. If our heroic troops during the Long March, and through the anti-Japanese war and the revolution had not been able to conquer their fear of death, victory would have been even more narrowly won than it was.'

'It is peacetime now. And the heroes we use in teaching died in peacetime.'

'We cannot ignore the possibility of another war. We must always be prepared for the possibility of that—and for that reason too we must learn not to fear death.'

'The other day we had a text about a young party secretary from an unspecified commune. He was hard-working, loyal to the party, and had the interests of the people at heart. All told, a good party secretary—as one would expect of such a person. But the thing which seems to have made him a hero was his death. Why?'

'Because he died for the benefit of the community.'

'I don't agree. I think that by his death he sabotaged the community. How can a saboteur be a hero?'

'I don't understand. How can you say he was a saboteur? He lived for the people, worked for the people and died for the people. What man can do more?'

'He was ill. He did not die as many other heroes have done, say by stopping a bolting horse that might have caused a catastrophe, or by conquering his fear and carrying out a dangerous piece of work. He had cancer, and it appears from the text that his heroism consisted of his refusing treatment.'

'That's right. He put on one side his own selfish interests.'

'But in this society a person's state of health is not just a matter of self-interest. He was an important member of the community he worked in. From an economic point of view, he was part of the community's resources, on a par with every other member of that community.'

'He decided to carry on with his work to the end instead of giving up, and accepting treatment. If he had accepted treatment he might have become a burden on the medical facilities of the commune, and occupied a bed in the hospital which could have been used for someone who needed treatment more than he.'

'He was seriously ill. He had a right to all possible treatment.'

'His comrades did try to persuade him to accept treatment, but he displayed his outstanding political consciousness by heroically refusing.'

'And that is why he died. Had he accepted treatment, he might have lived longer and done even better work. In fact what he did was to squander one of the valuable resources of the community. It corresponds, figuratively speaking, to throwing away a damaged ploughshare instead of repairing it.'

'I can't agree with you. On the contrary, he struggled with himself and changed his nature, overcame selfishness, fear and pain. He worked to the last in spite of great pain. This he did for the sake of the community.'

'And to the community's loss.'

'No, to the community's gain. He has shown that it is possible to triumph over one's nature. That anything is possible.'

'At the moment there is a national campaign being run called "Learn from Lei Feng". It is not that he performed miracles; as a matter of fact a lot of what he did was rather ordinary. But it is clear that if everyone were a Lei Feng, showed the same concern for saving and re-using things, the same public spirit, lived the same spartan life, and had in addition the same feelings of responsibility towards society, then it would, on a national scale, mean an unbelievable addition to, and saving of, resources. But yesterday I witnessed a scene which, in view of the campaign, had a different outcome from what might have been expected. A lorry was driving along the road outside here laden with planks. The road is uneven and the load shifted so that some of the planks fell off on to the road. The lorry stopped, but a cyclist got to the fallen planks first. I thought I was about to witness a Lei Feng scene, with the cyclist dutifully helping the driver to load the planks on again. But no, he put them under his arm and rode off in the opposite direction. The driver, who had got out, shrugged his shoulders, got in again and drove on.'

'I would make two comments about that. First there is a shortage of building materials at the moment, with everyone building earth-quake shelters. It is impossible to produce enough, but whatever there is is fairly and evenly distributed. My second comment is, why do you think we have to have this campaign? We *aren't* all Lei Fengs yet!'

The young Tai, who is our host during a visit I make to Xishuang-banna, is sitting in the front seat. His upper jaw appears to be full of stainless steel, blue-grey metal front teeth which are a bit too big. On his neck and arms he has tattoo marks, the edges blurred by age. The colours run into one another a bit and have no timbre. I have asked him through Liu, my interpreter, what sort of tattoos they are, and he tells me that they are religious symbols. His parents had them done in the past a long time ago, before liberation—that past which he and so many others tell me about almost daily, but which seldom comes to life because the stories are always impersonal. Just as the present is collective and the individual merges with his back-ground, so the past, in their accounts, is common to them all, enacted on a stage in which the good and oppressed appear opposite the bad and the oppressors.

And the faded symbols embedded in this Tai's skin are a relic of that earlier oppression. They are symbols and invocations which the monks used to order the parents to etch into their children's skin, promising that they would bring good luck and protect against evil spirits. He himself was a monk for a time, he says, but doesn't say when or for how long. It is difficult to find out when or how the monks finally disappeared from this area; whether it was a result of an administrative decision or whether the result of the new social consciousness. In any case, there are no visible signs of Buddhist practice here, such as are found in other parts of South-East Asia.

'The monks were bad men,' I am told. 'They did not work, they oppressed people spiritually and materially. They lived by the labour of others, and they lived well. They traded on people's fear of the unknown, on people's ignorance. We have learned from Marx that religion is the opium of the people. With them we had both material and spiritual opium—two scourges. Double oppression.'

'What happened to the monks? Where are they now?'

'Some left the district; those who did not wish to have to account for their actions. Many joined the reactionary Guomindang army, when it was driven away from here by the People's Liberation Army. Many have been re-educated, and are leading useful lives now. For the people. Look at me. As I said, I have been a monk. Most boys had to be for a time in those days. It was like conscription. Religious conscription, which it was difficult to get out of. It was a way of binding us to them.'

'Did you have missionaries here too?'

'I have heard that there were a few up in the mountains. Some people say they came from France. I don't know, I have never seen one myself. Nor do I know what happened to them. Perhaps they went home.'

'What were they doing up there?'

'I don't know. Well, they were missionaries. They used religion to oppress the people. They had been sent by imperialism. And most people were very frightened of them. They were foreigners. But at that time we were afraid of the Han Chinese too. They were foreigners to us. We were a minority group, and the Han came and ruled over us. The same as the landlords and monks. They were very hard times. We were very oppressed.'

'One of my students said that he had been told that in the past the missionaries were sent to China to carry out medical experiments on the Chinese people.'

'It was certainly missionaries who built the hospitals and such things in China. But not out here. We didn't have any doctors or medicine.'

'Do you think that any of them did good work, helped people in need, or anything like that?'

'Perhaps, but I have no experience of it. I only know what damage was done here in our district.'

'Priests and people like that can't be good people,' interjected Liu. 'It is a contradiction in terms.'

'Isn't that a rather sweeping statement. Don't you think that even a priest—putting his metaphysical misapprehensions to one side—could be a progressive person?'

'The two things are incompatible. One cannot be superstitious, believe in ghosts and that sort of thing, and be progressive. If one is religious then one must be a reactionary. And if one is a reactionary then one must be harmful to the people.'

'I have no axe to grind,' I say, 'but I must say that I know some priests, and have heard of others, who held progressive views.'

'How? I can't see how that could be so. One cannot be two colours at the same time.'

'There are people of different religious persuasions, including practising priests who, for example, believe in socialism, who admire what has been going on in China over the last few years.'

'One cannot be a socialist and a priest at the same time.'

'But I have met two foreign experts in this country who both come from strong religious backgrounds. One in fact has been a practising Roman Catholic priest.'

'Well he can't be any longer. He must have left his church.'

'Of course, he cannot practise as a priest in this country. Neither, as far as I know, is he interested in doing so. But they are both believers and at the same time members of the Communist Party in their own countries.'

'Then they are socialists, not priests.'

'I know that there were a number of foreign missionaries still in China after liberation, and I know that many of them expressed political opinions which were not in the interests of the new China. Those were the ones who were arrested or thrown out of China for subversive activities, espionage, and other things. But I know also that some of the missionaries remained here for a number of years—in fact they were asked to do so.'

'Who asked them?'

'At the beginning of the fifties Zhou Enlai issued a decree that the foreign missionaries who wished to co-operate and would work under the new conditions might remain. Provisionally, for an indefinite period.'

'I don't know very much about what went on in those days.'

'He did it because he recognized that many of these foreigners were carrying out valuable social, or shall we say humanitarian, work which, if looked at from a purely material point of view, was of value to the Chinese people.'

'I've never heard that,' says Liu, pursing his lips in a very sceptical manner; and perhaps it is unfair of me to quote a decision of Zhou Enlai which is really an argument against Liu. It would be difficult for him to declare himself as being in disagreement with his late prime minister. Our conversation lapses. But a few minutes later Liu, our host and the quiet chauffeur engage in a lively discussion in two Chinese dialects which, of course, I cannot follow. The chauffeur uses one arm to gesticulate with, our host turns right round in the front seat to talk to Liu who, from having been sitting back comfortably relaxed, is now sitting bolt upright, taut as a spring. After some heated debating over a mountain and a half, their discussion comes to an end and they all relax again. It is a very hot day. 'Superstition is incompatible with socialism,' says Liu, 'and it always will be.'

Even before the Cultural Revolution had taken shape and gathered momentum, there had been talk of radical changes being imminent. A new kind of citizen was to be created, more in line with the workers and peasants than the scholarly 'mandarin' type of the past.

The 'proletarian intellectual' was the rather incongruous name for this new socialist phenomenon who was gradually to replace the learned academic of the past. By the end of the 1960s, the first experiments were already under way in south China, where pioneers went out into uninhabited areas and built their own schools and universities. Their slogan was 'half work, half study', and these half-grown children of peasants, workers and soldiers were their own architects, builders, teachers, administrators and fund raisers. Building and teaching were carried on without any help from public funds, on waste-land which did not happen to have been taken over by a commune. The land was cultivated, buildings, small factories, workshops and electric power stations shot up, all built with very little money and almost no technical help.

It was not only for practical and economic reasons that this new intellectual was to divide his time between mind and matter. The distinction between the two kinds of work must be got rid of completely; the glory peeled from the academic, the contempt from the manual. This new idea, which gave many young people their first possibility of higher education, spread rapidly at the beginning of the Cultural Revolution. At times it almost developed into a smear campaign against academics of the old school and stories were circulated to show to what a great extent they had been out of touch with reality and therefore with the people.

One such story was about a professor of metallurgy at Qinghua University. He was a highly respected scientist, whose lectures and research were well known throughout the country. He had an assistant whose job it was to demonstrate the metallurgy specimens to the students as required during the lectures. One day, soon after the beginning of the Cultural Revolution, the professor was told that his assistant was an extravagance and that in future he must do his demonstrating himself. And then, of course, it turned out that as he had always had an assistant he had never actually handled the specimens and was incapable of finding the ones he needed. His assistant knew them all by sight, weight and touch and had never bothered to label them. He had the practical experience his superior lacked. The professor then had to admit that he had spent years out of touch with reality and solemnly promised to acquire a better knowledge of his subject through practical work.

This story may or may not be true, but it is certainly typical of a large number of stories which were circulating at that time. And so, in the long run, it became not only a question of creating a new generation of proletarian intellectuals, but also of re-educating the older generation. Their expertise should not be underrated, but their attitude must be changed.

And changed it was over the years, following the establishment of the 'May 7th Cadre Schools', which are really labour units connected, as a rule, with one's place of work, but often geographically remote from it. For a number of years now they have been used as places of re-education to which intellectuals of various categories are sent for a shorter or longer time according to how great their need is felt to be. The *Reader's Digest* would no doubt see these cadre schools as penal institutions, and detention there as the consequence of a harsh and unjust sentence. The reality is rather different:

I am sitting on a bench in Peking's Lotus Park, the place where one of the first visible signs of the public reaction to the fall of the 'Four' was to be seen. Here, soon after their downfall, one could see young men and women holding hands, arms round waists or even kissing each other—things which had certainly not been seen in public places for many years.

An elderly man is sitting beside me. He has an aristocratic profile, his small round glasses straddling a nose which is surprisingly un-Chinese. He does not use his hands as he speaks; they rest slender and refined, showing the brown spots of old age, on his knees. There is an air of resignation about him and he pays no attention to

the passers-by who occasionally stop and look at us—staring at a
Chinese speaking to a foreigner, which might have made him feel
uncomfortable had he been a younger man.

'Although I was here in the days of the Cultural Revolution,
being a foreigner who did not speak the language I felt, in many
ways, outside it. I have often wanted to know what was really going
on,' I say.

'So many articles have been written about the Cultural Revolution.
I am sure you have read many of them. Of course a great deal did
happen. There was the struggle between the two lines. A struggle
about whether China should continue as a socialist society, or
whether she should change her colour. It was a mighty battle.'

'I know, and I have done my best to understand the political
situation as it then existed. But I would very much like to hear a
more personal account. What, for instance, were your experiences?'

He smiles without looking at me, gazing at the gravel in front of
the bench.

'Personally? Well, so much happened. Were you never subject to
criticism at that time? Most of us were and had to defend ourselves
as best we could. It was sometimes very difficult. I am not a young
man any more. In fact, it won't be many years before I am seventy,
if I live that long, which I probably will. Fortunately my health is
good, though the doctor tells me that my blood pressure is too high.
Perhaps you know that a slightly raised blood pressure is common
among the Chinese. But I no longer work as hard as I did.'

'What happened to you during the Cultural Revolution? How did
you see it—as a step forward?'

'As I said, it was a major shake-up of the whole society. I think I
was already too old to be able to understand properly what it was
all about. I belong to a different generation. Like many others, at
one stage I was sent to a cadre school.'

'How long were you there?'

'Ah,' he laughs, 'quite a long time. It may be that I did not see
the need for it. Then. As I said, things happened very quickly. I
found it hard to keep up. I suppose it is easier for young people to
adjust.'

'Did you feel being sent to the cadre school was an injustice?'

'I don't believe there are many serious injustices in our society.
And if it was an injustice in my case, then it was an injustice in
thousands of cases—no, hundreds of thousands of cases, and I don't
believe injustice on that scale goes on in China. But of course it was

a revolution. And we knew from our beloved late Chairman Mao that a revolution is not a tea party.'

'Were you subject to criticism from your colleagues and students?'

'Most people were. That's what it was all about for a long time. And if it comes to it, I could see the justification for much of the criticism. Much of it.'

'What was the criticism in your own case?'

Again that distant smile which takes the place of words and avoids description of a reality which is too far away to be present, and too near to be described.

'I don't think I am a bad person, but, as I said, I belong to a different generation. Had I wished to I could easily have left China at the time of liberation. People who wanted to leave had nearly two years in which to do so, when the frontiers were still open. But I wanted to stay here and work for socialism, even though I didn't know much about it at that time. I am not a hero, nor a particularly good person, but I have done what I could to become so. During the first few years after liberation, I taught, because I had a trade I could teach. One could say that the reward for such work at that time was the feeling of pride in one's country it gave one. We did not get any money. There were no funds for that to begin with. But we got a regular ration of rice which was quite adequate and a roof over our heads. And the joy and excitement of helping to build a new China was very great. You could say that was our salary. And what more did we need? Before liberation most people were far worse off.'

'What was your background, your class, before liberation?'

He laughs aloud at my want of tact. 'I would have thought you must know us Chinese well enough to know that we do not talk about ourselves. Well, I think I can say that we were relatively well off, but we did not exploit people. I have always worked.'

'Did you have to work in the cadre school?'

'I was unaccustomed to the kind of work there.'

'What did you learn?'

'I learned that a peasant's work is very hard. And I learned that when one is getting on and has never tried it before, rice planting can be very painful. It is something to do with the fact that one's body finds it difficult to adjust to the working positions necessary. Apart from that I read and re-read Marx and Lenin and the works of Chairman Mao. Many times. I am very well versed in these works now. But I do find it difficult putting what I have learned into practice. Everything seems to move so fast these days I find it hard to keep up. I spent more than four years at the cadre school.'

'Was the Cultural Revolution necessary? Do you think it was a good thing for China, looking at what has come out of it?'

'It was necessary. I mean it happened, didn't it. But I suppose nowadays it must be difficult for people to make up their minds about it. Most have been affected in one way or another. I suppose I feel the same as many others I know. For me the Cultural Revolution is almost invisible.'

A group of my students has just returned from 'open-door school'— a form of practical work where they have an opportunity of putting into practice the subject they are studying. These particular students have spent several weeks in Canton at the biannual trade fair where they had jobs such as arranging accommodation and acting as assistant interpreters.

They are gathered in our flat at one of the pre-arranged visits we have from time to time, telling us all about it. They have, as usual, to be strongly pressed to take the tea, fruit and cakes we have provided for them. Their manners are impeccable, as they sit on the edge of the chairs, leaning forward in an attempt to follow the conversation which leaps round the room. They are not used to this situation, and they have to concentrate hard in order just to understand the words.

We have these gatherings at irregular intervals. They are one of the few possibilities we have of creating the linguistic milieu we so sadly lack at the institute. On these occasions we do our best to get away from the atmosphere of the classroom and to use the language spontaneously. With this in mind we ask them not to bring notebooks with them, which, of course, makes things more difficult for them. The school leaders have dubbed these sessions 'free speech'.

'How was it in Canton?' I ask. I have got used to calling it Canton again. There was a time, during the Cultural Revolution, when I was put right every time I used that name: the name of the town is Guangzhou, I was told; Canton is a bad English transcription, a mark of imperialism. Now most people call it Canton again, but I have had some difficulty in getting over the many corrections I had in the past.

'Very interesting,' one of them manages to say after half a minute of agonized silence waiting for someone to speak. There are certain things in their use of the language one has to get used to, and one is their interpretation of the word 'interesting'. When my students use it, it means 'peculiar' or 'amusing' with an element of the unexpected and the absurd about it. What was 'interesting' turned out to be the foreign businessmen, their behaviour and their preconceived ideas.

'I was in the group which allocated rooms in the hotels,' says one. 'It was very interesting to see the problems there were. Every year more and more foreign visitors come to the trade fairs and unfortunately there are not enough rooms to go round. And, just imagine, many of the foreign businessmen were *angry* at having to share a room with someone. That is very difficult for us to understand.'

'And there was one who thought it was only a question of money. He said he didn't care what it cost, he wanted a large room to himself. The room he wanted had been given to a foreign businesswoman. She said he could share, she didn't mind—so our leader asked if they were married. They said they were, so we asked to see the piece of paper which said they were married, otherwise they would have to go to the office in Canton where people get married. But they didn't want to. That was very interesting.'

'How do you conduct your business deals with the foreigners?' I ask.

A shy and serious young man who so far has not said anything is pushed forward. The leader, who always joins us for these 'free speech' exercises tries, in a quiet and unobtrusive manner, to see that each of them speaks at least once during the course of the afternoon.

The young man speaks like one of the textbooks it is our aim to get him away from.

'China's foreign trade is flourishing. It is a fundamental principle in all our business negotiations with foreigners that they should be conducted to the benefit and advantage of both parties. Our motto is, "Friendship first, business second." It is very important to cultivate friendly relations.'

He speaks with the steady monotony of one who has learned something by heart, hesitating occasionally to turn an invisible page with a wet thumb.

'Yes!' exclaims one of the others. 'We always begin our meetings with a banquet before talking business. That way we get friendship over on the first day. From then on it's business.'

Evening by the Pearl River

The big ocean-going ships are still anchored there, and the river which carries produce to the sea from the fields of the communes in the north and industrial goods from Canton in the south flows wide and deep before me. The huge hulls, with lanterns on their long derricks, lie there, and even after dark, invisible lighters chug their way out to them with goods for their holds. The water carries the songs of the workers and in the darkness one can hear the creaking of the oars propelling the sampans forward, and see the hurricane lamps dangling on their strings from the woven roofs.

The scene is the same. The time is different. Years have passed since I left Canton and here I am again, standing on the banks of the little island Shamian which lies in the middle of the city. I lived here for two years then, now I am on a flying visit.

In those days too I spent many evenings on this deserted wharf. I feel quiet of a different kind in me now, and in the city. Behind me stand the few large houses to be found on the island. Among them the former British Consulate built when the British ruled here, still bearing the monogram of George V on its wrought-iron railings.

There were the many working days when the young soldier, Lao Li, whose job it was, met me in the morning at the end of the foot-bridge and drove me to the school at the foot of the White Cloud Mountain. Afternoons and evenings were spent with pupils and friends visiting me here on the island. When it was fine we used to sit on the flat roof of my house with a view over the whole island and a long way up and down the river. All day it was I who taught them, practised with them, lectured to them, but in the evenings and in the holidays it was they who talked. About themselves, about China.

It gave me a certain satisfaction to be the only foreigner here. I had put Europe behind me and wished no more contact with it than I myself chose to have. It would have been crazy to have nursed ideas of any kind of integration here, but I was glad of the isolation from my background which gave me the chance to be anything but alone.

Then one day there was a girl. She was standing in the large empty hall which was on the ground floor of my house. She had ice-blue eyes and bright red lips under a lot of unruly curly black hair. She was the first European I had seen in many months. And there she was, standing just inside the door, as if she had dropped from the sky. I was on my way to work, and as I passed her she turned and said, 'I go too.'

Lao Li, who, as usual, was sitting on the bonnet of the car waiting, opened the door for me and got into the driver's seat. The door on her side was locked, and as I leaned over to open it from the inside Lao Li turned and took my hand away. He pointed to a car standing on the other side of the road, indicating that it was for her. She made it clear to me in a mixture of French and English that she had no intention of going alone, and finally Lao Li reluctantly let her get in. She did not speak during the first quarter of an hour, but sat with her hand on her red lacquered lips and stared out of the window.

Then, with a sudden movement as if she had forgotten something, she began feverishly searching in her handbag. She took out a long shiny object and moved it in my direction as if to give it to me, and as she did so, the blade of a flick-knife flashed.

'You have one too?' she asked.

'No, I haven't,' I said. 'I don't feel the need of any such thing.'

'I need,' she said, still pointing it at me.

'What for?'

She pointed it at Lao Li's neck and then at the people we were passing, making little chopping movements as if she were counting them.

'I don't think you will find it necessary,' I said. 'I don't think anyone has found such a thing necessary.'

She smiled, as much as to say that I did not understand, folded it up and put it away again. We completed the journey in silence.

At school I was told that she was a new teacher. Nobody could—or would—tell me anything about her. Probably they knew as little about her as they had done about me when I first arrived. But I was told that she had instructions to use her own car in future. It seemed to me rather extravagant to use two cars where one would do but that is one of the manifestations of the over-politeness of the Chinese to their guests. As far as possible one nationality is not obliged to accept the company of another.

She had the flat next to mine, but I hardly ever saw her. Apparently she never ate in the canteen in the house, nor did I see her in any of the little restaurants which had been rigged up in some of the nearby mansions. I didn't know her name nor where she came from. I was grateful that she did not threaten my isolation from the Western world with her presence.

A few days after my first meeting with her I was told that she had been suspended. Her methods of discipline had been unacceptable. Pupils who made a mistake she had sent outside, where they had to stand in the tropical sun and repeat the sentence they had got wrong over and over again. During her very first lesson she had asked one of the pupils to go out and cut a bamboo, which she used to bang on her desk every time anyone made a mistake. The school had requested her to refrain from such methods, and she had replied that she had the right to use whatever methods she thought fit. Following this she was suspended and we were waiting for an official from Peking to come and talk to her.

A suave official came, and was met by an explosion. She was waiting for him in her flat, and when he knocked she threw the door open, and I could see her from my flat chasing him down the corridor with a mop raised above her head and her hair full of strips of paper torn from the *People's Daily*. She shouted and screamed abuse at him, calling him a thief and a murderer, followed by streams of abuse of China and the whole of the Eastern world. After a time the house fell silent and some of the staff came to pack her things.

'She had a problem,' they said briefly to me later. 'Unfortunately we had to send her home.'

It was during the weeks following this incident that my way of life changed completely. I found myself totally isolated. One morning, as I was going through the door to go to work, the telephone rang. It was a call from the school saying that I need not go in that day. There was going to be a meeting, I was told. This had happened once or twice before, but during the course of the last few days I had had a feeling that something out of the ordinary was afoot. One of my best pupils, a girl of fourteen or fifteen, had for several months been giving me every week, secretly, a notebook with exercises in it which she had asked me to read and comment on. It consisted usually of several pages of writing—an essay, poetry, or a trans-lation—all of it over and above her normal school work. She was bright and keen to get on and did this extra work out of interest in the subject. In different circumstances, in another country, other

motives for this apparently furtive pupil/teacher relationship might
have been suspected.

In fact, there was no necessity for the secrecy. Everything she
wrote was perfectly innocent. I just assumed that she felt shy about
it. And then one day, when she usually gave me a book and got last
week's back with my comments, she took the one I handed to her,
stuffed it in her bag without giving me one in return, and said: 'I
haven't written anything this week, and it may be a little while before
I do again. As you probably know, a lot of things are happening in
the cultural field just now, and at this moment it is difficult for us to
know what we are allowed to write about. That's why I am stopping
for the present.'

This was my first intimation of the Cultural Revolution which
swept over us shortly afterwards. With it came my complete isolation.
I sat on my island, with no contact with my school, but could see
that *something* was happening. It manifested itself in the form of
parades through the streets with shouting and singing which I did
not understand. Next door to my house was an old Anglican church
which had been converted into a factory; the factory now disappeared, and long cords were stretched across the aisle on which
groups and individuals hung sheets of coloured paper with characters
inscribed on them. The whole aisle became a labyrinth of these
coloured papers which I could not read. I walked about blind and
deaf, and had no idea what was going on.

After another few days the growing revolution seemed to be
making its own rules. Door-keepers arrived at the church and all the
other large halls which were being used in the same manner and it
appeared that their sole duty was to keep out foreigners. But I was
the only one.

Some days later a man unknown to me arrived with my salary
and a message. The message was that I should keep calm, that there
was no need to worry and that I would be told before long what was
going on.

The little restaurants on the island had put up their shutters, and
the façade along the promenade, which stretched the length of
Shamian, was plastered with newspapers. Two of the cooks in the
house canteen prepared my meals and a new waiter who spoke not a
word of English put them silently on my table three times a day.

I spent most evenings down by the river. This revolution, which as
far as I was concerned had neither name nor face as yet, had not
affected the river people as far as I could see. The clusters of labouring

sampans which throughout the day either drifted with the current or struggled against it, still tied up on the wharf as dusk descended, layer upon layer, forming a vast area of boats on the black water under my window. Whole families lived on these boats, ate, slept, and multiplied in the space of a few square yards; thousands of them, each with its little lantern glowing in the dark. Perhaps they knew as little as I, or even less. I told myself that our common ignorance of what was going on was a bond between us. When some of them clambered up to the top of the bank where I was sitting, we would smoke a cigarette together, look at the river and smile. We had long since stopped trying to communicate by means of language.

In due course I received the promised communication. It was a masterpiece of non-information presented by a completely faceless individual. A colleague knocked on my door. I was glad to see him but he did not react at all as I had expected. He said briefly that there was a man who wished to speak to me and that he himself was there only to interpret.

In the little sitting-room of the house next door, with armchairs lined up against the walls, sat an expressionless man. He asked me to be seated and said that he had come to tell me what was going on. He did not tell me his name, or where he came from, and his statement and the interpreting of it went at such a rate that there was no chance for me either to ask questions or make comments.

'The situation is fine,' he began, and when I saw how tense he was and thought of all the things which had been going on round me in the last few days, I thought to myself that this was a masterpiece in contradiction for a start. He went on to say that this was to be regarded as an informal conversation and it would, therefore, not be necessary for me to take notes. Meanwhile, two young cadres, one on each side of him, wrote down everything he said, as is the practice at official meetings. Even my colleague, who interpreted coolly and efficiently, behaving as though he did not know me, wrote down every word he translated.

His informal account of what was happening lasted about three hours and told me nothing. He said that discussions were going on about educational reforms and that was why my school was closed. He did say that there was the possibility of changes in leadership in certain ministries, of which he could give me no details. Textbooks would have to be revised to some extent but everything was under control and the situation was fine.

He had, in the neatest possible way, avoided compromising him-

1. The friendliness shown by one's host when one pays a 'private' visit is often somewhat dampened by the presence of one's official companions.

A good interpreter can bring host and guest closer together by translating in the first person, while the distance is increased by the interpreter who uses the third person. The biggest barrier, apart from the language, is probably the crowd of local and visiting responsible comrades. 'You must take a picture of him,' they say, removing themselves from the camera's eye; but their presence is still felt in the little room, and they lead the conversation on behalf of the family who have been given the job of being the village's hospitable home.

An arid routine often seems to mark those homes which are liable to entertain foreign visitors. They must be the only houses in the village where the families regularly have to pick up burn-out flashbulbs and crumpled Kodak wrappers.

2. There are spectators in Peking.

In the streets at right angles to the wide Chang An Boulevard, between the Emperor's Palace and the main station, lie the ministries, shops and offices where foreigners do business. Round a parking place where chauffeurs are polishing their cars ready for high-ranking military people and foreign diplomats is a motionless but constantly changing crowd of onlookers. The place is an arena, a gathering point in Peking, which is no longer one big town but a collection of small ones.

Foreigners are still news, arouse curiosity and interest, not only in the people from far-off provinces, who are here to shop or are members of delegations to the capital, but also in the city's own inhabitants.

3. The tropical sun beats down on the bamboo shutters of of the cool room in which we sit drinking hot tea.

They are both directors of the same factory, a machine-tool plant and smithy near the Laos border. She belongs to one of the local minority groups, he to the great Han people, who are the majority in China. Even in this local context where he is one of only a small group, hers is still referred to as being a minority. He has been 'imported' from Shanghai to lead and direct the local industry. He says that he and his co-director are equal in every way: economically, culturally and politically. She agrees with a smiling nod when he says that differences in sex and nationality are of no importance. It is he who speaks. I only hear her voice when we say goodbye.

4. Children born since liberation are periodically told stories about the bad old days which they never knew. Assessment of the Cultural Revolution still hangs fire, but perhaps the day will come when it in its turn will be looked upon as a bad time, when there will be no one living who can remember the days before liberation, and the storytellers will tell stories about the Cultural Revolution to an audience which has yet to experience bad times.

5. *Supported on the right leg, the left alternately takes a step forward and a step backward on the narrow plank across the sampan. The oars, miraculously held together with only an incredibly short overlap, push the creaking little boat through the muddy water.*

Here, with one's back to the mainland, one is not aware of the Cultural Revolution. But a long finger from the big university on the other side of the river has picked out the Dragon Boat Festival as being a reactionary relic of feudal times. The river people have dragged their long painted boats on land and taken off the dragons decorating the bow.

The river is for work.

6. Shanghai trembles. It is the Cultural Revolution and battalions of demonstrators are marching through the streets, passing one another on the quayside, under the imposing buildings along the waterfront; mighty mansions, out of place here, so far from Victorian London.

It was these waves of people, from this town and that time, which produced the 'Gang of Four'. It was here that I came across anti-Semitism in China for the first time; strange, so far from my own part of the world. One of my hosts was telling me about the buildings and ended by saying that they were financed by a Jew.

'What nationality?' I asked.

'Well, a Jew,' he replied. 'A capitalist.'

7. 'In the new China, women are completely emancipated. A woman is no longer subservient to the man but is on equal footing with him. She is no longer solely responsible for those things which have been traditionally regarded as woman's work. In the modern family the man has the same responsibility for cleaning, cooking and looking after the children as the woman.'

8. Enemy of the People, 1977. Seen in the window of a state shop.

9. They were not playing football on the green that day, they were playing foreign politics. The enemy was · obvious in masks and well-reproduced foreign uniforms. The enemy was American imperialism, and the producers had made them up with bright green cheeks and large white paper noses. The bombs they carried in their belts were labelled US, and the soldiers of the Liberation Army who marched them round in front of us had heroic red cheeks. There was great applause in the huge stadium every time one of the enemy stumbled, or turned to his captors expressing cowardly fear.

It was not far from real life and outside the stadium children spat at the foreign soldiers, even though they were only on their way back to the dressing-room.

My students asked me to take the part of the capitalist in a school play we were producing. It was not a popular part. No one wanted it.

10. *A solitary soldier in civilian dress, without the red star on his cap
or the red rectangle on his collar, has slipped into the queue standing in
front of the street photographer outside the Summer Palace.*

*One is usually turned away if one attempts to take pictures of the
People's Army. One of the reasons given is that they are military secrets,
their large numbers and obvious presence everywhere notwithstanding.
But it is difficult for them to object when they are themselves standing in
front of a camera.*

*On the streets one gets the impression that the uniform in itself is a
hindrance to the friendly, if reserved, attitude, mixed with curiosity,
which one meets among civilians. It is difficult to catch the eye of a
soldier, or get a smile from him.*

11. During the first days of the Cultural Revolution.

The weekly concerts of Western classical music which took place on the banks of the river have been discontinued. They say the sounds are decadent. I can hear the music of the revolution coming from the buildings opposite my verandah. There is a congress of musicians of the revolution going on and they are practising. The instruments are traditional Chinese, but the cadences are too harsh and not really suitable for them.

Following the morning concert, the police use our traffic-free island for a parade ground and target practice. They march in rubber-soled shoes and respond to quiet commands. The only sound audible from their weapons is the metallic click of the flint along the row of men, rather like the roll of a drum.

Up and down the streets of the neighbourhood. the first big wall newspapers flaunt their exclamation marks. It is difficult to know what is going to happen, but somehow one does not feel that these white jackets represent the state arming itself against the people.

Later, Red Guards and civilians took over many of their functions.

12. *She is about the same age as revolutionary China.*
   In her time Liu Shaoqi has been honoured and thrown out. Lin Biao has
been honoured and thrown out. Deng Xiaoping has been three times
honoured, twice thrown out. Jiang Qing has been honoured and thrown out.
   She is carrying her baby on her back; in her basket she has food. In the
streets round her there are placards hailing China's new leaders.
   It is a long way to Peking, and the seat of power.

13.There is a difference between the support given by a family and that offered by the community as a whole.

Life in big cities is often lived on doorsteps, in doorways, where, with home at one's back, one can observe and follow what is going on outside. From the doorstep one can quickly take cover if a foreign camera comes too near.

One of the side-effects of the earthquake has been to drag people half-way out of their houses. Second dwellings, rows of clay huts, have been built by the city people along the pavements. Perhaps it is this new development in private life which has led the authorities to put notices on the emergency buildings, asking for moderation in sexual activity.

14. He does not understand the treatment, but he knows who made it possible. With great concentration he sits at the classical instrument, the 'butterfly', which is a cross between a xylophone and a harp.

He is demonstrating for us, at the school for the deaf, that acupuncture has reduced his congenital deafness to the extent that he can now distinguish one tone from another. Every morning he has needles inserted behind his ears, and he himself directs the therapist to the right spot.

After his solo he bows respectfully to the portrait on the wall. He has no doubt about who has given him his new-found hearing.

15. *A student says: 'We can learn a lot from the peasants. We can learn about practical work, about the past and about self-sacrifice. At the same time we must not lose sight of the fact that the peasants still have a great many old-fashioned ideas and customs. We must be on our guard against private enterprise creeping in among them and we must see to it that the broad masses never lose sight of the target.'*

This student has two pairs of leather shoes and a Swiss wristwatch. He has learned a foreign language which will enable him to earn his living in the future. In a few years he may be selling the products of the peasants to foreign businessmen and be buying technical equipment for the peasants' fields. Those fields in which he will hardly ever set foot again in the early morning mist, with pails of night soil dangling from his carrying pole.

16. *'Let it be possible for every woman who can work to take her place on the labour front, on the principle of equal pay for equal work. This ought to be carried out as soon as possible.'*

—*Mao Tse-tung*

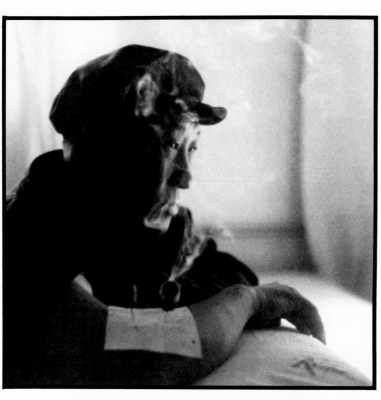

17. The case notes, written in exercise books, are lying on a little table outside the clinic. My students laugh in amazement when I tell them that in the West these notes are regarded as confidential between doctor and patient.

'Why on earth should illness be a secret? It isn't as if there was anything to hide.'

None of the patients in the clinic take the slightest notice when we roll up to watch the examinations and treatment. Modesty, confidentiality, lie in other fields.

18. In the cool temple of the past, a worn statue of Buddha and an old board game played by old men.

Outside, a mass meeting condemning the 'Gang of Four' beneath a clear warm heaven. In their time, chess was decadent and bourgeois, as was the use of a knife and fork, leather shoes, foreign music and foreign customs.

Now one can play chess again in public places.

19. 'I belong to the Bo-lan minority. In the past I was a serf, but since the liberation of our region I have my full rights. Before, I was afraid of the Han people, I had always been told: "Never take a stone for a pillow or a Han for a friend."

'When the Liberation Army came I fled to the mountains—it took time for me to realize what good they brought. My nationality was the most despised, and I must never speak to strangers unless they first spoke to me. And if I did speak to them I had to address them as "Mother" and "Father", even if they were only children. We could not marry any other nationality. We can now. If a Han marries one of our minority group, the children will be considered as belonging to the minority group. If a man from one minority group marries a woman from a different minority group, their children take the nationality of the father. That is our custom.

'But it is not often that a member of a minority group marries a member of the Han people.'

20. *'The underlying motive of many socialists, **I** believe, is simply a hypertrophied sense of order. The present state of affairs offends them not because it causes misery, still less because it makes freedom impossible, but because it is untidy; what they desire, basically, is to reduce the world to something resembling a chessboard.'*
—*George Orwell*

self, or giving me any information. He ended by saying that if I had any questions he would be glad to try and answer them at our next meeting. But, he said, he would prefer to have them in writing a few days in advance. I could hand them to the 'relevant competent authority'.

The pillar of stone with the human face got up, his stenographers put their pads in their pockets and they all left, together with my friend who had acted as interpreter. I spent the rest of that day, and all the next, trying to make up my mind whether he had said anything or not, whether, if I peeled off the layers of camouflage, I would find any real information.

That peace which I had begun to find as a result of my now fairly prolonged stay here began to tremble. During the day I had walked round the town and had bumped into several little processions headed by one or more people wearing dunce's caps and with placards hanging round their necks. I got out of the way when I met them for it was quite clear that I was not meant to see them. I was not to know what it was all about.

One day there were two of us at my little round dining-table. She was from somewhere in Europe and had had the same kind of job as I somewhere else. Some time before all this began she had asked for a transfer. Having been, like myself, out of contact and work for many weeks, she was suddenly informed that for the moment she would be transferred to Canton until things had settled down. She might or might not be working here. She was low and dispirited when she first turned up and we had exchanged identical questions. What do you know? What is going on? Is it true that there are riots in Peking? Have you had any contact with your unit? How long do you think it will go on like this? We had both found someone with whom we could share our ignorance.

We kept ourselves to ourselves, went our separate ways during the day, met at grossly luxurious meals in the canteen, exchanged small talk of no value to either of us; both felt we were in a way outraging public decency by walking round the town like political peeping Toms, without the satisfaction of being able to see anything. We neither saw anything nor were caught in the act.

We were still the only occupants of the twenty-bedroomed house. The cooks prepared food for us and the staff remaining there to wait on us, including a couple of lift attendants who had nothing to do because our flats were on the first floor. A corner of the former bank premises had been equipped as a hairdresser's for the people who should have been living there. There were receptionists at the long empty counter, a number of cleaners. There were some gardeners belonging to the house who looked after the flowerbeds and some handymen, electricians, carpenters and blacksmiths standing by in case something should need repairing.

One evening in one of the unbelievable rainstorms which indicate the change of season in the tropics, we went for a walk round the island. One of the white-coated girls from the reception desk who was standing in the doorway shook her head at us as we passed. In weather such as this things are transposed: the dull tarred roofs of the sampans glisten, while the river which normally reflects the light becomes dark and dull. Some of the boat people had climbed ashore as usual that evening and were sitting in groups round a hurricane lamp, playing cards on the wet gravel under a canopy of crumpled oilskins.

We walked along talking as usual about what a difference it would make if only we had access to Western newspapers. Neither of us wanted to go home, to leave China. We both felt heavy as falling rock and at the same time as if floating in a vacuum. We touched one another under a banian tree which was no protection against the rain, walked on ankle-deep in water and ended up knee-deep at the bottom of some steps behind the church. There was an enamel sign furrowed with thirty years of rust which informed us that behind this shuttered door one could buy the *New York Herald Tribune* and *Life International*. And in that little cave we clung convulsively to one another's wet bodies, leaning against the rusty railings. A few hurried movements which blanked us both out, and moments later we could walk back to the house and nod to the white-coated girl who had not stirred since we left.

This evening I walk into the hallway, but see none of the faces I knew in those days. The church has become a factory again. People are sitting about in the sultry evening, with their trouser legs rolled up, and gaze intently at the passing foreigner. George V's monogram is still there, but only the corners of the *Herald Tribune* sign remain.

Journey Home, the Day After

I am sitting outside the sheds where the institute's lorries are kept, chatting with Zhu. He is a young teacher who has not yet been given any pupils. He is stripped to the waist and has a cloth tied round his head to stop the sweat running into his eyes. He is busy making moulds for the concrete rafters to be used in the new single-storey dormitories which are under construction. About fifty moulds stand drying in the sun, and behind us, on the other side of the dusty sports ground, several hundred students and teachers are casting the foundations for the buildings. The big trumpet-shaped loudspeakers, which can reach every corner of the area, are buzzing idly in the noonday heat. Someone has forgotten to switch them off.

Zhu explains the reason for building the new dormitories. It is the earthquake again. The colossus behind the factory which houses more than a thousand students on four floors has only one staircase. The new building will have only one floor.

'It will be much safer like that because it would be possible to get out of the windows if it happened again. The last time, when there was the big earthquake in Tangshan, some comrades living on the top floor wanted to jump out and had to be restrained by force.

'And we are responsible for the safety of the students. Many are still afraid; that is why we are speeding up the construction of the new buildings. The danger is not yet over. But there is a shortage of building materials. Imagine how many new buildings have to be constructed—the whole of Tangshan will have to be rebuilt. But we have a great advantage in being a socialist country.

'If a catastrophe of that magnitude had happened in a capitalist country there would still be the same shortage of building materials; there would be no difference there. The difference is that with us there cannot be a black market in the necessary materials. We are all equal here and it is up to the central government to apportion the materials available and to get extra production going.

'In a capitalist country, the catastrophe would bring increased wealth to a few, the demand for whose products would suddenly escalate, and increased hardship to the many who had already been hit.'

There is a lot of talk about earthquakes these days, although we have managed to put some distance between us and the 'Big One'. We discuss signs and portents, not in theoretical terms, but quite concretely. A whole system of observers has been built up, tens of thousands all over the country who, while doing their daily work as usual, keep an eye open for the little signs which, from experience, are thought to mean sudden changes of a geological nature. Certain animals are known to be particularly sensitive: pandas curl up and cry and animals which normally live in burrows or go into hibernation emerge, all—according to the latest theories—in sufficiently good time to alert people.

But it seems that, for one reason or another, the 'Big One' was not predicted. Zhu continues:

'There are some who say it could have been. But the "Gang of Four" deliberately opposed an alarm. The rumour goes that they knew there was a big earthquake on the way but thought it would be politically useful. I don't know if this is true; so many things are said about the "Gang of Four". It is also said that they were opposed to rescue work—but we are told that the rescue work was put in hand immediately and was carried out very efficiently. How that goes with the "Four" opposing it I don't know. But rumours are often contradictory.

'As a matter of fact, I happen to know that it went ahead quickly. I am from Tangshan myself, or nearby at least. I wasn't at home when it happened, I was here at the institute. We were nearly thrown out of our beds in the teachers' dormitory. There were some who cried and a few who panicked, but by and large it went all right.

'We got everyone out and the institute's doctors went round giving first-aid. No one, in fact, was badly hurt; it was mostly reassurance they were in need of. There was one death. An old teacher who wasn't quite quick enough and was hit on the head by falling masonry as he left the building.

'Then there was a long wait. We all had to sit outside until it got light and then we were told what had happened—that it was Tangshan which had been hit. I was very upset and wanted to go home at once to try and find my family and see if they were all right. We Chinese often say that we fear nothing, and no difficulties will stop us. I suppose that is true if one is speaking of us as a nation but, naturally, as individuals we do feel fear and unhappiness.

'Well, I wanted to go home. I tried ringing on the institute's phone to find if there was any possibility of getting through to Tangshan, but of course there wasn't. All lines of communication were broken and if any other than the radio had still been open, they would have been reserved for the use of the rescue workers.

'One of the students found me here on the square in the early morning. He wanted to go home too; he also came from Tangshan. He cried a lot and I felt responsible for him, both as a teacher and as a comrade.

'He asked me what I thought he ought to do. I didn't know what to do myself. I was miserable, and wanted to cry, but I found strength to help him. "Come on, we'll walk," I said, and he cried even more and said we couldn't possibly walk all the way to Tangshan, it's more than a hundred kilometres, and I said that if Chairman Mao and Zhou Enlai at the head of the Liberation Army could walk and fight for more than ten thousand kilometres over the roughest and most difficult territory in China, then we two could walk those few kilometres to Tangshan.

'Perhaps we were putting our own interests above those of the community; perhaps we could have been of some use in Peking. We didn't know how much damage had been done here. But we did know, without knowing any details, that it was Tangshan which had been worst hit.

'We began to walk. The young man had wanted to bring some things with him, but I told him it would be a long and arduous journey. We had to go as we were without taking anything with us.

'Even that morning, only a few hours after it had happened, people were hard at work on the roads out of Peking building earthquake shelters. Some were mixing mud for bricks, others cutting bamboo and felling trees. On the roadside, people were at work with spades and baskets full of earth, and temporary shelters were being made out of tarpaulins.

'We did not even try to take the train. The boy suggested we should go to the station first in case there was a train, but I knew that either the lines would have been destroyed or, if by a miracle they were intact, then the trains would be for doctors and nurses and other people doing rescue work. He understood, and of course I understood him too. He was very unhappy and thought only of his family, whom he loved.

'When we had walked for some hours, big military lorries began thundering past us, but in the wrong direction. We learned later that they were transporting the casualties from Tangshan to Peking, and I thought to myself that if they were driving full to Peking then perhaps they would be driving back empty later. Some hours later convoys did begin to appear going in our direction, but they were full of rescue teams. Eventually, when we had been walking for most of the day, a couple of empty lorries passed us and one picked us up. The driver explained that he could only get to the outskirts of Tangshan, many kilometres from our destination, because all the roads had been destroyed. After that we would have to manage as best we could. It was not a very long lift we got, but it gave us a little rest.

'We were put down late in the evening. There was not a house to be seen, only ruins. I told the boy he must pull himself together, because we would have to walk the rest of the way now, and it would be hard. There was nothing left of the road. We had to scramble over piles of rubble and there were no lights. It rained. He was very quiet. I tried to keep his courage up but in the middle of the night he said he couldn't go on any more. He sat down and began crying terribly.

'I told him that he couldn't give up now. I had to give him a little political pep talk about it never being time to give up. I talked to him about the heroes he had learned about as a child and young man, and in the end I got him to understand that we wouldn't get anywhere by staying where we were. I was tired too and I was frightened. I wanted to sit down beside him and cry too. I thought a lot about my family, wondering what had happened to them.

'It was almost impossible to make any progress in the dark and we must have gone in the wrong direction many times, but we kept on walking and when it began to get light we were able to find our direction. Late in the course of the second day we arrived. We were both very lucky to find our immediate families unharmed, and although we had both lost close friends and some relatives, nothing had happened to our parents and brothers and sisters.

'Our village had been very hard hit; most of the houses were in ruins. But of course they are the responsibility of the community, not of the individual. And something most extraordinary had happened on the night of the earthquake. You know it often happens that in small towns or villages there is someone not quite right in the head who is made fun of, although when people get to know him, then the teasing isn't usually malicious. Well, there's somebody like that in my village. He is very strong and very helpful. He's always there when there is any hard work to be done. Otherwise he goes about on his own. He is rather shy, but that might be because he is deaf and dumb.

'Well, about ten or eleven that night, when everyone had gone to bed, he ran round from house to house, went inside the houses and pulled people out of bed. A lot of the villagers got very cross with him, abused him for disturbing their sleep and went back to bed. But he kept on pulling them outside until he got so tired he had to give up. And a few hours later the earthquake happened.

'We've never been able to explain it, but as I said he is a bit odd and he's deaf and dumb. Anyway he has been working like a bulldozer rebuilding the village.

'I have often thought about my fears that night while we were on the way. Naturally I was anxious about my family and there was the uncertainty and all that. But I think also that from time to time the thought crossed my mind, "What if we run into bandits here?" and I have a feeling that my companion was thinking the same. But neither of us said anything.

'We heard later that there were people whose bad characters showed up after the earthquake. There were some cases of looting. There was one man in Tangshan who appeared to be a true hero. He led a group of rescue workers going from ruin to ruin trying to find the wounded and get them out. It was dangerous work; many of the ruins were liable to collapse on top of them and this man always insisted on going in first. He worked day and night, did not eat or sleep and sometimes was the only one who dared enter a basement under a pile of rubble. On the third day, when he was on his way out of a partly ruined house, some bricks fell and broke his collar-bone. His comrades carried him to the nearest first-aid post, although he protested vigorously. And when the first-aid people removed his shirt, they saw that both arms were covered with wrist watches. A grave robber concealing his dirty work with a camouflage of heroism.

'But we shouldn't be surprised by that. We know that class enemies exist even in socialist societies. And without socialism I think Tangshan would have been in a much worse state. A capitalist society might perhaps have been able to employ more technical help, because your part of the world is better equipped in this respect. But what we lack in technology we have in our highly developed organization and our socialist consciousness.'

As Zhu was telling me his experiences of the catastrophe, I was thinking of a text which had just been printed at the institute. It also dealt with the earthquake and personal contributions to the rescue work. Zhu did not say it directly, but he had hinted that he felt that perhaps he had cheated his community by not being in Peking to help. The text the students are working on now is about a man in Tangshan who did not happen to be at home when the town was hit. He rushed out to help with rescue work and continued for hour after hour. Eventually one of his neighbours found him and told him that his own house had collapsed and that his daughter was trapped in the ruins. The story ends:

> 'That's all right,' said the man, 'there is sure to be someone who will help her. My help is needed here.' The eyes of those standing near filled with tears at hearing the man express such selflessness and total devotion to the community.

Law and Order

Since the middle of the 1960s, when the Cultural Revolution abolished substantial parts of the law and its administration, it has been very difficult to get any information about Chinese criminal law and its enforcement as practised today. Even visiting professionals— lawyers, sociologists and so on—find it difficult to get permission to meet their Chinese colleagues. And it is very seldom indeed that any foreigner is allowed to visit institutions such as prisons, reform-through-work camps and establishments for re-education. Even as a resident here it is almost impossible to find out the details of a great many current laws, rules and regulations. One begins to wonder how much of the law is actually written down.

Since the coup in the autumn of 1976, when Hua Guofeng became leader of the country, there have been some signs of organization, as well as a significant tightening up of such laws as do exist, and in the administration of the law, which for some years has been some-what confused. At all events, it certainly was confused to a large extent during the early years of the Cultural Revolution, when one could justifiably have described China as being in a state of legal anarchy.

We are now seeing a general tendency towards increased discipline in all fields, most marked among the young having higher education —the same generation as those who, at the height of the Cultural Revolution and apparently with Mao's blessing, took the law into their own hands. Their excesses were many, and their 'selection' and persecution of social (read political) offenders were in many cases quite grotesque.

But if the public is ignorant of the law in detail (in the sense that few people have an opportunity of studying the criminal code or police regulations), there is little ignorance of the law in general, as everybody knows what is permitted and what forbidden. This is partly due to the fact that whereas in the West we are used to regarding the law as being a series of prohibitions and restrictions, in China it works in reverse. Everything is forbidden unless it is expressly permitted.

This, of course, simplifies matters considerably: it is much easier to administer and disseminate knowledge of a few permissions than endless prohibitions. But it may offend some foreigners with a different concept of justice.

On the whole, however, it is of little importance what foreigners think about Chinese legislation, apart from the fact that it may detract from the positive view that one might otherwise have of Chinese society. In other words, it may have negative public relations value, as does the reluctance of the Chinese to allow foreigners to have a clear view of what is going on in China.

If one wishes to piece together a picture of how the law works, one has to rely on private Chinese sources and eye-witness accounts, supplemented by the information which can be got from the international press agencies or special correspondents stationed in Peking. These last sources, however, must be scanned with a very critical eye. Tall stories circulate endlessly in the small foreign colony in Peking, and I have myself been present when someone deliberately started an improbable story which, sure enough, found its way into the Western press a few weeks later.

At about the same time as, but of course independently of, the fall of the 'Gang of Four', the Western press gave accounts of the prosecution and even the execution of homosexuals in several Chinese towns. Some foreigners raised the question with the Chinese authorities as to whether homosexual practice was prohibited. But seeing that, as has been said, the law is not expressed in prohibitions, the question is wrongly phrased and the answer should be no. It is not prohibited but on the other hand it is not permitted. There are no laws applying to homosexual practice or other possible forms of 'sexual deviation', but the long and the short of it is that the only form of sex life which is explicitly allowed is that which takes place within the narrow context of a heterosexual, legally registered marriage. That is where the boundaries are, and everything outside them is liable to prosecution.

Incidentally, these cases of prosecution of homosexuals which I have discussed with Chinese friends do seem to have put an end to the stupid, and unfortunately often heard, claim that homosexuality is a symptom of decadent capitalistic morals and *does not exist* in China.

The case of the execution of a homosexual, which I was able to confirm and which the Western press turned into a whole series of executions, was not because of sexual preferences or attitudes but because it was a case of homosexual *rape*. It was the violence rather than the sexual choice which led to the death sentence being passed.

As far as one can see, the attitude to capital punishment has changed considerably in the last ten or twelve years, changed in the direction of greater severity. In the past the death sentence was seldom passed, although capital punishment has existed on paper ever since the People's Republic was founded. On the occasions on which it was passed, the condemned person was, as a rule, granted a stay of execution for three years, during which time he had a chance to show his willingness and ability to resocialize. After this, in most cases, he was reprieved.

A number of things now seem to indicate that this is changing. There appear to be an increasing number of death sentences—or at least more have come to our knowledge than did before. And to a far greater extent than before, execution takes place immediately after the sentence has been passed. Often such a short time elapses between the pronouncement of sentence and the execution that there is no possibility of appeal.

This is particularly the case in the sensitive area of violence towards foreigners. China is interested in guarding and maintaining the respect and goodwill that she now enjoys internationally, including in those circles which, politically speaking, are far removed from China. Therefore no lenience is shown to any Chinese citizen who lays hands on a foreign visitor. There have even been cases of assault over the last few years in which the criminal has been summarily executed on arrest. This includes cases in which there has not been an actual assault but only attempted assault.

In one of these cases, of which I had personal knowledge, the reason given for the execution on arrest was that the criminal had 'ideological problems'. It must be said, however, that this may have been an interpreter's slip and that 'ideological' should have read 'mental'—if that makes things any better according to our way of thinking.

For many years, since 1949, China has rightly been proud of the low incidence of crime, although exact figures have never been published. The accounts of public honesty which made locks and keys more or less superfluous would not appear to be just propaganda. What little crime there was was always said to be a relic of the murky past, and an indication of the fact that it is difficult to change old habits and social attitudes quickly. Crime was considered to be due to the social order at the time or to the conflict between new and old.

According to private Chinese accounts, this presents something of a problem, because if crime is related to social order how does one account for the significant, even if not alarming, rise in crime today? And should not the conflict between old and new have been resolved by the growing up of a large post-revolutionary generation? More than half the population of China today is under twenty-five. New China is almost thirty.

And so, in the case of a death sentence, the criminal is absolutely certain to be described as being the child or relative of a landlord or other member of the ruling classes of the past; it being understood that it is only members of that corrupt and vicious group who commit crimes, not the ordinary working people. This is demonstrable in many cases but one does ask oneself if it can be as generally applicable as it is made out to be.

But more important than what Westerners think of the administration of justice in China—whether they judge it from a moral standpoint, from political sympathies or antipathies, from knowledge or ignorance—is what the Chinese think of it, how it works in China for the Chinese, and in what ways it encroaches on, or improves, their daily life. And I suppose from their point of view what is even more important than the death penalty, which in any case is still comparatively rare and has certainly not reached the alarming figures sometimes suggested by the Western press, is what spearheads of permission have been driven into the massive wall of prohibitions and restrictions surrounding daily life.

The police force, which in practice has been given a good deal of judicial power (that same police force which was suspended for long periods by civilians, mainly Red Guards, in the late 1960s), has widespread powers as far as the ordinary Chinese population is concerned. If, for example, a family has guests for the night, they must inform the local police and give the names and addresses of their visitors. The police can at any time demand entry into a private house; ideas like the sanctity of the home and search warrants are unknown here. When out late in the evening I have often seen the few cars about being stopped and searched. This happened particularly frequently during the time following the seizing of power by Hua Guofeng, and the rumour was that this was because of an attempt on his life on one of the roads leading north out of Peking. According to this rumour, his Red Flag limousine had been riddled with bullets. But in the general unrest at that time, there was an extraordinary display of state, military and police power.

One of the things which has happened as a result of the campaign for stricter discipline which has been going on for several years is that the police are allowed to levy fines on the spot—a power they did not have, or did not exercise, before. There are fixed penalties for traffic offences, which for the most part apply to cyclists, who form the bulk of the traffic—fines which range from one to five yuan. For purposes of comparison, a student or apprentice has fifteen to twenty yuan a month, on which he has to live; a young worker or teacher thirty-five to fifty yuan, and veteran workers and other more senior people between one and two hundred, sometimes more. However, it is not so much the presence of a fining system or even of the fines themselves which the Chinese I have spoken to find open to criticism. It is the fact that there is no appeal. There is even a regulation to the effect that if anyone complains about a fine it is automatically doubled. Even a well-grounded protest is regarded by those in authority as complaining. One of my students was fined two yuan for a minor offence. He had nothing smaller than a ten yuan note on him and politely, but firmly, denied that it was his duty to walk several miles to the nearest place where he could get it changed. His refusal was immediately deemed to be defiance of the law, and the fine was summarily raised to ten yuan, two-thirds of his monthly income.

I am not suggesting that Chinese police are corrupt or sub-criminal, and indeed in this respect there are light years between the old days and the China of today. But one cannot help wondering what these police powers might lead to in the future, if there were a change in the political situation and with it a change of attitude. And I think of the stories I have been told about the Shanghai police before liberation. In those days the police were completely corrupt and had devised many ways of supplementing their incomes. One of these was very well known but seemed impossible to stop. Police who were in charge of the manually operated traffic lights at intersections would change from green to red just as a lorry was on its way over the crossing, so that witnesses could testify that it had been crossing against a red light. The lorry drivers, therefore, always had a mate sitting on top of the driver's cab, whose job it was to throw something of the cargo—fish, fruit, vegetables, or some other bribe—

to the policeman so that he did not change the lights. Unless this was done, one could be certain of a fine.

The practice which was relatively widespread during the Cultural Revolution, of parading those whose political views were unacceptable round the town with sandwich boards detailing their crimes—a practice which many Chinese considered unnecessary and offensive—is reappearing. Now and then young 'criminals' are marched from one institute of education to another, partly as objects of derision, partly as a warning to others. Nowadays, however, the fervour which made them so distressing in the past is lacking. As a rule, they are rather tame affairs done as a matter of duty, and many people would like to be spared having to witness them. They are often received with concealed yawns and the furtive reading of newspapers during the hour-long sessions in which the young offender is harangued.

Criminal law penetrates the whole of private life—or that part of life which the Western world has defined as being private. If, for example, civil law has laid down certain sensible and progressive rules concerning such things as the rights of women in connection with marriage, divorce and abortion, criminal law takes the anti-quated and hidebound view that adultery, for example, is punishable with up to ten years in prison for both parties concerned. In a parti-cular case of rape in 1977, in which there was no doubt as to the guilt of the offender and the innocence of the victim, *both* parties were sentenced—the offender with ten years' imprisonment and the girl with five. This was not because she was considered to be partly guilty but because she was said to have taken part in an immoral act.

A woman I met in Peking once, who had an astonishingly relaxed attitude to these matters and to talking about them, told me that she herself had been before a 'morality tribunal' for adultery. Her sentence was relatively short, but the consequences were long. At her unit's weekly meeting, in which everyone gathers for political studies and which always closed with general criticism and self-criticism, she repeatedly had to acknowledge her guilt and receive criticism from her colleagues. This had been going on for a number of years. On my asking how long it was likely to continue, she said: 'No one knows. Perhaps for ever. Probably.'

Reports from different parts of the country suggest that there are great differences in the sentences passed. This is not necessarily owing to lack of co-ordination in high places, but rather a positive result of flexibility, a flexibility which is understandable if one bears in mind the fact that China is, both historically and culturally, a vast heterogeneous nation. The morals of Peking would look peculiar to the people in the once strongly Muslim province of Xinjiang, 3,000 miles away, or in South Yunnan where, apparently, there has always been a much more relaxed attitude to sex.

Going back to the case of the unfaithful wife, it is worth noting that, under the present judicial system, having served a sentence does not mean an automatic settling of accounts with society. In most cases, a sentence will be a great burden socially, not only on the guilty party but also on his immediate family. It can be very hard for them to live with the social pressures which leave a mark as permanent as a brand. Very often, on the release of the criminal member, an entire family will, if it is able to do so, move to another place. In other cases, and these seem to be many, the family is required publicly to wash its hands of the offender and show its social conscience by taking part in the endless meetings of criticism directed against him.

But the fact remains that by far the greater number of rules and regulations have never been printed. Much depends on evaluation of the situation and on precedent. Even something as simple as customs regulations, which after all are of no practical importance to the vast majority of Chinese, are relatively open. Decisions are made depending on who the traveller is, under what circumstances he arrived or departed, and the degree of friendliness between the traveller's home country and China.

But in universities and places of higher education, there are rules which are strictly enforced. The time when students and teachers were on equal footing is long since over. The regulations require the students to obey their teachers and the teachers to respect their students—a giant stride backwards from the rather more egalitarian ideas which flourished during the Cultural Revolution. One paragraph in a set of university regulations expressly forbids students to fall in love. Some will perhaps read into this a modestly worded prohibition of the sexual activities which are liable to follow falling in love, but it has been made clear to me that it is a definite prohibition against 'the arising of feelings of love between students of the opposite sex'.

One of the few legal documents which is freely available is the constitution, just revised for the third time. It is probably more exactly set out than most constitutions, and if one follows the revisions of it since it was first written, one observes restrictions on personal freedom creeping in. The earlier constitution gave the citizen the right to private correspondence—confidentiality of letters —while the present constitution allows the citizen only 'the right to send and receive letters'.

The present constitution was written under the leadership of Wang Hongwen, who was the most protocol-conscious of the 'Gang of Four'. Now the question is whether to scrap it since he assisted in drafting it, or let it stand, which would indirectly imply that he had done something good.

It is perhaps not quite by chance that, since the liberalization of cultural life which occurred last year and which brought with it the greater possibility of reading foreign books, the most popular reading among my students and colleagues has been English and American detective stories. Most of them are second-rate, but they nevertheless go the rounds from pocket to pocket, becoming more and more dog-eared as they do so. The need to read light literature after so many years of literary puritanism is understandable, but I find it in many ways significant that it happens to be whodunits which are the most popular.

And in this connection it is also worth noting that a disproportionately large number of the questions I am asked in my weekly lectures are about law and order in the West. How do the law courts work? What are the prisons like inside? What happens to people when they get out, what are the powers of the police, and so on. I am seldom asked about possible social motives for crime, its background in general, or whether there is any social stigma attached to having been a criminal.

Possibly some of my students are as interested in learning something about our legal system and its consequences as we are in learning about theirs. And perhaps information flows so sluggishly in both directions because both parties find the subject equally difficult.

Images and History

Together with some of the village leaders I have just finished a delicious meal, consisting entirely of local produce—strong, well-grown produce, tended, gathered and skilfully prepared.

It is noon and very hot. We are sitting in the large cool meeting hall of the village. The cicada are chirruping outside the open doors and the breeze passing through is cooled as it eddies up under the stout timbers of the roof. We are seated at one end of the long hall, which is used as canteen, theatre, political forum and evening school, and is the place where agricultural matters, such as the reclaiming of land and new methods, are discussed. It is also used for storage purposes and as a drying place. On the long strings stretched the length of the hall, some big freshly dyed pieces of cloth are hanging up to dry. At one end hang twin portraits of Mao and Hua.

I ask my hosts if I may take some pictures of the hall. There is something about the construction and dimensions which intrigues me. They say there is no objection and I set up my camera in the corner from which I think I will get the best possible view.

My companion from Peking comes over before I have taken the picture and says he would like to have a look. His eye screwed up against the viewfinder, he eventually shakes his head. 'That won't be a good picture,' he says. 'You will have to move the camera.'

'It will be a very good picture,' I object. 'From this point I can get nearly the whole of the hall in.'

'The washing on the line hides part of Chairman Mao's face,' he says. 'That is not a good picture. Please take it from another angle.'

'But I don't want a picture of the portraits, I want a picture of the construction of the hall.'

'We would appreciate it if you would make sure that you get the whole of Chairman Mao's face in the picture.'

This little exchange is typical of the formal, almost religious attitude most Chinese have towards pictures and photographs. It took me some years back in time and made me recall several episodes in which I was involved with pictures.

Shanghai, Spring 1967. I had just come from the casualty ward in a big municipal hospital where I had spent a couple of hours with the female guide and interpreter who had been assigned to me for my stay in Shanghai. Together with the headmistress of my school in Canton, Madame Li, and my escort from there, Fu Yukang, I was on a round trip of China during the Cultural Revolution. A pilgrimage to the holy places of the revolution, they called it, because our route covered many places which had been put on the map by the Red Army in the course of the Long March up to Yenan in the north, where it ended and the first revolutionary base was established.

We were in the Shanghai of the Cultural Revolution. Fu and Li had a meeting in the imposing British colonial-style hotel where we were staying while I wandered round the town with my guide. At the hospital we had seen one of the colossal meetings of the day on TV. The meeting was directed against one of the town leaders who was made to stand on a platform with bowed head, receiving devastating criticism from the people for hour after hour. Shortly before this the British consul had been driven from his residence, and everywhere in this, the largest city in China, one could feel unrest rippling beneath the surface. The power struggle was in one of its decisive phases, there had been local riots and a deep split expressed itself in the endless flag-waving columns and battalions of demonstrators marching through the city.

On the kerbstone behind one of the big shops which I had been visiting with the guide, an old woman was sitting. Her blouse, tightly fastened at the neck, was of the shiny black material typical of peasant wear; the surface of the material glistened almost as if it had been lacquered. She was squatting on the edge of the gutter, her unkempt grey hair falling in a cascade over her wrinkled forehead. She had a little board on her knee and on it were small pieces of dried ginger. Street-sellers were an unusual sight in the large cities in those days. Her face, furrowed by age and hard work, had an appealing look. She smiled. I took a photograph.

I had only walked a few steps down the street when I was tapped on the shoulder from behind, something which immediately makes one think one has lost something or done something wrong. It is only someone who has found something, or a policeman, who taps one on the shoulder like that. And in China one quickly gets unaccustomed to physical contact of any kind.

There were two men, one middle-aged, the other quite young. They said a whole lot of things to me in Chinese. I looked at my guide who looked rather serious.

'These men are angry that you took a picture of the old woman over there,' she said. 'They don't think you should have done that. They are insisting you hand over the film.'

My immediate reaction was that Shanghai at this moment was not the place in which to make a fuss and stand upon one's rights. The few days I had spent there had been enough to show me that one does not get very far with that. I opened the camera immediately, pulled out the film and gave it to the older man. He stuffed it unceremoniously into his pocket and the two men turned on their heels and walked off.

My guide and I walked on too, calm but filmless. Half a minute later, just as we were turning a corner, another two men came running after us. Again a hand on my shoulder and a flow of words. It appeared that they had witnessed the incident which had just taken place and did not think the other two men had any right to demand the film. They had taken it away from them and come running after us to restore it to its rightful owner. They regretted the fact that of course it would be no good any more because it would have been ruined by exposure to light, but felt that, as a matter of principle, I ought to have it. It was mine, and in their eyes I had done nothing wrong.

While I was standing listening to all this, together with apologies for the bad manners of the others, the first two men reappeared. There was some pushing and shouting because they wanted the film back and did not realize it had been returned to me. By now I was anxious that things should not go any further and gave them the film immediately. I tried to make them understand, through the interpreter, that I myself felt I had broken an unwritten law that one does not take photographs of people without their permission.

'It is not a question of permission. You are an enemy of China and have taken that picture to use as anti-Chinese propaganda. That is illegal.'

At this point I saw that my interpreter was becoming uneasy and I myself suddenly realized the potential danger of the situation. A serious charge had just been levelled against me. Words like 'enemy' and 'anti-Chinese' were not used lightly in those days and implied the possibility of very serious consequences. And, at this moment in time, Shanghai was in a state of revolution. There were no police and the enforcement of law and order was in the hands of the people.

There I stood with my interpreter, who was visibly shaken by this sudden development, facing two counsel for the prosecution and two for the defence, while a jury was rapidly building up around us; hundreds of people crowding round my claustrophobic dock to hear what had happened and take sides. I don't think I was afraid of any physical violence, although considering the sort of things which were happening at that time it might have come to that too. But a prickly panic rose in me at the sudden imprisonment by the crowd, which grew and grew, and at the incalculability of the consequences.

The discussion began to get heated. More and more people joined in, taking sides for or against. There were outbursts of angry words. And of course in this situation all interpreting stopped. She had enough on her plate.

Eventually she said shortly: 'Come on, we'll go. The car is just round the corner.' But the crowd was unwilling to let us go, and one of my prosecutors was holding me by the arm. I was on no account to go. To this day I do not know how she managed it, but she got my two original prosecutors to agree that the matter could not be settled in the street. The traffic had gradually come to a standstill, people were pouring out of the buses at the intersection where we stood. With my prosecutors leading the way we pushed through thousands of bodies, through an avalanche of words, and with heavy breathing down our necks we eventually got to the old Russian car, with its unsuspecting driver sitting and waiting for us.

Part of the crowd was in front of us, which made it difficult to get in. However, we eventually managed it and sat down, sweating and trembling from the adrenalin pulsing through our veins, and with that odd feeling of relief one has when one has just had a minor accident and doesn't yet know that one is bleeding.

Once in the car the two men pulled out their little blue identity cards by way of introduction. In those days if one had an identity card it meant that one also had authority. And as the car made its way slowly past the faces pressing against the window, my interpreter took up her role again. We were once more in an official situation in which her job was to act as middleman between two parties who lacked a common language.

The younger man was a docker. He showed me his tattered card with a faded picture and many dark red stars stamped on it. He gave his name and said that he represented the revolutionary masses and had only been doing his duty in arresting an enemy of China. The older man was a university lecturer, but of course the universities were closed at the time, and he gave a similar reason for helping to arrest me.

I had no identity card at that time, but I told them my name, that I was a teacher in Canton and added that I had done my best to avoid things getting to such a pitch. My two defendants had decided at the last minute not to accompany us, so I had to plead my own case.

The guide took out her little notebook, opened it and began reading aloud in a clear though strained voice. When she had finished, she turned to me.

'I read aloud parts of the talk you gave at the meeting the other day to show them that you are neither a counter-revolutionary nor anti-Chinese. I always keep a record of my official interpretations.'

As we slipped into the entrance hall of the hotel we saw Madame Li and Fu standing by the hotel kiosk inspecting the local souvenirs. They looked at us in astonishment and it must have been obvious to anyone that this was no ordinary meeting. My interpreter went over to Madame Li and explained to her briefly what had happened. And the expressions on her and Fu's faces told me that they were not particularly pleased. I was told by Madame Li to go to my room and remain there until further notice.

Nearly seven hours went by. All through the burning Shanghai afternoon I sat at my window watching the demonstrations on the Nanking road below. At times I worked myself up into believing that the next column was one which was coming to 'struggle' me, as it was called in the jargon of the day—that strange mixture of the extreme and the restrained; oversized and understated. I spent most of the afternoon composing my speech for the defence, piling argument upon argument to satisfy them of my fundamental innocence and the insignificance of my crime. I could not even begin to imagine how far it could go. The mayor with hanging head whom I had seen on television that morning was probably still standing there in front of those thousands of people. True enough, my crime was not of the same magnitude as his, but in those days one really could not make valid comparisons.

I tried to visualize the scene in the cool foyer below me—whether anyone had joined the group, and what direction the discussion might be taking. I was used to discussions being endless, and the fact that no one had authority to bring them to an end. In central China on the way here, we had had to wait twenty-four hours for a train at one point because some members of the Red Guard claimed the right to travel free. They argued that the train is the property of the people and therefore no one had the right to demand money from them. The counter-argument of the train staff was that they were employed by the state to collect money from passengers and they could not fail in their duty and neglect their responsibilities. And the train did not leave the station until the Red Guard had been convinced by discussion to pay or leave the train. This was repeated at station after station.

And here I was, waiting for the outcome of the parliamentary debate which was going on down there in the hotel lounge. Finally Fu rang me on the house telephone and told me to come down. The discussion was over. Not knowing what was awaiting me, and therefore with an uncertain expression on my face, I entered the conference room which the hotel had put at the disposal of the meeting. My two prosecutors stood up. They smiled and came to meet me with outstretched hands, competing with one another to shake mine. An iceberg lifted from my heart and I looked across at my interpreter, Fu and Madame Li. They were all leaning comfortably back in the big deep armchairs, obviously relaxed in the knowledge that they had managed to get out of what could have been a very difficult situation. We all sat down and the interpreter took up her task again. The young docker acted as spokesman.

'We shake you by the hand and call you our friend, and at the same time we will begin a serious and frank self-criticism. We have transgressed against one of the supreme instructions of our Great Helmsman, Great Teacher and Leader, Chairman Mao. He has clearly and correctly pointed out that "without investigation, no right to speak". This is of immense significance in the Great Proletarian Cultural Revolution which is being carried out at present by the whole of the Chinese people in order to further and consolidate Chairman Mao's correct line.

'We jumped to conclusions without investigation. We assumed that you were collecting negative material about China for use in the reactionary foreign press, whose only interest is to falsify information and slander our country—but we failed to investigate before jumping to conclusions. Since we have talked the whole thing over with the comrades from your area, we now know that you are not an enemy of China, that you meant no harm but were only a bit tactless. And tactlessness should not be treated as a serious crime, as long as there is no evil intent.

'Therefore we would like now to declare our sincere friendship and beg your forgiveness for our unpardonable behaviour, resulting from not following the supreme instruction of Chairman Mao.

'To show how sincerely we mean this, and to complete our self-criticism, we have decided that tomorrow we will go back to the place where it occurred. We will stand there all day and tell the passers-by about the serious error we made today. When one makes a mistake one must not be afraid of admitting it and we must never be afraid of self-criticism. This has been an important lesson to us, and by practising public self-criticism we can not only help ourselves to put the matter right, but also help others to understand how important it is to follow the supreme instructions of Chairman Mao.'

Today, after a long delay, the illustrated paper featuring Mao's funeral is out. There are large headlines and numerous pictures. The long queue of prominent people filing past his bier, the huge crowds throughout the country holding funeral services of their own, the cascades of flowers, and the official pictures of the party and state leaders, their heads bowed, standing before the people. But in the pictures of the leaders there are some gaps. Four persons have been scratched out and in their place spray and brush have produced a blurred background effect. Wang, Zhang, Jiang, Yao—non-persons whose absence disturbs the symmetry of the pictures.

The retouching has not been very well done; here and there the knife has cut too deep into the emulsion and it has been difficult for even the finest brush to reproduce the uniform grey tone of the sea of people in the background. It turns into fine lines, which dissociate themselves from the equally fine dots of the emulsion. This is not falsification in the sense that anyone is trying to create the impression that no one ever stood there. Everyone in China knows exactly who stood there, and my colleagues can put their fingers on the splotches and say, 'That was where Jiang Qing stood, and there is Yao Wenyuan.'

'Why have they been removed?' I ask. 'We know, all China knows, indeed the whole world knows, that they stood there.'

'It is enough that we know. The hate and anger of the people is so great against them that we do not wish to see them. They have been removed from power, they must also be removed from history. Such people belong on the dunghill of history.'

'The dunghill of history is at least a *place*,' I say, 'but they have been removed completely. Can one deny historic facts, what actually happened, and say it never did?'

'There are different ways of looking at history. We cannot give them a prominent place they do not deserve.'

'But is that not falsifying history?'

'As I just said, people do not wish to see them. Particularly not Jiang Qing, who feigned grief at the passing away of Chairman Mao, while deep down she was feeling devilish joy. That alone is an insult to the entire Chinese people.'

Again a jump in time. When the first placards with criticisms of well-known leaders began to appear, many of them were illustrated with portraits cut from newspapers. In order to make it clear to people who was loved and respected and who was an enemy and a traitor, a tradition quickly grew up that pictures of the latter category were crossed through with a large red cross going from corner to corner—a clear recognition of the fact that here was someone who really did exist but with whom one did not agree. The magic sign was rapidly extended to names, which were allowed to be put up provided that each character (most Chinese names have three characters) was crossed through. While I am not aware that there was any retouching of the kind done today, it is perfectly true that even in those days printed matter which carried pictures of non-persons was filed under lock and key, or simply went out of circulation. I find the crossing-out method, which does not affect facts, more respectful to historical reality than the erasures of today.

Not far from Chairman Mao's birthplace in Hunan province, in the village of Shaoshan near Changsha, one finds, as might be expected, a museum of the revolution. The birthplace itself, a large and spacious farmhouse in the middle of beautiful countryside, is of course another such museum, a national shrine which has been visited by hundreds of thousands, probably millions, of people over the years. A railway has recently been built, but in the sixties one could only get there by bus from Changsha.

At this shrine of the revolution I had a discussion with the young girl who showed me round. Probably, like many others before and after me, I was surprised to be shown the rather large farm where Mao had been born and at the same time to be told that it had been the home of a poor peasant family. I was shown the fields and lakes where Mao worked as a boy and which were owned by his rather gruff father and wondered how so much land could be the property of a 'poor peasant'. I did not think it fitted with the socio-economic divisions of old China, in which poor peasants are described as landless or with only a little rented land, and lower middle peasants as owning a little land, but having to supplement their incomes by working as hired hands for the rich peasants and the landlords.

The attendant insisted that Mao came of poor peasant stock, and I asked her if she had heard of Edgar Snow. Yes, she had, she said, and added that many Chinese people had read parts of his book *Red Star over China.*

'But in that book,' I said, 'surely Snow refers to a conversation with Mao in the Yenan days in which Mao did *not* describe his family as poor. On the contrary, he said that they employed hired labour, although they all had to work themselves as well. That suggests to me that they were somewhere in the region of "middle peasants".'

'Edgar Snow is a good friend of China and a personal friend of Chairman Mao,' said the attendant. 'He is a progressive foreigner, but he is not a Marxist.'

'Maybe he is not a Marxist, but his information about the child-hood of Chairman Mao came from the Chairman himself.'

'As I said, and without wishing to say anything derogatory about Edgar Snow, he is not a Marxist. And perhaps he is not always a reliable reporter. Perhaps there was a misunderstanding.'

I thought later I might have been unfair. It is quite possible that in the translations of Snow's book the parts about Mao's childhood had been left out and that I had used arguments the attendant was not in a position to counter. And I must add that in China, if official history says something, then that thing is an unshakeable fact.

The same sort of thing occurred some years later when I revisited a museum of the revolution which I had first been to in 1967. In a showcase in this museum one of the long curved bamboo poles with a notch at each end is an exhibit. It is a traditional carrying pole which, slung over the shoulder, is in use to this day for carrying baskets of earth from trenches, vegetables home from the fields or any heavy load, using the special tripping gait which is necessary to make the pole swing in the right rhythm.

The pole on exhibition was, in the past, said to have belonged to

Lin Biao, and was a witness to the fact that he, along with everyone else in the early years of the revolution, had done manual labour—which he doubtless did. Lin Biao was, in those days, hailed as Mao's close comrade-in-arms; he held the second highest place in the state hierarchy and was looked on as one of the leaders of the Cultural Revolution. So it was not surprising that his carrying pole should have been prominently displayed among other relics of the revolution.

But on returning to this same museum today, some years later, during which time Lin Biao has been written off as a traitor and arch fiend following his dastardly attempt to flee to the Soviet Union, one does not find that his pole has gone as a result of the campaign to remove him from history. It is still there, still in its prominent place, and the attendant, in passing, will remark that this pole once belonged to one of the heroes of the Chinese people, the late Marshal Zhu De. If one remembers and thinks it worthwhile one can point out that ten years ago the pole belonged to someone else, to Lin Biao.

'That is correct,' the attendant will reply. 'It was exhibited here as having belonged to Lin Biao, the renegade and traitor, who tried to take over power. But during the process of exposing his crimes we discovered that this pole had never really belonged to him. He had used it, that is correct, during the early years of the revolution, but it is now established that he had in fact stolen it from Marshal Zhu De. It has only recently been placed in its true historical context.'

But on the other hand, things which have been erased from history can emerge again with the same ease as that with which they originally disappeared, although attracting greater attention.

At Zhou Enlai's death it was Deng Xiaoping, Zhou's second-in-command who, on behalf of the party, made the official funeral oration. Shortly after that he was denounced and removed, so it was with the keenest interest that we awaited the documentary about Zhou's death and cremation. It was awaited with eagerness for several reasons. Zhou was, without doubt, one of China's most popular leaders, and rumour had it that the film had been sabotaged and kept back by the 'Four', who were said to be sworn enemies of Zhou.

For several days before it was released there was constant talk about how it would deal with Deng's speech. There were mutterings about the possibility of his return to power being imminent, but officially he was still 'dead and damned'. On the other hand, most people considered it would be impossible to make a documentary about Zhou's funeral without making some reference to the most important speech made.

In the discussions we had about it, there seemed to be four possible ways of dealing with the problem. One could show the film with Deng making his speech. Not many reckoned that as being likely. One could hear Deng making the speech without actually seeing him, or one could have someone else, an anonymous voice, making the speech off-screen. Finally, one could leave out any reference to the speech at all. There were very few who thought the last possibility likely. But, whatever happened, in whatever way the problem was finally solved, most people thought it would give some kind of indication as to whether Deng was likely to return or not, about which there was a great deal of speculation.

And then, when the film was finally released, there proved to be a fifth solution which none of us had thought of. At a certain point an anonymous voice said that a speech had been made in which, among other things, 'it had been said'—and then followed a precis of Deng's speech, the authorship of which no one in China had any doubts about.

But that did not help any of us to guess what was going to happen to Deng, although many things at about that time pointed strongly to his return.

Stine has broken off her course for the present and she is taking part in the open-door school: manual work for students. It is of special value to her as a foreign student because it gives her a chance to practise speaking. She has been assigned work at a printing press, where among other things they print the large portraits of Chairman Mao. She is working there with a veteran woman worker who helps her to get the hang of things, and does it with great warmth.

Her work consists of going through the portraits of Mao as they come off the press and discarding any which have any blemishes on the face owing to smudges on the block or spilled ink. Even the slightest speck means that it must be discarded. Stine's colleague tells her that she has been doing this important job for many years.

There are various places in Peking which are considered particularly good background for snapshots, the best, of course, being national

shrines and monuments. There is a whole ritual to be gone through
before either friends or the professional street photographer is
allowed to take a picture. Pictures are always posed and seldom
smiling. Young couples take endless pictures of one another with a
great deal of giggling, turning away, and general excitement during
the introductory manoeuvres, culminating in a moment of great
seriousness when the picture is finally taken.

In this puritanical country there are almost sexual implications in
the whole procedure, from the long foreplay to the climax—and
the same embarrassment at there being witnesses.

One day in Canton a young artist came wandering into my flat.
His unannounced arrival was as un-Chinese as was the attractive
silk scarf he had round his neck. He had a drawing-pad under his
arm and some bits of chalk behind his ear. He did not appear the
least embarrassed at having come into the wrong flat; he just grinned
and sat down. With the help of gestures and the few words we had
in common, he made me understand that he was a member of a
conference of artists which was going on in the building next door,
and he asked if he could draw a picture of me.

I had had a tiring day and was slowly dissolving in the tropical
heat, slouching in my chair, as usual. As a stereotype the portrait
was perfect and his technical ability was obviously very great. It was
a masterpiece of its kind, depicting me with head held high, gazing
into space with a resolute, steely (but friendly) expression, my chin
up in righteous indignation and a breeze of banners and purpose
sweeping back my hair. He signed it 'to my friend in revolution'.

Ritual

Peking winters are frightfully cold. I resisted for a long time the admonitions and exhortations of my students and colleagues who have been trying to make me buy myself some warm clothes. But I have at last had to give in and have been to a shop in the city and bought myself a nice blue quilted circus tent of a coat. Xiao Wang praises me and says that it was very sensible of me to have done so.

Xiao Wang has just replaced the helping hand of Zhang Zai. Wang is a newly fledged teacher who has not yet done any teaching, and I have a feeling that he is a bit scared at the thought of beginning. He is good company and, after the first few days' inspection of one another, we have discovered that we are on the same wavelength. He has wit and can laugh at himself—Chinese qualities which appear when one is tête-à-tête, but seldom, in my experience, in a group situation.

He is not very confident about his English and is laboriously and erratically working his way through a syllabus of his own. He always sits silent and slightly turned away when the dean, Zou, or other teachers come to talk to me, but I observe that he constantly jots things down in his notebook. When my guests have left he comes over with questions about new words and phrases he has heard during the conversation. He has an admirable habit of not pretending that I have made something clear if, in fact, I have not.

When he has nothing urgent to do he often disappears for half or a whole hour at a time. Several times a week he has to go to one meeting or another. Meetings seem to take up a disproportionate amount of my students' and colleagues' time. But he quite often comes back and tells me that he has been over to see Lulu at the nursery school. She is all right, he says, and calls him 'uncle'.

About once a week he accompanies me to the nursery school in order, he says, to help, should there be anything the staff want to say to me or I to them. On one of these occasions when I was talking through him with the leader about some signs of aggression on Lulu's part, he said: 'Please don't take offence, but the leader says you have not the slightest idea of how to bring up children. You should stick to your students and see that they learn English and leave Lulu to her. She will see that Lulu develops all right. In fact,' he continued, taking a thoughtful puff at the cigarette which he always holds between the very tips of his fingers as if he were afraid of burning himself, 'in fact, you can't take it as an insult because she is right!'

One day he comes sauntering into the office, sits down at his desk and says,'OK?' Pause. He introduces all his requests or messages with this 'OK?' followed by a pause, so that I have time to finish what I am doing. I put down my pencil and look at him.

'I expect you know that tomorrow it is one year since our dearly beloved Premier Zhou Enlai passed away. It was a great blow to the whole nation. We were full of grief but on account of the "Gang of Four" we could not, at that time, express our sorrow. That we will do tomorrow and I have come to ask you, on behalf of the leaders of the institute, if you would care to take part in a memorial meeting we are holding tomorrow. We would appreciate it if you did.'

Such an invitation it would be highly improper, even insulting, to refuse. In fact one would only do so if one wished to make a conscious political gesture. It is true that the invitation was put in such a way as to make refusal possible; it was not an order. But at the same time I felt in the air that to refuse would be an unheard-of piece of rudeness.

He explained that on account of the memorial meeting there would be no teaching on the following day. In other words, there would be no work for me; if I chose not to take part I could stay at home.

Early next morning the students come out of the main building, forming slowly expanding wedges, and huddle together in small groups trying to keep warm on the big empty parade ground in the icy morning cold. They are all wearing large quilted overcoats and those of them who have come here after having done their military service are still wearing their khaki uniforms and soft caps, but without the felt rectangles on their collars and the red plastic stars on their caps. I go down and join one of the groups. The few words which are spoken linger in the cold air, suspended in white vapour. Xiao Wang comes across the coarse crackling grass, his hands deep in his pockets, his shoulders hunched. He tells me that I am with the wrong group and I follow him across the parade ground to a corner where the middle-aged and elder teachers are assembled motionless and expectant.

The group formation is obviously standard. Everyone knows who belongs where and each group has its own unmarked point of assembly. There is no sound except that of the frost crackling underfoot and the sky is that pale washed-out blue it is the whole winter through.

There is no signal, no sound nor sign as far as I can tell, but at a certain moment the little groups of students and teachers mingle, then disband and form new groups. Suddenly everything takes shape and long straight columns of people, three abreast, form with military precision, each column separated from the next by a few yards. Xiao Wang and the others I have been standing with also move quietly into place, but I have never taken part in such an exercise, have not been told anything about the morning's procedure, have no place in a column. I attach myself hesitantly to that in which my closest colleagues are standing marking time. We are then one too many and the symmetry is broken. I am not keen on marching in formation but would feel even more out of place marching apart from a group.

And again, without any obvious signal, first one column begins to march, followed by the next, which falls in behind them, then us, so that finally the whole institute is marching like a mighty army over the frozen ground, across to the huge film studio with the vaulted roof.

Some of the people in the columns have little camp stools hanging over their shoulders; there are not enough seats in the big hall. The entire institute is there, including the score or so of workers who are attached to us; the cooks have their own column, and the doctors and nurses from the clinic, with the red cross on their brown bags, have theirs. The only people not present as far as I can see are the heads of the institute—the president, vice-presidents and the administrative heads.

The hall is in icy half-darkness. Left over from the days when it was still a film studio are two enormous parabolic lamps high up under the ceiling, inadequately illuminating the windowless hall with a pale ghostly light. Everything goes on in complete silence. The long rows of benches which take up the greater part of the hall fill symmetrically as the columns march down the middle aisle, divide, like planes flying in formation, and drift to each side filling up row after row.

In front of us a little platform has been constructed. It is full to overflowing with paper flowers, and in the middle of this formidable arrangement there is an easel with a large black-and-white picture of Zhou Enlai's wise and forceful face. Immediately in front of him, in a little clearing in the sea of flowers, a microphone stands waiting.

While we have been marching in and shuffling sideways along the benches, the loudspeaker has been playing a muted long-drawn-out funeral march. Low tones predominate and dragging repetition of the same few themes at low volume. There are two spotlights focussed on Zhou's face in such a way that the frame does not cast a shadow. We sit and wait; the hall is full.

One of the leaders of the unit enters through a side door, walks up to the microphone and mumbles a few words into it.

'We must stand,' whispers Xiao Wang to me.

With a silence one would not have thought possible for 1,500 people, the whole hall rises at once and as they rise remove their caps with their right hands. The leader takes off his own dark blue cadre cap and holds it with his arm straight by his side. He bends his head at an impossible angle, from the nape of his neck, not from the shoulders. One and a half thousand heads are bowed in the same way, faces parallel with the floor.

The muted music is now turned up slightly and I am aware of movements as of shuffling feet behind me in the centre aisle. A moment later the top leaders pass us with slow deliberate tread. Between them they are carrying an immense wreath of paper flowers, mounted on a wooden frame with handles so that they can carry it like bearers at a funeral. They put it on the floor in front of the platform and two young students step forward slowly and lift it up to its place in front of Zhou's portrait. The leaders take off their caps and bow slowly from the hips until the upper halves of their bodies are parallel with the floor. They then stand slowly upright and take up the same position as the rest of those in the hall, head bent forward from the neck, chin almost touching the adam's apple. Here we stand. Nothing happens. The only sound in the high-ceilinged hall is the droning from the crackling loudspeakers. There are not the usual accessories, no swinging censers or chasubles, but there is something familiar about the whole ritual and it occurs to me that mourning, and its expression, is perhaps more truly international than anything else we know.

The president climbs up and stands in front of the microphone.

In one hand he is holding his cap, of better quality than most, his arm by his side, and in the other hand he holds a manuscript. He begins speaking in a steady monotone but, in the circumstances, Xiao Wang does not think it appropriate to interpret. During the speech some of the people round me begin to cry aloud. It is mainly the young who cry. For them this is probably the first big common sorrow, national sorrow, in which they are united since Mao's recent death. The older people who have lived in the China of the past have experienced much more. If China's history has not made them resigned, it has made it difficult for them to give outward expression to their deeper feelings.

He is followed by four other speakers, representatives of the cadres, teachers, students and workers who, in that order, mount the podium and deliver long moving speeches. Some of them have difficulty in controlling their emotions, their voices trembling behind the melodious, precisely articulated words. All four go through the same ritual. They mount the podium, bow that awkward right-angled bow from the hips, facing the portrait of Zhou, stand motionless in this attitude of deepest respect for a few minutes, turn to the microphone and speak. The voices come over clearly; the acoustics in the studio are good.

It is cold standing still. The floor is concrete and the hall is not heated. Outside it is more than twenty below zero, and the cold creeps up, paralysing one to the ankles. But there is no sound of uneasy shuffling, no fidgeting or restlessness, in the many hours we stand here. There is only the sound of the sniffing back of tears and an occasional outburst of sobbing. A hall with 1,500 grief-stricken next of kin.

I think of another hall at another time. The big light theatre with the well-upholstered seats under the glistening blue-glazed roof in the Zhong Shan hall in Canton, built as a memorial to Sun Yat Sen, founder of the Republic.

The year is 1966. China's leaders had just fallen, but we were not there to lament their fall. It was a cultural propaganda evening, a theatre evening which was to strengthen everyone's support of Mao's line and to condemn the revisionist lackeys who still held some positions of power in Peking and elsewhere. A short time before this I had been to see one of the last performances of the traditional Peking opera—which was now banned for its 'glorification of figures like gods, emperors, beauties and ministers'; for referring to the ruling classes of the past and for its depiction of that extravagant way of life which was never part of the daily life of China's peasants and workers. The new opera and ballet of the revolution, under instructions from Jiang Qing, was beginning to find its feet.

'The old opera will return,' said my escort that evening. 'Just wait. The new cannot compete with the old. They all say that the old was never popular with the masses, but that's not true. Just wait, ten or twelve years and it will be back.'

The statement that traditional opera had never been popular was something I also found hard to believe. On the occasions I had attended traditional opera the vast majority of the audience appeared to be attired in overalls, military uniforms with only two pockets, indicating the rank of private, or stripped to the waist—having come straight from work. There were relatively few military uniforms with four pockets, or bespectacled intellectuals. But now, apparently, everyone accepts that the old opera was not popular and must therefore go. The truth is, perhaps, that it was *too* popular.

On that particular evening we were to be introduced to the new cultural revolutionary theatre. But it was not so much theatre as an endless string of stirring monologues which the touring theatre group presented. They were recited in the rather exaggerated diction one is accustomed to hearing on the wireless and which is supposed to make what is said easier to understand. And for those Canton people who did not speak standard Chinese there were subtitles in the form of hand-written slides projected onto vertical screens hanging on each side of the stage.

The individual numbers consisted of dance sequences set to revolutionary music, and introduced by actors in pale grey, well-pressed uniforms, whose smiles revealed shining white teeth framed by shining red lips, and round-rouged cheeks. Each fresh number was introduced with a request to the audience to stand to attention, and the two ideal beings on the stage conducted a forest of clenched fists with forward-turned knuckles, whose rhythmic beat seemed to form a second ceiling above the heads in the hall.

A swinging shout of '*Wan Sui, Wan Sui, Wan Wan Sui*' emphasized the wave of rising and falling fists. 'Chairman Mao, long live, long live, long long live!'

I found the thing with the clenched fists difficult and decided from the start that I would not participate and agreed with myself that while it would be provocative to remain seated when the rest of the audience were standing, it was up to me whether I expended my adrenalin on raising a clenched fist or not.

My escort was hesitant too. He rose as I did with the rest of the audience and with a sideways glance at me murmured a barely audible '*Wan Sui*'. I glanced at his right hand and though he clenched it when the others did, he never managed to get it higher than the back of the chair in front of him, nor did he relax it completely. It seemed permanently half-clenched and half-lifted.

Like so many other of my colleagues, in the months following this, he had to account to his pupils for his political attitude and one of the charges brought against him, I heard, was that for years he had used the wrong tone when saying Chairman Mao's name. It is the rising and falling tones in Chinese which determine the meaning of the word, and he had pronounced the name in such a way that it meant 'Chairman Cat'. That was only one of the charges brought against him. Whether his indecisive fist and feeble voice had been observed by others and added to his list of crimes, I do not know.

On another occasion when we were discussing the importance Chinese propaganda attaches to physical fitness, one of my pupils mentioned the marvellous example many of China's leaders had set by taking up swimming. That was before Mao's historic swim across the Yangtze, but flocks of youngsters used to train daily in rivers and lakes, swimming in formation with fixed bayonets, machine-guns and flying flags.

'Yes,' said one of my colleagues, 'since we are talking about swimming, you all know the word "swim"; you learned that a long time ago. In English there is an expression to "swim with the tide"— there are many who are good at that. The same words can be used to express many different ideas. You should be able to work out what that expression means.'

My colleague with the uncertain attitude and unexpressed protest swam neither with the tide nor against it. He trod water, and drowned as a result.

When the service for Zhou Enlai is over we leave the studio in the same regular formation as before but break up once we are out on the parade ground again. Out in the sharp winter light, hard to adapt to after hours of semi-darkness, the small groups we first started with stand and stamp to get the circulation going again in their frozen feet. A feeling of relief comes over the gathering—not because the ritual is at last at an end but because grief, it seems, is a personal feeling which may be publicly expressed. Later, when talking to some of my students who were asking me about funeral ceremonies in my own country, I tell them that among other things, there is one part of the country where the custom after the burial is for everyone to shake hands with the bereaved and wish them a 'happy mourning'.

'I can understand that,' says one of the students. 'It warms the heart to be able to express one's feelings.'

A new text is lying on the desk in front of me. It has been written by the students after a few weeks' stay in a people's commune and is an account of their experiences, living and working with the peasants.

While they were there two campaigns were going on simultaneously. One was a campaign to change old habits and ways of thinking, the other to make a contribution to the national effort to save timber in middle and north China, which is poorly afforested.

Among the older peasants the question of death and burial is still very important although, over the years, propaganda has undoubtedly done a great deal towards reducing ancestor worship. Nevertheless, it still remains important to the older peasants that their earthly remains should be interred in a way which conforms to tradition. This has meant that they sacrifice much time and money during their lifetimes in order to buy wood and employ carpenters to make coffins, which are then stacked in their houses ready for the day when they will be needed.

Both nationally and locally, this custom is now regarded as a terrible waste of precious raw materials, and the object of the campaign is to enlighten and educate people so that they no longer do it. Unfortunately, there is a deep-rooted prejudice against cremation. Mao's body was embalmed and will be in the memorial which is being built in Peking, but Zhou Enlai was cremated. Everyone knows that this was done on the orders of the 'Gang of Four'. They hated Zhou, and were afraid of the love the people had for him, and wished to destroy him so that the people could not make pilgrimages to his grave.

The students give a description of how the campaign was conducted in this particular commune. They describe day-long meetings, during which old peasants who had piled up coffins for the entire family in the largest room in the house were criticized for squandering the wealth of the country and therefore of the people and, in addition, of depriving the commune of valuable land which, if not used for a burial ground, could be cultivated.

The carpenters in the commune were in the vanguard of those supporting the campaign. 'From now on,' they said, 'we will not have anything to do with this kind of conservatism. From today we have decided we will never again make a coffin. But we will, free of charge, help to dismantle and put to better use those coffins which are already standing in many homes. We must expend our resources and our energies on life, not on death.'

But they had difficulty in getting this point of view across to many of the more tradition-bound peasants, who argued that it was comforting to know that one was going to be properly buried, that cremation had never been a tradition in China, and that wanting to be buried in the time-honoured manner had nothing to do with ancestor worship or anything like that. They looked on cremation as being disrespectful to the dead, while claiming that they had no reactionary religious ideas about life after death.

'Then suddenly an old peasant gets up,' the report goes on. 'He says that he too has his coffin waiting for him at home, but that since he has been sitting listening to the discussion he has begun to see things differently. With great seriousness this old uncle says that he would like to volunteer to be the first to be cremated. And all the other members of the brigade praise him and applaud his decision.'

The whole account is fascinating, even if it is written in rather clumsy English. But one of my jobs is to help the students put the text into correct English so that it can be used for teaching purposes. I suggest that we must alter the bit about the old peasant's change of heart, and am met with violent protests.

'Well,' I say, 'it is true that as far as the language is concerned there is nothing wrong. But there is something wrong with the logic. Can you see it?'

'He is a true hero,' says one.

'You quote him as saying that he volunteers to be the first in the commune to be cremated.'

'That shows how progressive he is. His is an example to be followed.'

'He is not dead yet. Who says he will be the first to die?'

'We cannot change his words. He said that and in so doing he demonstrated something very important—that one can change one's opinions, that one can change one's attitudes to old ideas and accept new. He is the first of a long line of heroes who by their deeds will help to convert the whole of China and consolidate the revolution.'

I stand corrected, an old pedant who had been concerning himself with formal logic when the basic concept was quite clear.

To the picture of ritual also belong the days during the Cultural Revolution when every unit in the country had its own altar. In the block where I lived the staff had put up a life-size picture of Chairman Mao. The 'little red book', which had come out under the auspices of Lin Biao, was in everyone's hands and every morning at seven o'clock we all had to attend what were called meetings of 'devout seriousness' in front of the icon. One by one we had to step forward holding the little book in its bright red plastic cover, and with clenched fist raised, stand in front of the picture of Chairman Mao and swear eternal loyalty and devotion. Furthermore, we had to say what actions we were taking that day to forward the Great Proletarian Cultural Revolution. In the evening the ceremony was repeated and everyone made a 'solemn report to the Great Helmsman, the Great Teacher and the Great Leader Chairman Mao' about what actions he or she had taken during the course of the day. The ceremony was accompanied by introductory and closing singing of songs. It was exhausting to take part and difficult to decline. When one day I asked a colleague, with whom I was on very good terms, how far he thought all this was really necessary and if looked at closely whether it really conformed to socialist thinking, I was told that it was absolutely necessary.

'At the moment China is in a state of crisis. A tremendous struggle between the two political lines is going on and it is in order to show our whole-hearted support of Chairman Mao's correct line that we hold these daily meetings.'

'But where is the other line? I don't know anyone who does *not* take part in these meetings.'

'They conceal themselves among us and wave the red flag to destroy the red flag. Hypocrites are to be found everywhere.'

The Honey Man

From the garage window we can see the upper reaches of the Mekong River, the evening light casting long grey shadows across it. Here, where it eats its way through Yunnan, it is not yet the Mekong. Only on the other side of the blue mountains on the horizon where it dives into the belly of South-East Asia does it change its name.

There are washing facilities in the garage, and every evening there is hot water for about an hour. This is not because there is any shortage of water but because there is no electric pump in this compound and the water has to be pumped by hand into the big tank on the roof—which takes nearly all day.

It is the washroom for the long-distance lorry drivers, but they have hospitably invited Liu and myself to share it with them. I stand under the hot shower and look at Liu, thin and bird-like, and compare him with the lorry drivers standing there with their well-built bodies, the muscles rippling under the dark skin. I look at the purely physical difference between the intellectual and the worker, between the refined academic from Peking and the massive manual labourer from China's southernmost corner.

China does not consist only of intellectuals and clever careerists, but a large part of *my* China does. Liu is no careerist; he is a very hard-working man who does the job he has to do with great conscientiousness.

And I think of many of those I have met during the course of the years here for whom the critical fact has been that they were intellectuals. There is still so much odium attached to being an intellectual that it is not something people usually brag about. Once, however, I had a guest, a young teacher to whom I offered coffee with an apology, saying that it was probably not to his taste if my ideas about the Chinese and coffee were correct. To my surprise, he replied, 'Yes, please,' adding that he came from an intellectual background. 'We intellectual Chinese like coffee, red wine too, which most Chinese can't stand either.'

Some time ago, in a class in which we were discussing national characteristics, I asked my students to draw the Chinese flag for me. Naturally, there was no difficulty about this, and a regulation flag was soon waving across the blackboard—the red background with the four small golden stars in a half circle round the big one. I then asked the students to explain the flag to me. This was not a problem either: the background colour represented the revolution and socialism, the big yellow star in the corner the party, and the four small stars the workers, peasants and soldiers.

'That only makes three,' I said. 'What about the fourth?'

There was a rather bewildered silence, followed by a short discussion in Chinese. Eventually a spokesman for the class explained that the fourth star represented people from other walks of life; that is, people who are not workers, peasants or soldiers, but patriots in some other way.

Some days later a little delegation from the class came to see me and asked if I remembered the problem about the flag.

'We have asked some of the older teachers,' they said, 'and they have told us that the fourth star represents the intellectuals. But it is important to remember two things. First, it doesn't represent all intellectuals, only those who are progressive and support socialism. And second, one must remember that the flag was designed many years ago. Many things have happened since then. It must be regarded as an expression of things as they were in those days. And Chairman Mao himself said that without the active co-operation of the intellectuals the revolution could not have been successful.'

'Am I to understand you as saying that if such a flag were designed today the intellectuals would not be represented?'

They could not answer that question. It was purely hypothetical, a silly question about a situation which did not exist. And besides, answering it could have far-reaching consequences which no one felt like risking.

Ten years ago my pupils had no doubt whatsoever as to what the fourth star represented. They were growing up in an educational system which made a sharp distinction between manual workers and academics. Most of them came from an academic background and it was obvious that they did so.

Probably the young I am teaching now come from much the same sort of social background, but because of the Cultural Revolution a blotting out of the social category of the professional intellectual has occurred. The requirements for admission to higher education have shifted from the academic to the physical.

There is a conflict here because while it is said to be impossible for a former exploiter of the people ever to change his class—the most he can do is to 'change his class cap'—the Cultural Revolution allowed an intellectual to achieve peasant or worker status by doing manual work for a period of time.

If one asks the present group of students to what class they belong, one is invariably told that she or he is worker/peasant/soldier. But, if one has the chance to go deeper and find out what their parents are or were, one usually finds that the class to which they say they belong is not the class into which they were born; it has been acquired by two or three years' work in a factory, commune or military unit.

On the floor above me there is an elderly teacher. He has encyclopaedic knowledge, even outside his own professional field: is arrogant to the tips of his well-kept fingernails and enjoys great professional respect.

But during the Cultural Revolution his status did him no good. He was violently attacked by the students and, like many others, made to run round the sports ground half a day at a time with three strapping students at his heels who, as they ran, poured ink over him. His arrogance had shown itself, among other things, by his refusing to eat at the institute canteen. He preferred to bicycle home to better food. He was re-educated by having to come to the canteen every mealtime, when rice and vegetables were dumped on the floor in front of him and he was handed a pair of chopsticks.

Possibly the establishment of the cadre schools should also be looked on as an attempt, through lengthy separation of the groups involved, to resolve the strong and bitter conflict—which had been brewing for a long time—between the students and their teachers. Perhaps it would have been difficult, though it did happen in a good many places, for the teachers who had been 'struggled' by their students to face the same group again. That may be partly why some, particularly many of the older teachers, spent several years in distant cadre schools.

But most of them are back again now. One does not speak of 'rehabilitation' but of 'modification' of their ideas and attitudes which has been sufficiently successful to allow them to carry out their pedagogic duties again. And the sophisticated old teacher on the floor above is in full swing again. He earns the same salary as before, nearly four times as much as most of his colleagues, and has even had back pay for the time during which teaching stopped and he was hounded round the cinder track.

In the village where our institute towers in secluded grandeur and to whose inhabitants we have closed our pompous gate, hard work is going on. For hundreds of years this northern part of the city has been Peking's rubbish dump, and it was not until some years after liberation that efforts were made to reclaim it layer by layer, bring in top soil, mark out fields and build irrigation schemes. A small energetic community has grown up here. Every autumn they dig up the fields and with the earth 'cast' high vertical banks which are roofed over and used as forcing-houses during the winter. And in spring, when they have harvested the crops in these forcing-houses, they return the walls to the fields, ready for summer cropping.

The village has its idiot and also its cripples, a couple of crooked old objects who, from ill-treatment or an accident many years ago, are now so disabled that they have to drag themselves along the road with their hands done up in rags.

There are a couple of young men who, with incredible virtuosity, cycle up and down the road. On the back of their bicycles they have big oil drums fixed and in their hands they hold a shovel. They are the manure collectors and their job is to follow the horses and carts, shovel up the droppings and deliver them to the commune. They have brought it to a fine art, so that they can bicycle at high speed, lean under the handlebars when they spot a prize, and like polo players on their elegant steeds, shovel up the muck as they ride and with an upswing fling it over one shoulder so that it flies into the tin behind.

And the village has its old grannies too, hobbling about on their bound feet, attired in the traditional high-necked black peasant blouses, open to the wind, exposing their long flat breasts—long and flat from the sucking of many babies trying to find nourishment where, in the end, there was none.

And finally the village has its intellectuals: an old couple about whose past I have not been able to find out anything. The only thing I know about them is that they were intellectuals once and that they were called to account by the people for some unspecified crimes. It is not as a punishment for these crimes, because work is not punishment, nor is it in expiation of their sins, but in order to improve and reform them that they have been given the job of village 'honey men'.

With a pair of donkeys pulling the cart, they have to go from house to house, to the village hall, canteen, clinic and institute, and pump the latrines into the large tank strapped on to what is euphemistically known as the honey cart.

It *is* honey, indeed gold, for the fields, and if one asks if it is not a rather unpleasant, or at least not very desirable job, one is told that the work is valuable, that it is important that it should be done and that Chairman Mao has said that no work is better or worse than any other.

'If that is the case, why do these old intellectuals, whose crimes I don't know, have to do this particular job? It does look as though they have been given the most unpleasant of all the jobs that can be found—even if one does believe that no job is better or worse than any other.'

'For some people such a process is necessary. Different methods of re-education have to be used in order to change people's way of thinking from negative to positive.'

'Do you think, then, that if a person is, or has been, an enemy of the people he becomes a friend by being given work of this kind?'

'It is not contemptible work. As I said, it is very valuable.'

'For the fields, yes, but for him and her? And for the community? If, for example, they were first-class scientists, would it not be more valuable to the community if they worked at their profession, teaching and doing research?'

'I don't think it is wise to question the decision of the people or their methods of re-education.'

Liu and I have just finished our evening shower. A makeshift curtain has been hung up to separate off a small corner of the big washroom for the two of us. Whether this is in deference to the assumed bashfulness of foreigners or from a deep-rooted feeling that people of different social status should not see each other naked I don't know. The curtain is inadequate—the lorry drivers can see us and we round-shouldered intellectuals can see them.

On another occasion Liu and I are walking with some of our local hosts in the streets of Xishuangbanna. Outside the little hospital a small group of people is standing waiting for us. They form a half circle round us and we shake innumerable hands. There is a second outer ring of people standing looking at us. An old woman manages to break through from this outer ring, between the members of the delegation of welcome, and catch me by the arm with a large wrinkled hand. Her head on one side, she only just has time to put three fingers of her left hand to her lips, the well-known gesture for 'eat', and murmur a few words in a quiet gentle voice before my hosts realize what is happening and quickly, but quietly, turn the handsome old woman round and put her outside the inner circle, which then closes behind her.

Without a moment's hesitation, Liu turns to me and says, 'She said thanks to the party and Chairman Mao.' There his improvisation comes to an abrupt end and the circle round us begins to move in order to take us inside.

But her gesture was unmistakable, and I could hear that she spoke the local Tai dialect, not standard Chinese, which is the only Chinese Liu understands. But in most other cases his improvization would have been correct because this is by far the most common introduction to any speech. And of course I can understand the embarrassment which must have been felt by most of those involved in the situation. They are about to show to a foreign visitor an example of the enormous progress which has been made, and which is genuine enough and needs no embellishment, and a beggar appears! Here in China, where the social progress which has occurred as a result of the revolution has done away with the causes for begging. I do not believe this woman was begging from poverty, from hunger she had no other means of satisfying. It seems much more likely that it was the result of a life-long habit going back to the poverty of the past, a reflex which made her approach an obviously well-to-do foreigner who had suddenly appeared in the town.

And in the same way as the curtain in the shower room is an attempt to shield me from the realities of life, so my intellectual escort attempts to shield me from the realities he does not wish to believe are there.

The Students' Peasants

My newly built house has five rooms
Which contain tables, cupboards, and good furniture.
Beside the wooden bed there is a sewing machine.
In the courtyard pure water runs from a tap
And our 'Flying Pigeon' and 'Red Flag' bicycles have shelter.
My household raises chickens, pigs and sheep
And my radio welcomes me home with music.
My brand new clothes are of nylon
And with three meals a day of rice and bread
—Delicious to taste and served piping hot—
I have not a care in the world.
On my private rose tree there are no thorns
And the revolutionary cause has blown from my mind.

These words, with their mild sarcasm, meant to point out one of the dangers of the present relative material wealth enjoyed by the peasants, were heard and written down by one of my students. They are the words of a song sung during work in the fields, an unusual phenomenon, a 'critical work song' directed against those members of the brigade who, in the opinion of others, are in danger of forgetting that the revolution goes on for ever, and no one can ever relax.

And it is at this time, when the new leaders of the country are talking of reintroducing bonus arrangements, increasing the supply of consumer goods and generally raising the standard of living—all things which were revisionist treason in the ears of the ascetic leaders of the Cultural Revolution—it is precisely at this time that this song is being sung; perhaps rather loudly in some quarters.

The song was quoted in a joint essay written by some of my students about a political study visit to a particular commune, and they added a footnote: 'This song reflects the narrow-mindedness of the peasants. They can see no further than their own liberation.'

Bearing their essay in mind, and using the song as a point of departure, I have had several discussions with them about what it means 'to be a revolutionary'. Among students it is a commonly expressed opinion that peasants, by and large, are distinctly conservative in their attitudes. Expressed in a revolutionary peasant society like China, where it was the peasant armies which fought their way to liberation, this opinion would be very disparaging to the majority of the population and bordering on heresy were it not for the fact that Chairman Mao has said exactly the same thing.

But it is quite another thing when students, with a stroke of the pen in a two-line footnote, describe peasants as narrow-minded and imply that they are lacking in political vision and insight. It can only mean that they see themselves as better revolutionaries than the peasants. This is particularly surprising considering that they are represented by the fourth star on the flag and therefore belong to the intellectuals, who for the last ten years have been more or less disowned as a class.

And though the students frequently talk about the importance of joining the peasants and workers in order to learn from them the true revolutionary spirit, at the same time they are liable to speak of them in a very condescending manner, giving the impression that they see themselves as being the ideological teachers of the peasants.

These days, there is a phantom standing in the wings. No official announcement has as yet been made, but the bush telegraph is buzzing with rumours that it can only be a matter of days before Deng Xiaoping returns. For most of those with whom I can discuss the matter, the only question is how high a post he will get. And his return or otherwise will give a clearer indication of what course China will follow than did Hua's seizure of power last year. Supporters of Deng have already begun discreetly to make their positions known, at the same time underlining the fact that they have held this attitude all along, even during the violent anti-Deng campaigns which have broken out from time to time.

'Not long ago,' I was told by a colleague, 'a student said to me that I had obviously forgotten the party orders to carry on the campaign against Deng to the very end and as far as he knew this order had not been rescinded. He called me a secret supporter of the traitor. There was only one thing I could say to him: "If you say Deng Xiaoping to me, I will say Jesus Christ to you!" '

And another colleague stood up strongly for Deng saying (in spite of the fact that he is unmarried): 'Deng will be a good leader for us. He knows and understands the wishes of the people, and he is prepared to realize them. When he was last in power he made a move to put an end to the unreasonable arrangement whereby a married couple are often separated from one another for long periods, sometimes for life. He had just managed to get it through the Academy of Science when the lies and treachery of the "Gang of Four" got him out, but there were many who were very pleased that he had tried. We Chinese always maintain that the splitting up of families does not worry us as long as it is in the interests of society and the revolution, but naturally married couples want to live together. That is why they get married. Deng understands this and that is one of the reasons many of us would like to see him back.'

During this period of uncertainty, a teacher comes in one day and describes to me a toy, of which he wants to know the English name. It is, he explains, a little doll with a rounded base made of lead so that it always stands up again no matter how hard one tries to push it down.

'Is there any special connection in which you want to use the name of such a toy?' I ask.

'Possibly, soon,' he says.

It is during the intervening years, the years in which daily life, routine development and the predictability of things have gone awry, that a great change in the relationship between the students and the peasants—or rather in the attitude of the students towards the peasants—has taken place.

The students I am working with now are approximately ten or twelve years older than the pupils I had ten or twelve years ago. They therefore belong to the generation I saw plunge head-first into the Cultural Revolution and which I now see emerging from it, at a time when the Cultural Revolution, as one of my students with unconscious irony put it, has been declared by the party to be 'victoriously dead'. There are several striking differences between those I worked with then and those I work with now. In Canton I had pupils who saw themselves as being in danger of becoming the forerunners of a 'professional' and arrogant academic class. Much of their criticism of the educational system was to the effect that they were to a large extent dissociated from the realities of life, and in particular from the realities of the life of the peasants. It is true that now and then they were sent to work in the fields as a mobile labour force when extra hands were needed at harvest time and so on, but many of them regarded this as an empty gesture, a short stay which gave them only a glimpse into the harsh realities of life outside their 'academic hothouse'. It was a declaration of solidarity with the peasants which did not carry with it any personal sacrifice. I think most of them felt genuine warmth and admiration for former poor peasants and were disappointed that their contacts were so limited. It was an occasion for them when, as sometimes happened, an old peasant visited the school to describe the 'bad old times'. They regarded these 'recall the past' meetings as of the utmost importance.

'You have to remember,' they would say, 'we are young, we were all born after liberation. We have never had any experience of the old days, and imagination and speculation are not enough. It is necessary that we are constantly reminded how badly off people were in the old China that we do not forget and get too pleased with ourselves about the new.'

They put up posters asking why they were given polished rice when the peasants had to eat unpolished, and recalled the fact that it was not so many years ago that many peasants had only the polishings or millet, roots and berries to live on.

And when they spoke of solidarity with the peasants it was not just a declaration that on principle they were on their side. In many cases they went further—as far as saying that they did not wish to go on with an academic career but to go out into the country, settle among the peasants and work with them.

There was at one time an official programme being carried out intended, it was said, to get the 'educated' youth out of the towns and into the countryside where they would learn from the peasants. In this case it was probably a mass and not entirely voluntary movement of some of the young who, for a few years, had led the Cultural Revolution with a mixture of chaos, order and great determination. There were without doubt many who did not wish to leave the towns, and there appeared roving bands of young people who had made off from their agricultural jobs and were trying to keep body and soul together by other means. These bands which, to some extent, must have contributed to the rise in the crime rate do not, however, appear to have been alarmingly numerous.

But the fundamental respect and loyalty of the majority of the students for China's revolutionary masses, the peasants, was never in doubt.

At one time in the late 1960s, when the antagonisms and clashes in my school seemed to be cooling off, the pupils and teachers who remained collected together after the school as such closed down. Although individual pupils had left the school, the town and even the Cultural Revolution itself, the larger part were still here. The climax of the internal dissensions had been when some pupils had barricaded themselves into various school buildings and fought out their political battles with sticks and stones. There were other institutions where it had been even more violent, to the point of using stolen firearms and home-made ammunition.

Following this climax, when it became apparent to the two warring parties that physical violence would not resolve ideological differences, they all went by train and boat to the big island of Hainan in the South China Sea. There they joined a commune, worked at fishing and agriculture, tended rubber plantations and apparently made no plans to resume academic work. They settled down for an unspecified time in order to learn from the peasants how to put into practice the political theories they had learned about in abstract from their endless weekly study groups.

And here, unfortunately, there is a gap in my personal observations. I would very much have liked to follow their development during the years on Hainan, but must be content with trying to find out what the results have been, because, even if my present students are not the same as those I had then, they have, broadly speaking, had the same experiences, and those I saw in the 1960s disappearing into a mighty reform campaign I now see emerging from it.

The Cultural Revolution has its blind spots; it is impossible to describe it in any detail and no official statement about it has yet been issued. But it seems certain that the 'invisibility' which shrouds it, putting any personal and often painful involvement on one side, is due to the fact that an overall assessment of it would inevitably mean a further evaluation of its protagonist and 'protector'—Mao. For this and other reasons, it is a cautious generation which is now emerging from this chain of historical events; cautious and stamped with weariness and uncertainty. Where one of the powerful instructions of the past was, 'We must never be blind and uncritical slaves of orders just because they are orders and come from our superiors', the same generation is now stamped with a resignation which gives rise to the exact opposite policy: 'For the sake of unity it is important that we do everything our Great, Glorious and Correct Party prescribes for us.'

I see the youth of China today as a generation worn out by the struggles of a decade—struggles not for personal independence, but to help their immediate community battle with a distant and, in many instances, evasive and unknown authoritarian power. I believe ten years' devotion to leaders and their ideas — only to be told that the ideas were all wrong and the leaders themselves traitors in disguise—has gradually reduced these revolutionary storm troopers to the point of being unable to take a stand about anything. It may be a relief to them at the moment but in the long run it can be very dangerous.

During the last ten years they have seen leaders thrown out, apparently as the result of broad popular demand, and they have seen others replace them. But as the process repeats itself over and over again, they have become resigned to the fact that when all is said and done, it is not *their* influence, not their battles, which are responsible for the changes.

At the onset of the Cultural Revolution we had to discard many of our textbooks, almost from one day to the next, because a large number of the texts contained eulogies of Liu Shaoqi, the president whose name eventually became synonymous with the whole of the right-wing revisionists of the revolution. When Lin Biao first appeared it was as Mao's close comrade-in-arms and successor, and a few years later he was shot down over Mongolia while trying to escape to the Soviet Union, after an alleged attempt at a coup. Jiang Qing, as Mao's wife, became the guarantor for the carrying on of the correct line and was rhetorically hailed as the spokesman for everything good (although she is the only one of China's leaders I have known to be the subject of sniggering and derisive laughter from a newsreel audience, safely concealed in the darkness of the cinema, and I find it reasonable to believe that she never enjoyed great popularity). Zhu De managed, before his death, to regain his position in the exclusive group of three consisting of himself, Zhou and Mao, in spite of the fact that he had been the target of much criticism during the Cultural Revolution. Deng Xiaoping has been alternately praised and reviled, but there is not much ground for believing that campaigns whether for or against have had much effect, one way or the other, on the individual person's attitude to these people.

A colleague tells me, with amazing candour, that he is sick and tired of political studies and that for years now he has spent several hours each week on the collective nonsense which is called 'studying the works of Chairman Mao'. He adds that it is only since the fall of the 'Four' that he can tell me how every day for several years he has had to sit staring at the leader in the *People's Daily* trying to appear deeply interested.

'Most people in the study group were in the same boat,' he says, 'but none of us dared admit it to the others.'

'Why didn't you discuss it with each other? That kind of oppression didn't exist during the Cultural Revolution.'

'I suppose we were all afraid of being criticized. Everything has been so difficult. We couldn't speak freely.'

'And now?'

'Now, fortunately, it is different. Now we can criticize the "Gang of Four" freely.'

'And the present leaders?'

'Why on earth should we criticize them? They have liberated us from the "Four" so we are all right now.'

'But the "Four" had liberated you from Lin Biao and Liu Shaoqi, who in their turn tried to liberate you from something else.'

'That was different. It was not the same with them. They tried to make us believe something. In reality they were all reactionaries, only we didn't see it in the beginning.'

'And are there no reactionaries in the party now?'

'I suppose there will always be a few, but now that they have been cleared out after the evil influence of the "Four" the party is on the right course again.'

'But hasn't it always been? After all, you have always referred to it as the Great, Glorious and Correct Party.'

'Well, we had to, didn't we?'

And so we could go on without ever getting to the core of the matter: that is, whether there has been a strengthening or a weakening of Mao's words that 'rebellion is justified'. Personal attitudes in these post-revolution years have tended to become laissez-faire, wait and see. The older generation, who were the object of attack, feel in many ways resentful and the younger generation has lost its original dynamism and is exhausted. The general impression that students give is that although they still have a kind of built-in sense of duty to show the right sentiments by collecting writings, experiences, and information from the peasants, to whom they are less and less often sent, they feel even more the need to confirm their ideological superiority over a conservative peasantry.

If one looks behind the rhetoric and the platitudes, one finds a young generation who are deliberately cultivating the traditional arrogance of their class and cementing it fast. The requirement that candidates for higher education must have done a kind of 'national service' by doing manual work is, to all intents and purposes, only an attempt to disguise the true situation. Thus the Cultural Revolution has not only turned full circle, it is back on a 'lower level'.

Examinations have just been reintroduced. At present they are in the form of half-yearly tests of general proficiency, but everyone is convinced that this is only a preliminary to bringing back the 'old bourgeois examination system', as it was described at the time it was abolished in the mid-1960s. It was one of the first things achieved by the Cultural Revolution, one of the first practical results, and discussions on this subject had breadth and depth.

After a number of pleasant lunches with leading cadres where the talk was free and friendly, I have been excused from taking part in the examinations. Or, more correctly, I have not been invited to take part.

I am anxious to find out why exams have been reintroduced and what this means in terms of the Cultural Revolution.

'Before the Cultural Revolution we had a set of old-fashioned bourgeois exams. They were used to encourage book-learning, a stick and a carrot for the careerists. The new examinations will not have this function. Their sole purpose will be to judge the student's ability.'

'What is the difference? An exam and an exam cannot really be two different things. And strictly speaking doesn't it depend, not so much on what the purpose is, as on how the students see them and make use of them? Don't you think they will see and use them in the old-fashioned way?'

'I don't think you quite understand the difference between the old-fashioned bourgeois exams and the new socialist ones. The students certainly understand it. They have been trained and tempered by the Cultural Revolution. They have had a change of heart. We have come much nearer to eradicating the tendency towards individualism.

'What is the purpose of the exams? The teacher who is with his students every day can estimate their standard far more precisely than any outsider. And what happens if anyone fails?'

'There will be no failures.'

'Isn't one of the objects of an exam to decide whether or not people should continue with their studies?'

'Yes, certainly, and that is one of the objects of the new exams too. But this year we have decided to set the pass mark so low that everyone will pass.'

'And next year?'

'We shall have to decide that next year. The standard will probably be raised.'

'With what consequences?'

'There is talk of possibly repeating a class. We don't know yet. It will depend on what our experiences are this year.'

'And you don't think that good marks and career factors will rear their ugly heads under these circumstances?'

'As I said, there has been a change of heart. Young people now think more about the common good than about their own individual interests.'

And that must be correct. In our institute, as in all others in the country, every morning from now till the end of the exams letters are read out on the loudspeakers. Letters from students, whose names are given, who are about to graduate from the sheltered life behind these high walls and go out into the world to put their knowledge to good use. They are moving epistles which reverberate over the sports ground and echo down the corridors, asking for the most menial jobs that are to be found, asking to be sent to folk communes, factories, and other types of manual work where they can show their will and ability to take part in the building up of socialism.

The anxiety which prevails outside the examination room is not noticeably different from what I witnessed in the old days. Several of the twelve- to fourteen-year-olds wept buckets during oral exams, even though we had decided to make it easy for them. In fact, it turned out then that the exams were not marked in the usual way. In the first round, realistic marks on a 1–100 scale were given, but these were not final. When they had all been examined, the teachers got together and went through the individual marks. There might be one who came near the 100 mark but who, according to general opinion, might not be able to keep it up and would be in danger of getting too self-confident; his or her marks were then significantly reduced. On the other hand, there might be one who had begun to realize how hopeless he or she was and was about to give up the unequal struggle; such marks were significantly raised. Both ways the changes were supposed to serve as a stimulus to the students involved.

But while we daily hear the excerpts from these letters requesting menial jobs, there are some teachers who receive little notes from their students—the same students whose letters have been heard on the loudspeakers—containing discreet requests for office work in a ministry, or to be allowed to continue with academic work. In some of the letters there are also references to the writer's relatively high status by virtue of family background or place in society. But I have not seen any which declare themselves as part of what is theoretically the most elevated group of all, namely that of the peasant, or even as worker or soldier.

The new socialist examination system is quite different, I am told, from the depraved and corrupt bourgeois system as practised in the Soviet Union. In the past, when students from China were sent to universities in the Soviet Union, if they passed their exam they had to suffer the indignity of being given a fountain pen, a diploma and a leather briefcase in which to carry their diploma and other private papers. With these visible signs to bolster up their conceit, they returned to China feeling themselves to be superior persons.

On one occasion during the Cultural Revolution, one of my students said: 'We are treated like Peking ducks. That is why we are protesting against the educational system. Peking ducks are force-fed. The school offers us only one goal, our career, but for us it is more important that we should have an opportunity of joining with the peasants, who are the backbone of China.'

Daily Life

When, in the summer of 1965, old Director Li met me at Peking airport and I stood, open-minded and ignorant, faced with an incomprehensible China, we drove to Tien An Men, the main building of the Imperial Palace which, with its tumultuous colours, watches over the huge grey Place of Heavenly Peace. There I saw my first stone lions and my first calligraphy on their home ground; there my air-conditioned nostrils had their first whiff of Peking's fragrant talcum-fine dust; and there an endless sea of possibilities stretched out before me. And as I stood there knowing I must begin shedding all the Western ideas I had brought with me, with shivers running down my spine at the thought of all the unknown to be weighed and measured against the known, the smiling old man pointed to a passing bus and said, 'Look, there's a bus. It is Chinese. We made it ourselves.'

And I stood there trying to see such a common object as a crowded bus with new eyes.

'We are no longer dependent on imports from other countries. We are our own masters even in the matter of transport. It is a great step forward for the Chinese people. All the time we are making giant strides in the direction of self-sufficiency.'

What Li expressed that morning was brought home to me more and more by everything I experienced as time went on. A tremendous sense of achievement at having got so far, but always with fresh goals to aim for.

One day, immediately after the fall of the 'Four', I was being driven through Peking by a young chauffeur. Most of the drivers speak no foreign language. If they do, the older ones speak Russian, the younger English. This one spoke English sufficiently well for us to converse and as he drove skilfully and energetically through Peking's anarchistic bicycle traffic, he told me about the latest accusations against Jiang Qing (what the other three had done was still veiled in mystery). He was an experienced chauffeur and drove with studied elegance, his left arm resting on the car window. It is characteristic of many of the chauffeurs that, while they spend an awful lot of time looking after the outsides of their cars, they drive, to the horror of most foreigners, like the cart drivers, with no feeling for the moving parts.

We were in a Shanghai car, a private car which has been the proto-type for Chinese production for some years, the newer models of which are showing more and more the influence of Germany and Japan.

With old Li's pride of ten years ago in mind, and in the knowledge that I was sitting beside a representative of the new China, I asked him how he liked being given a Shanghai car. I myself thought it a splendid vehicle. He pursed his lips, his free hand hit the roof of the car, and he shook his head.

'No good,' he said. 'Better give me a Mercedes Benz. One of my friends drives Mercedes. German car. Much better.'

At regular intervals meetings are held in my office. I act as host be-cause mine is the largest office in the building and the only one which is heated. There is central heating in our house, but this particular winter the production and transport of coal has been in a critical state. Enormous efforts are being made to re-open the mines in Tangshan and get production back to normal, but we must expect a winter of rationed heating. In the institute's north-facing offices and classrooms it is down to three or four degrees below zero these days, but of course we are not the only ones suffering as a result of last summer's catastrophe.

At this moment, our meetings are mainly concerned with working out more effective teaching methods. They are brain-storming meet-ings in which we try to get together a stockpile of ideas, twist and turn them, in an effort to 'increase production and improve quality'.

In the course of our discussions I have discovered that the in-stitute has at its command no less than a complete audio-video set— TV camera, tape-recorder, mixing table, monitor and tapes. None of us have had any experience of audio-visual teaching but we all have ideas and suggestions. It transpires that none of this equipment has ever been used—partly because there is no one who knows how to use it and partly because, as one of them said with a smile I could not quite interpret, it was a personal gift from Lin Biao to the institute. Possibly it is the latter which, in the light of later events, made the gift such an embarrassment that it could not be unpacked and put to use.

At any rate, these things have been standing in one of the store-rooms for seven or eight years and have never been unpacked. I am now asked to write a little sketch to illustrate points in the use of the language, suitable for performance by ourselves and some of the students. The group responsible for getting the whole thing going suggests that I should take as my theme the life of the hero Lei Feng who at the moment is having a renaissance as an exemplary national hero. He was the young soldier who, during his short life, learnt to put self completely behind him and only thought of (and practised) devoting himself to others and the community.

While the audio-visual team sets about finding an unoccupied room to use as a studio, I write a simple little scenario. With every-thing organized we meet to try out the system before we begin recording.

It seems that Peking's hot summers and icy winters, combined with extremes of dry and damp, have been more than the sensitive apparatus can stand. Strange things appear on the screen and the sound refuses to come out properly. We do our best to improve matters but with a signal lack of success. I suggest we will have to let the project rest until we have had the apparatus repaired. It is im-possible to use it as it is.

'I think it will be difficult to get it repaired,' says one of the group. 'None of us have been trained to work with that sort of thing. We have skilled technicians in our tape-recorder workshops, but they would certainly not dare start on this. It is a Japanese machine and very sophisticated.'

My next suggestion is that the institute should contact the tele-vision section of Peking Broadcasting House because, by chance, I happen to know that in addition to their Chinese cameras and machines they have some Japanese equipment. The group thought this was a brilliant idea and they promised to put it to the 'relevant competent authority'.

After a week of waiting, I am informed that it is regretted, but Broadcasting House is Broadcasting House, and we are us and there is no direct line of communication between the two units. I protest, and even suggest they should try and make contact just the same, but am told, very definitely, that this is impossible.

Then I suggest Tsinghua University. From having visited there I know they have a department which not only does research in TV technology but, as a sideline, produces equipment for colour television. They should have both the theoretical and practical knowledge, as well as the tools with which to do the job. But again I am told: Tsinghua is Tsinghua and we are us and there is no direct line of communication. One of the teachers says he knows someone there and I see a chance: 'Ring him up and ask him if there are not a couple of students in his department who would like to come and do a service to another institute.'

He looks at me in astonishment and laughs.

'I can't just ring up Tsinghua!'

'Why not?'

'Because they will immediately want to know who I am; they will ask my name.'

'If they do, tell them your name.'

'I can't do that. I have no authority to ring Tsinghua.'

There is some further discussion from which it appears that all possibilities are impossible. The group resigns itself to the fact that we shall just have to carry out the project with defective equipment— there is no other solution.

'It was a story about Lei Feng you asked for, wasn't it?' I ask.

They confirm that it was and express interest in the result.

'About Lei Feng who, through initiative, industry, and self-sacrifice, showed that anything is possible, provided that people help one another, who never let himself be discouraged by apparent impossibilities and therefore was able to accomplish things other people could not.'

But maybe my sarcasm was misplaced, because if the system says it is impossible to contact others outside the regular channels, I suppose not much can be done about it. But it may be that my irritation was not even understood.

Hitherto unseen and unthinkable books are circulating in the institute, one of the first obvious results of the expected liberalization following the departure of Jiang Qing and Co. Some of the books, judging by their appearance, have been concealed for many years; others are brand new. There is a lively exchange going on but I have yet to meet the owner of a book. They have all been borrowed. Who the owners are and how the books came into their hands remains a mystery, but most of them seem to pass by my desk for comments on their quality.

The need for light literature after ten years of asceticism does not surprise me, but I can't express unqualified approval of those I see. Most of them are poor-quality English or American paperbacks of the detective or war-story genre. One such book has come completely out in the open, however, because someone has, somehow, got hold of a tape-recording of British actors doing it as a serial. It is a detective story about an English village policeman who is trying to catch an escaped prisoner who has been wrongly convicted and who is competing with the police to find the man who framed him. The book and tapes go the round of the more advanced classes, and every day I can hear sounds from yet another classroom of a well-spoken British bobby tracking down his man.

This is not to say that the doors have been flung wide open to foreign light literature, and that other things have given way to it, but the number of well-worn books increases daily and they are carried about sticking out of people's pockets with increasing casualness and little or no attempt at concealment.

One day Xiao Wang is sitting in the office reading a tattered book with a shiny cover. He asked me if I know it and says he thinks it is good. It is a war story by an author named Sven Hazel. I tell Wang that I do not know that particular book but have read another by the same author, that he is Danish like myself, that I think he writes trash and is an author strongly tainted with Nazism. I can suggest other equally exciting books which I can really recommend.

'But he seems to be very anti-Soviet,' I am told, and with that I have to agree. But this remark makes me reflect on the sad situation in this country today, in which something need only be anti-Soviet to become automatically acceptable.

However, following my comments on Hazel and his writing, Xiao Wang does tell me that he doesn't feel like finishing the book.

On another occasion I go into a colleague's office to deliver some finished work to find him sitting in deep contemplation of his fingertips.

'I am neurotic,' he says, seeming very put out at this discovery, which certainly comes as a surprise to me.

'What makes you think you are neurotic?' I ask.

'I can see it by my fingertips; they tell me I am neurotic.'

'You have got hold of the *Reader's Digest* again,' I say with great conviction. 'What did it say about your neurosis?'

'How did you know I had been reading that?' he asks in great surprise.

'Because in the first place you are not in the least neurotic and in the second the *Reader's Digest* is the only periodical available here where they fill people up with such shit. How did they make you think you were neurotic, and what has it to do with your fingertips?'

'There was an article which said that if the little patterns in the skin of the fingertips are the same on both hands it is a sign that you are neurotic. What does neurotic mean?'

I try to explain as simply as I can, and as I myself understand it, that being neurotic is something to do with anxiety, associated with insecurity and lack of adjustment to the society in which one finds oneself. Where my comments on the low standards and reactionary attitude of the *Reader's Digest* had not made the slightest impression, my suggestion that neurosis might have social causes results in an outburst from my colleague.

'That's a load of rubbish,' he says, nearly flipping his fingertips off. 'I am not in the least neurotic.'

A usually quiet and soft-spoken teacher knocks on my door one day and asks if he may ask me a question. He is just writing a contribution to the English wall newspaper and he wants to be sure that his use of language is correct.

'Is it correct to say the "witch and female bitch Jiang Qing"?' he asks.

I tell him that, as far as I am concerned, he may call her what he likes, but I do have a couple of comments about the wording. First of all, 'female bitch' is tautology since the word bitch in itself determines the sex. Secondly, I would like to comment on the terms themselves. I am sure he would agree with me that if one finds it necessary to use terms of abuse about someone it is in principle important to use terms which do not depend on the person's sex, but on their actions.

My intention is an edifying little lecture on discrimination against women—something which is still found in China, and often has a clear linguistic side to it. Echoes of the Western Women's Lib movement have reached a few ears in China, and we have a long discussion on how language can be used to boost men and do down women. He tells me that the same kind of campaign is going on in China too, and how it is still necessary to keep things to do with the oppression of women constantly before one. Although he thinks, from what he has heard, that in this respect China has made a good deal more progress than the West.

'It is only in country districts that there are still some difficulties. For example, it is still unusual there to divide the housework equally. It is a little better among young people in the country but the greatest progress in this area is undoubtedly in the towns. For us it now seems perfectly natural to share the chores. It is unusual to hear talk of men's work or women's work. That is a great improvement on the old days.'

I would like to believe him, and can only agree with him that it is a great step forward from the China in which a man had the same rights over his wife as over his horse: 'to whip or to ride her as he chose'. But I am a bit surprised to hear that people in towns have advanced so far when I think of the loud laughter with which my students greet the information that it is I, and not Stine, who does the cooking at home.

'Unfortunately,' he goes on, 'there are still many youngsters who are not quite as mature as they may appear. Perhaps they are still clinging to old-fashioned ideas in spite of the advances we others have made.'

We end our conversation by thanking one another warmly for our valuable meeting. On the way out he turns: 'By the way, concerning the question which originally brought me here. Would it be all right if I call her a witch and an ambitious bitch?'

It was only a few hundred miles from Canton to the Vietnamese border, on the other side of which the war with the United States was going on. In the Children's Cultural Palace there were life-sized figures of President Johnson and Vice-President Humphrey. The children tested their strength by grasping the necks and seeing how fast they could make the eyes rotate. Between classes they walked about the corridors with phrase-books in their hands and practised sentences like: 'Come out with your hands up, we treat our prisoners well.'

Every night there was anti-aircraft practice in the black tropical skies over the town. Droning propellered aircraft crept round up there, allowing themselves to be picked out by the long fingers of the searchlights. There was no doubt about who the enemy was, and the words 'American' and 'United States' were never used without the qualifying words 'imperialist' or 'imperialism'.

It is therefore an almost unbelievable experience to arrive in Peking a few years later and see the Stars and Stripes waving over a big building in a corner of the diplomatic quarter—the American Liaison Office. Ordinary 'after you' politeness comes to a startled halt when one nearly bumps into Hubert Humphrey coming out of the swing doors of the Hotel Peking. And when on a long lonely walk along the Great Wall one finds a squashed Coca-Cola tin it is with feelings of embarrassment.

But the really depressing thing about this change of attitude is the unctuous admiration for so many of the worst things about America. Once again, it seems that as long as you are sufficiently anti-Soviet you can be as far to the right as you like. That the doors have been opened on both sides is no bad thing in itself, but one frequently has to ask oneself what has happened to China's political attitude and where is her consistency?

It pains many of my colleagues that Albania—to everyone's surprise —has suddenly raised her voice in criticism of China who, since Albania broke with the Soviet Union, has been practically her only friend. The two countries had entered into a blood pact it seemed, sworn eternal loyalty to one another; and China, with her relatively large resources, has been a big economic prop to Albania. One of the commodities which Albania exports to China is cigarettes. The fact is, however, that in order to fulfil their export obligations the Albanians have had to farm out the larger part of the production to the sister country—China. This means that this year the cigarettes are being produced in Shanghai, made of Chinese tobacco, packed in Chinese packets by Chinese labour, but, according to the trade agreement, have stamped on the package: 'Made in Albania'.

That is only a small matter but is mentioned as an example of China's willingness to help the loyal Albanians with advantageous commercial deals both directly and indirectly. It was taken as a national insult, therefore, when the Albanian Embassy in Peking— quite without precedent—began circulating a translation of a long political leader in *Zeri i Popullit* attacking China's policy after Hua's coup. The leaflets circulated in my unit too, and were read and discussed, but in a curiously flat atmosphere. I had the feeling that if one had been able to discuss it confidentially there would have been many who would be inclined to agree with the Albanians, but one of the difficulties here is the near impossibility of confidential discussion. We are limited to half-hearted discussions about facts and cannot concern ourselves with underlying principles. There was speculation as to whether it was likely to come to an open diplomatic break, and there was an unconfirmed rumour from one of the language institutes that all Albanian students had been sent home in a hurry.

The only clearly expressed opinion I heard was from a young man who summarily dismissed Albania's criticisms of China with the words: 'They can't criticize us. Do you realize that there are more people in Peking at any one time than in the whole of Albania?'

Quite apart from the fact that this is no argument, I must say that it is one of the worst examples of brainless chauvinism I have ever met.

'Just imagine, one of the "Gang of Four" gave his daughter no less than seven Japanese colour television sets as a wedding present. That kind of extravagance with privileged valuables cannot be tolerated.'

At this time, when the background of the 'Four' is being revealed layer by layer, every day produces a new scandal to add to the general picture, and the stories are being retailed with a mixture of horror and respect. Naturally I agree with my informant that it was gross extravagance, and that it seemed rather unnecessary to have seven television sets in the same house. But I also wondered where he had got them from. You cannot buy Japanese TV sets in Peking or, as far as I know, anywhere else in the country.

'He got them from people who wanted an audience with him. Representatives of delegations who wished to speak with him had to send money or gifts before he would see them.'

I thought that was even worse than having given them away, and expressed surprise that I had never heard the charge that he had accepted hundreds of expensive wristwatches, a small fortune in cash, the imported goods mentioned and masses of other goods as well.

'I think that is a very important point of criticism against a man who is supposed to be a leader in a socialist society. In my eyes it is much worse than many of the other charges.'

The explanation I got was that it is, after all, common practice. Naturally most people did not approve of it, but that was how things were. It was definitely not regarded as bribery and corruption —it was a tradition which had been carried on. This explanation raised a question in my mind which I felt would be too scandalous to ask.

Among her many crimes, Jiang Qing had been accused of pestering the old and sick Mao into letting her have a small fortune to pay for the life of luxury she was said to lead. Many times during my stay in China I had been told that my salary was higher than that of Mao, that he got 400 yuan a month while I got nearly 500. I have too great a respect for Mao to see him as a miserly two-faced man, but the question inevitably presents itself: how did he come by the fortune which the gossips say Jiang Qing got out of him?

The question of what will happen to the 'Four', or what may already have happened, never seems to have aroused much interest. The two things which were important in the case were the crimes they had committed and the fact that they were no longer in power. Whether they would be executed, exiled to a distant province, or imprisoned for life did not appear to be a matter of much concern. Most people's immediate reaction to the question was that there hardly seemed grounds for execution and they said that anyway there is no tradition for the execution of political enemies who have fallen from power.

There was only one person among those I asked who showed strong feelings on the matter. It was not at all in his nature (as I knew it), nor quite in keeping with the 'Chinese character', that he gave way to a violent outburst.

'I would like to see them tied to four lamp-posts on Tien An Men and we should all be allowed to go and beat them to death. They don't deserve to get off any lighter than that.'

This was an exception to the generally expressed more moderate view, which was that the best thing would be that they should be forgotten but their crimes remembered.

Another China, Far from Power

The first glimpse of China's incredible efficiency—which I had almost forgotten—is the foyer of my hotel in Rangoon at the end of a few weeks' tour of South-East Asia. As I get up from breakfast, a young Chinese attired in a four-pocket cadre uniform approaches me and says: 'Denmark Kunming?'

I confirm that I am from Denmark and am on my way that very afternoon to Kunming where Director Li from my institute will meet me at the airport. The young man says that he is from CAAC, the national Chinese airline, and his job is to see that I catch the plane.

Naturally I ask him how he knew where to find me and from that moment he is unable to speak English. Nor for that matter Burmese, which I also try, getting the receptionist to act as interpreter. He indicates with signs that I should be seated and sits down himself with a faraway look in his eyes. Now and then he looks at his watch but does not appear impatient. One of the hotel boys brings my luggage down; otherwise there is silence in the hotel in this silent town.

After a time the CAAC man gets up, goes over to the reception desk, picks up the telephone and dials a number. While he is waiting for an answer he turns to me and says one word: 'Limousine'.

He does not appear to be getting any answer and after one or two further unsuccessful attempts he comes back. 'Car,' he says now, and the difference between that and a limousine is obviously that his vehicle is a Land-Rover.

In complete silence and at a furious speed he drives me the twenty kilometres or so to Rangoon's deserted traffic-free airport, approaches a gate and hoots. A man comes out, swings the gate open and we drive on to the apron. My chauffeur points and says, 'In there.' I grab my bags and go where he tells me.

There are four Chinese diplomats from the embassy in Katmandu and myself. They have Japanese-made electric fans with them, large pale blue blades on a chromium-plated stand. I assume they are on their way home at the end of their time in Nepal. The plane we are waiting for is the day's only arrival and departure from this airport.

Out on the apron, two men are squatting, painting a transparency. There is something in Japanese and Burmese on it, and in English it says, 'Welcome to the Japanese Prime Minister'.

A few hours later I land in Kunming. Liu, prototype of the correct and perfect middle cadre, is standing at the foot of the gangway. I had hoped he would bring Xiao Wang with him; that would have been an experience for us both.

There are six customs officers to relieve me of my single bag and, as usual, it happens without any fuss. I wonder what they do the rest of the week. This is the only international connection and I wonder if there are ever any more passengers than there are today, bringing to mind all the talk about 'fewer troops and simpler administration'. One of the customs officers tells me that he knew I was coming today. Their colleague, whom I have been teaching in Peking, had written and told them. He had hoped to be here himself, but apparently had not been able to make it. I remember him well. He was delighted that I was going to visit his home province and spent a long time in my office telling me about it.

Kunming has certain resemblances to Peking. The inner part is planned along the same lines. There is the same big bare square which indicates a centre without, however, being surrounded by a densely built-up metropolis, and a long main thoroughfare crossing the square from east to west but without Peking's cars and lorries. It is a town without Peking's pressure and numbers of people, one which seems to be waiting to be occupied. Kunming is in repose.

In spite of the fact that a foreigner is an unusual sight, one can walk in much greater comfort here than in Peking. Among other things are no parents seizing their children by the arm, pointing and saying, 'Look, a foreigner.' Kunming is an overgrown village, a provincial capital where the symbols of power—squares, government offices, avenues and public buildings—are out of scale.

Liu does not like me to go out alone, and our programme is so tight anyway that I haven't much opportunity to do so; but if, as happens now and then, I have an hour or two between trips into the surrounding country and I want to go for a walk, Liu is by my side in an instant. I don't know if this has to do with my personal safety (I don't feel at all at risk) or because he is afraid I might get involved in something or just disappear. Still, I can understand it. He has been given the responsibility of meeting me at Kunming airport, going through the programme with me and seeing that I get back to Peking, safe and sound, on a certain date.

But it is not Kunming we have come to see. We are on our way south to the region which borders on Burma and Laos, to one of China's big minority areas. Bad flying weather is holding us up. Chinese pilots have a commendable reputation for not taking off unless the weather is crystal clear and calm over the whole route, and the first leg of our journey takes us over high mountains, down to a microscopic landing strip in a remote valley. This valley is so narrow and surrounded by such high mountains that we cannot land from a straight approach. The little two-engined Antonov has to work its way down in a spiral which gets tighter and tighter, until it becomes possible for it to straighten out and touch down on the short runway.

Once in Zemao, Liu and I have a common bond. Here we are in the same boat: we are both foreigners. Neither of us has been here before. We are both lost as far as the local dialect is concerned, and Liu, my interpreter, has to have an interpreter himself. We are both in the same situation of being dependent on the explanations of others, even if Liu is one step nearer than I.

Our host in Zemao is a man of commanding presence and with a devilish-powerful handshake. He chain-smokes, gesticulates and laughs a lot. In spite of the fact that he is the official host and I an honoured guest, he insists on speaking the little English and the smattering of French he has at his disposal. He laughs at his clumsiness in the use of the languages, but still insists on getting round Liu interpreting.

'It takes so long if everything has to be translated twice,' he says.

Our host is a 'true' Chinese in that ethnically he belongs to the Han people, who make up by far the largest proportion of the population of China, the small percentage which is not Han being composed of about fifty minority groups. And it is one of these autonomous, or at least partly self-governing minority areas we are on our way to visit: Xishuangbanna.

As was always the case when I was sent on journeys by my school or institute before, everything is paid for: transport, lodging, local guides, cars, theatres and whatever other expenses there are—apart from food, which I must pay for myself at about 1.50 yuan a day. At first glance this may seem ridiculous. My unit is paying thousands of yuan for me and my escort, sending telegrams and having long telephone conversations to ensure that everything goes all right, and yet they insist on my paying this absurdly small sum for food myself. But if one remembers that this is a country in which until a few years ago it was a struggle to get enough food just in order to survive and where death from starvation has been an ever-present threat for generations, one realizes that there is good reason for having a rather special attitude towards food. Food is not something to be given away, it is something which has to be worked for. I work, so it is only proper that I should pay for my food. It is perhaps a reflection of the daily struggle for survival in the past that the Chinese for 'good morning' or 'hello' is: 'Have you eaten?'

From Zemao to Xishuangbanna is a day's journey. We have a small private car with a red pennant on the bonnet, and a jeep in front of us as escort. The journey is through rain forests on roads which have been carved out of the mountainside with pick and shovel—impossible hairpin bends and long tough climbs up the precipitous mountainsides. En route we pass an endless stream of lorries, all with cooling systems on their wheels, which would otherwise get red hot from the braking required on the long descents into the valleys. Here and there is a clearing in the dense forest where groups of men stand with two-handled saws, cutting long tree trunks into perfectly even planks.

Soon after leaving Zemao the blue cotton jackets and short-sleeved white shirts, characteristic of the Han people and the city dwellers, disappear and are replaced by multi-coloured clothes of extravagant design, long black hair surmounted by Turkish towelling turbans, resembling great lumps of soft dough, ornamental belts, jewellery and big silver earrings, all of which are home-made. At first sight one might think they were theatre groups or crowds of people on their way to a celebration on Tien An Men. But the long columns on the edge of the road balancing the yokes on their shoulders and with agricultural implements in their hands clearly indicate that these are work teams on their way to work in the fields, and that these are their ordinary working clothes.

After a drive of nearly ten hours, through small villages of thatched houses built on stilts, we stop on the last hairpin bend halfway down the mountain. Below, brilliant green and glistening wet, lies Xishuangbanna, in China's southernmost valley.

Liberation in this part of China did not coincide with the establishment of the People's Republic in 1949, nor did it happen by any sudden seizure of power. It was a gradual process of reform over a period of five or six years. The land belonged to a few feudal lords who had more power and ruled more harshly than in most other parts of China. Here, the saying was: 'He who sets foot on the land is a slave.' Head tax had to be paid on a newborn infant, and poor peasants and hired peasants could not expect to be paid more than one-third of the value of their labour, and out of this they had to pay tax to the Kuomintang army, offerings to the temples and road tax to the landlords for the use of the paths they themselves had constructed.

It was a minority area and gross discrimination went on. The people were divided into three main groups. The few resident foreigners, mainly French missionaries, formed an elite. Next came the Han Chinese who had been stationed here by the government to look after its interests. The local population regarded them as immigrants or colonizers, but it was in their hands the power lay. Then came the Tai nationals who ethnically and linguistically have links with Thailand, but are regarded as an integrated Chinese minority. In addition to these groups were about twenty-five to thirty small minority groups among whom there was no particular classification, but who all had to observe certain conventions with regard to the other groups so that they knew their place. Thus, inferior people had to address the Tais as 'father' or 'mother', and had no right at all to speak to anyone superior to the Tais.

There were a few schools but the cost of being educated was so high that the possibility only existed for the sons of the feudal lords; their daughters were not able to avail themselves of it because the law required that one had served a form of 'monastic' conscription before attending school in the then strongly Buddhist province of Yunnan.

In one respect it is not very different from other parts of China. Wherever one goes one gets the same informative account described by the interpreter, quite incorrectly, as a 'brief introduction'. It is informative in that one is given information about people and statistics, comparing the past with the present. The bad old days when 'the privileges of the landlord were as many as the hairs on a cow' and the poor peasant paid for 'water to drink, paths to walk on and earth to cover his face when he died', are thus contrasted with the gradual transition to common ownership and liberation. From, as a local expression puts it, the days when 'the big heaven was light, but the little heaven was still twilight' to today when, according to what I am told, everything is fine.

It would be unreasonable to expect these downtrodden people to answer questions about whether there was anything in the past which had any positive qualities or, on the other hand, whether they have any problems now. This attempt to see both sides of the question in order to put the past in a more favourable light as compared with the present has been made, in the bombed-out name of objectivity, by many travellers. But in China one gets nowhere with this. The past was bad and the present is good. There is not enough doubt about that even to allow for discussion.

And certainly from the purely practical point of view, there is no doubt but that things *are* much better. In the sparsely populated area of Yunnan which was formerly ravaged by epidemics of malaria, smallpox and plague, the health of the population has improved out of all knowledge. Only a few years ago between 50 and 90 per cent of the population suffered from malaria; the figure is now below 0·6 per cent. Sceptics who doubt this are reminded that it is no longer considered necessary to recommend visiting foreigners to take anti-malaria pills.

And, where formerly education was a privilege limited to a few males, now 80 per cent of the population attend school full-time at primary and secondary levels. That it is not 100 per cent is due to geographical difficulties. Certain minority groups still prefer to live in groups of only three or four families high up in the mountains. For the children of these people, a system of peripatetic teachers has been organized. They go from house to house, from one group to another, giving the children basic instruction.

And whereas in the past, owing to its situation and lack of roads, Xishuangbanna was cut off and had no access to industrial goods, there is now a growing system of roads serving the whole vast area.

They have introduced a system which, financially speaking, is unusual. Whereas the cost of transport for necessary commodities is not added to the cost of the goods—the state foots the bill for that—everything in the category of consumer goods has a proportion of those transport costs added to it. This means that some goods if bought here will cost up to three times as much as in their place of origin only a few hundred miles away. A packet of Kunming cigarettes, for example, which in that town cost 45 fen, cost twice as much here, and a litre of beer which in Kunming costs 52 fen costs 1·50 yuan here, nearly three times as much.

But quite apart from the cultural, economic and historic differences from those parts of China I have gradually begun to feel I know, one feels here, to a marked degree, that one is far from the centre of power. Whereas in Peking one can as it were feel the presence of power, which in many ways seems to stamp the people with the same dusty grey as the town itself, so here one feels the physical distance from the centre and that power. The only bright colours in Peking are those connected with the system of power itself, and the historic monuments from the imperial past. The rest of the town is contained within a narrow spectrum of sand grey and sun-yellowed chalk. Not even the road surfaces are an unambiguous black but pale and pastel-coloured.

From the days when the Han Chinese were regarded as immigrant oppressors until today when, although still immigrant, they are regarded as liberators, the attitudes and feelings of the local population must have undergone a colossal change. Many of those I speak to remember being told, 'Never take a stone for a pillow, nor a Han for a friend.'

Most of my questions to the local inhabitants are directed at finding out how they got over their intense hatred of the Han in such a relatively short time, what problems they had and what processes they had to go through in order to be able to live in such comparative peace with their former oppressors—or rather with the ethnic group to which their former oppressors belonged. The questions were either not understood, or were considered irrelevant, because the answer was usually that naturally one could not live in enmity and mistrust with the people who had liberated one and who by their actions had shown themselves to be brothers and sisters.

I was told, however, that as a result of Kuomintang propaganda about the Communists, there were many who fled into the mountains when reports reached them that the Liberation Army was on its way. This probably had less to do with the fact that they were Han than with the reputation of terrorism and banditry with which anti-Communist propaganda and general ignorance had invested them.

At one of the formidable banquets through which, as a traveller and honoured guest, one has to work one's way in this hospitable and food-loving country, I sat beside one of the highest-ranking cadres of the region, the leader of the revolutionary committee. He was an intelligent and very amusing man who carried out his duties as host with great *savoir faire*, and was a diverting central figure without being in any way self-centred. He discoursed with wit and verve and was obviously very knowledgeable. He had that aura of 'having been away', that indefinable almost physical increase in personality which I have noticed in some of my colleagues who have travelled abroad. I did not question him about his background and he observed the Chinese convention of never referring to one's personal affairs even though one may be occupying a central position.

Some days later, however, talking about him with one of my other hosts, I asked what his background was and whether he was an 'imported' Han who had been posted to the job of local administrator.

'He belongs to one of the large minority groups here,' I was told. 'Before liberation, he was one of the biggest landowners in the district. Now he is a good Communist and one of our most respected leaders.'

This is something I cannot understand at all. An earlier oppressor and exploiter who, as a result of the revolution, has been appointed leader of his former serfs and tenants. It is not that I am against the idea on principle—if the man is intelligent and in general has the right attitude, there is no reason not to make use of his abilities in the new context. But it goes against everything I have seen and heard in the rest of China. I have often been told that one can never change one's class, only the outward signs of it; one may change one's 'class cap' but one cannot change one's nature. Once an exploiter always an exploiter, even if one shows oneself to be progressive and, in any case, no longer has the practical possibility of exploiting anyone. And in most cases 'class nature' is regarded as being hereditary.

I thought of an unfortunate meeting I unwittingly brought about in the summer of 1966 in south China. I was visiting a people's commune where I had been invited to stay for a few days in the main village. It was a village which did not often have foreign visitors so my stay was not punctuated with the routine lectures and information sessions one can usually expect in the more important communes. There was no fixed programme either, we just let one thing lead to another and had plenty of time for everything.

At one point it occurred to me that I had never met a class enemy —I had only been told they existed and that one had to be on one's guard against them. So I asked if it would be possible for me to meet one of the former landlords of the district, not from any sympathy for what he represented but out of curiosity, and to get his reaction to a number of questions.

The leaders of the commune discussed it among themselves. They did not seem overpleased with my request but they would let me know. And the same afternoon I was fetched from the family where I was eating lunch and told that 'an important meeting' had been arranged.

There they sat, in the large wooden village hall, three weather-beaten old men whose discomfort was written all over them. They were sitting beside one another along the front row of the hall's hard wooden benches. Immediately in front of them, with his back to them, sat my interpreter at a little table. He had paper and pencil with him and sat waiting. On the low platform which served as a stage, a comfortable chair was awaiting me. I was shown to my place and told that I could begin my interrogation.

This was not what I had intended at all and I did not wish, nor did I feel that I had the authority, to sit there like a prosecuting counsel asking these old men questions about their anti-social activities of fifteen or twenty years ago. But the stage was set and it was impossible to get out of it now or to make any alterations.

One by one they were introduced to me and made to stand while a list of their crimes was read out. As far as I could make out none of them had been big landowners; they had belonged to the better-off section of the peasant group, had done a little money-lending with usury, had gambled, and a couple of them had smoked opium. One had been well enough off to have a second wife, but none of them had been a really big shot.

My questions were through the interpreter who sat between us. He was deliberately rude, and when they mumbled something which he did not quite catch because he was sitting with his back to them, he snapped his fingers over his shoulder without turning round and demanded a repetition.

I asked them mainly about their present status in the community, and they told me that they enjoyed none of the privileges that society otherwise affords its members but that they worked on an equal footing and for the same pay as the others. But whereas the others were paid if they were ill, these ex-landlords were not paid and had to borrow money. This applied to their nearest relatives also.

'Do you find it difficult' I asked, 'to work side by side in the fields with the people who were once your hired hands?'

'I don't understand the question,' the man I asked replied. 'We do the same work as the others and do it as well as we can.'

A little later I tried to find out about the loss of rights, how long was it likely to last and would it apply also to the following generation or even longer.

'I have got some of my rights back,' I was told, but these were not specified. 'But that does not apply to my wife. She is an evil influence and takes every opportunity to stir up trouble in the commune. She will never get her rights back. The same I suppose is true of our children, but I don't know.'

'And their children?'

'I don't know. I don't understand the Party's correct line in this matter.'

'But you think the Party's line is correct? Are you content with things as they are?'

'The Party's line is correct, but I don't understand it.'

The liberation of Yunnan province differed in many ways from that of the rest of the country, partly because there was no spontaneous uprising in support of the conquering army, and partly because the army had to tread carefully in this ethnically and linguistically foreign country they had come to liberate. That was why it was a gradual process, during which the Communist army sought the help and support of those feudal lords who were disposed to be co-operative. One of the most important jobs for these lords was to act as interpreters between the liberating army and the serfs and peasants they had come to liberate.

My host, the previously mentioned feudal lord, had, I was told, shown his willingness to co-operate by interfering with and sabotaging some of the interests of the Guomindang army. I was not told, however, the nature of the sabotage which put him in such a favourable light in the eyes of the liberators.

So it would appear that the consequences of one's actions are not always the same, even in united China.

Wherever one goes just now one gets a detailed account of how much, and by what means, the 'Gang of Four' have sabotaged production and growth everywhere. This is noticeably absent in Yunnan. The 'Four' are never mentioned, and when at a tea factory far out in the mountains, for the sake of something to say, I ask the workers if they have noticed the evil influence of the 'Gang of Four', they reply casually that they think they have. 'Last year our production was 6 per cent less than planned. We put that down to the negative influence the "Four" have had all over the country.'

'In the old days our world was bounded by the mountains we could see. Now we have been liberated and know what is on the other side of the mountains. We have been liberated economically, culturally and politically, and the little heaven as well as the big heaven is full of light.'

One should not lay too much emphasis on the use of the passive form 'have been liberated', and perhaps when it comes to the point it doesn't much matter whether liberation occurred through one's own efforts or as the result of intervention from outside.

But one has the feeling here, all the same, that behind the mountains they can see lie range after range of other mountains.

And Peking is infinitely far away.

A No to a No

The demarcation lines are slowly beginning to shift—those un-defined lines of demarcation which have encompassed our work and limited our possibilities of expressing ourselves. But it still remains a question of feeling how far we can go before we find ourselves in the no-man's-land between the acceptable and the unacceptable.

But every day since the fall of the 'Four', we feel that the ice-floes are beginning to break up. No new instructions have yet been issued —or at least none that we are aware of—but many things indicate that discussions within the Party are taking place at every level. And it is not student committees, teacher committees, deans, or other educational groups in my institute who will lay the tracks on which we are to run; it is the local Party office. I have tried to work out how the Party decisions filter out into the exercise called teaching and whether feedback takes place.

The Party has a cramped little office two doors from mine. Except when there is an important or confidential meeting, in the summer months all the doors in the building stand open, but those of the Party office are kept permanently closed. It is clearly an area which is not meant to be any concern of mine—not directly anyway. I have been very briefly introduced to a couple of the staff, and it was clear that it was as Party members, not as teachers. Not one of them speaks a word of any foreign language and only one, who has been pointed out to me as being the Party Secretary, is also a teacher.

But from the way our daily work goes I can be pretty certain that it is in that little room that things are vetoed or okayed. I have noticed time and again that while new projects under consideration, such as new texts and teaching methods, are put through a very fine political sieve, very rarely does one find any evidence of an educa-tional argument backing the decisions.

It so happens that during the years I have taught in China I have never had the experience of a 'policeman' in the classroom or lecture theatre, an observer of the ideological propriety of what I was saying. It would, of course, be quite superfluous anyway because, even if I wished to, it would be virtually impossible for me to indulge in any subversive activities. The students, even the schoolchildren, are so politically conscious that it would soon be stopped, either by their drawing the notice of the authorities directly to it, or by discussing among themselves the unexpected and hitherto unheard of things I had said. And in most cases in this country discussion means public discussion.

But recently the leadership of the institute, which in the last analysis means the Party office, has accepted one of my suggestions. It involves my giving a kind of general talk about once a week to the third-year students. It is not intended to be part of their course in the ordinary sense but to provide them with a better background knowledge against which to use their English. We are agreed that the students' general knowledge about such things as Western, and therefore British, history, culture, daily life and political systems is sadly lacking, and that it would be reasonable to try and give the students at least some superficial knowledge about these topics in connection with their study of the language.

I have been given a kind of carte blanche to prepare a series of talks. It is not a real carte blanche of course, which I hadn't expected anyway. It is conditional on my submitting a list of titles for approval at the beginning of the month. It was not possible to find out how much discussion there was about the subjects I suggested, nor what level they reached in our internal system, but judging by what I knew or guessed, it is reasonable to believe that they had to go to the Party office before they were finally approved.

It is now several months since I began this Saturday morning activity. In addition to my own suggestions, which I have never had any difficulty in getting approved, the students themselves have made suggestions. Specific down-to-earth topics such as: 'How does one eat, and what are considered good table manners?' 'How does the (so-called) parliamentary democracy function?' 'What is it like going to school in England?' 'What is it like travelling in Europe?' And so on; relatively harmless and uncontroversial questions, unless one had in mind to use them as springboards for more controversial subjects. These mornings in which I go through partly questions like these and partly my own more rambling topics, seem to work well and according to plan. It gives us the possibility of creating what we so desperately need—a milieu in which to practise the use of the language. For all of us it is a relief to get away from the prescribed texts, even if it does make great demands on the students in terms of their having to concentrate very hard in order to follow what is being said. If I use words or a construction to which they are un-accustomed, they are still so hampered by the stilted methods we use in our daily teaching that they find it very difficult to guess the meaning from the context. They are terribly restricted by the rigid teaching methods, which do not encourage imagination, initiative or independent thought. There appears to be great enthusiasm for changing the system, but I find it difficult to make out how much change would be allowed. I don't know how much is dependent on the political system in general—probably a great deal.

Even though I have been given a fairly free hand in this work, there is still a barrier between us. Naturally it is partly a problem of language, which means that we have to move slowly, but at least we move! But in addition to this there is the ritual respect with which I am treated and which I find a great hindrance to getting together.

Every one of my talks begins in the same way. As I enter the large lecture room all three or four hundred students and teachers rise to their feet and a student seizes the microphone and calls upon the audience to 'Welcome Expert Mr Jan' with a round of applause. After that, a second student, a different one each time, makes a short speech in perfect colloquial English, thanking me for doing them the honour of coming here to speak to them. The unhappy speaker, who is usually ready to die of fright during the speech, generally manages to include a few of the everyday expressions he has learned in the course of the previous week and written down in his 'colloquial' notebook, and eventually ends by suggesting yet another round of applause. I suppose the idea is to help as many students as possible to get over the hurdle of what is known as speaker's nerves. Difficult at any time, but particularly so in a language in which they are not very sure of themselves. As such, it may be a valuable exercise, even if it is usually only cliché piled upon cliché.

But apart from this, and the fact that it is sincerely meant as a polite gesture, it widens and emphasizes the gap between us each time it happens, a gap which is already a great deal wider than that between a Chinese teacher and his students. I have come here to do a job of work, not to bask in ovations as if I were a visiting state dignitary.

During the lecture, which I try to conduct in as relaxed a manner as possible, a Chinese colleague stands behind me and writes on the blackboard words which the students do not know. He writes them in English followed by a Chinese translation. We have had long discussions about this. I am very much against it, because it seems to me that it confirms the students in their tendency to treat the language as a collection of formulae. They compile dictionaries on scraps of paper, in exercise books and on the backs of their hands and for the most part are not able to use the words and phrases outside the context in which they first heard them.

And while I clown about and chat and try to forestall my un-wished-for interpreter by explaining, acting or drawing the words and ideas which are new to the students, I have learned to spot the next victim of our weekly ritual. The one who has been picked for the closing vote of thanks is always sitting on the front row, and as we approach the end of my talk I can see the increasingly glazed look in his or her eyes. He or she gradually stops taking notes, and sits paralytically still. As I begin to round off my two- or three-hour session, the 'thanker of the day' gathers together his or her scraps of paper and edges towards the microphone.

I always feel very sorry for both the opener and the closer and have my doubts about its helping them to learn the language. And I sometimes wonder whether the distance created between the students and myself is not deliberate.

Today something has gone wrong. It is ten days since I handed in my monthly list of titles, with a short résumé of the contents of each one, for approval. There had been no comments other than the usual, that they were looking forward to hearing them. The teacher who is my line of contact with the higher authority which has to approve is a man of my own age whom I really can't quite make out. As far as language goes, and probably in other fields as well, he is very knowledgeable, talented and well oriented, and we often have dis-cussions which I hope are as stimulating to him as they are to me. But there is something about him which makes it difficult to feel relaxed in his company. Polite without being oily, one might say that he gives the impression of there being too much surface for too little substance. He has got into the habit of coming to my office several times a day and always opens the proceedings with an almost identical little speech about how touched he is that I can be bothered to waste my time on him, how much he admires my matchless gifts and what an invaluable help I am to everybody, particularly to him who, of course, has no gifts at all.

It is true that politeness and self-effacement are traditional aspects of Chinese behaviour, but I have begun to find it a bit tiring having it repeated two or three times a day. So the other day I very discreetly timed his opening manoeuvre; it was a little over a minute. When he had gone I multiplied this by the number of daily visits on work days and the number of work days in the two years I am to be here. I have tried before, in various ways, but without success, to get him to stop; now I thought I had found a method which must be successful.

'Zhou,' I said to him next time he came in and before he had time to begin, 'I have made some calculations about your amazing politeness which we have so often talked about, and have come to the conclusion that in two years you will have spent no less than some thirty-odd hours thanking me and telling me how clever I am and I, of course, will have spent an equal amount of time listening to you. Why don't we stop it here and now?'

He burst out laughing at this formidable figure, went over to the blackboard to work it out for himself and got roughly the same answer. 'I must say,' he said, 'I have never thought about it in that way. I am most impressed; not only are you a very gifted teacher of English but you are also a first-class mathematician.' He then went on to his usual introductory talk.

But today, as I said, something has gone wrong. It is a different Zhou from the usual flattering conversationalist.

I have been sitting for several days working on the notes for today's talk, the first of this monthly series. I do not like the formality of a manuscript but have a pile of notes written on scraps of paper to jog my memory as I go along. With this sheaf of absorbent recycled paper in my hand, I get out of the car at the back entrance of the institute and walk the few hundred yards to the large lecture-room which, with a small gallery, hangs like a polyp on the main building.

As usual I can see Xiao Wang bringing in my armchair, which I never sit in, my ashtray which I never use, a jug of water and a glass. But as I am about to enter the hall I see Zhou standing by the door. He has come cycling from the opposite direction and reached the door before me. He is standing against the door, seems rather nervous and agitated and tells me that my talk has been cancelled. I look over his shoulder into the crowded hall where everything is ready as on every Saturday morning, students and teachers sitting waiting.

'It doesn't look very cancelled to me,' I said. 'I can see them all inside.'

'The students have other work to do today. It is cancelled.'

'What are they going to do instead?' I ask.

'Something else. They have an important meeting. There is not time for your lecture today. Another day perhaps. I am very sorry about this inconvenience. I am sure that, as you always do, you have done a lot of preparation for it. And unfortunately it is my fault that you have wasted your time on it.'

I try to calm him down, telling him not to worry because it isn't a waste of time if it is only a case of postponement.

'It *is* only a postponement, it is only today and until further notice. I hope you aren't very angry with me. I am very sorry for all the trouble I have caused you. But it can't be today.'

He accompanies me to my office and a few minutes later Xiao Wang comes in with my chair, ashtray and glass which he had only just taken down to the lecture-room. He puts the things in their places and leaves. Xiao Wang is, among other things, very tactful and always disappears when we have to discuss confidential matters in my office. Either he senses it or he has had orders.

Zhou remains only a few minutes, and uses them to continue with his apologies without giving any clear answer to my questions. But I'm not really surprised. The only thing which surprises me is that it has only happened at the last minute. My subject for the day was to have been European opposition to the Common Market, particularly left-wing opposition. I had put it first on my list and had awaited comments, questions, agitation or silence about it. As I had heard nothing in the last few days I assumed, somewhat to my surprise, that it had been approved.

Zhou leaves me and I sit alone in my office trying to work out what has happened. I try telling myself that there really is a valid reason for this sudden cancellation. It does happen, particularly during these politically unstable times, that meetings to discuss sudden new developments are called without warning. The students, teachers and I have all got accustomed to this state of affairs and try to plan our work so that it does not matter too much if it has to be interrupted. But, apart from the fact that they were all sitting there, and that all my usual requisites had been taken in and had to be taken out again only a few minutes later, coupled with Zhou's un-characteristic nervousness; something gave me the feeling that this was no ordinary cancellation.

One or two of the veteran teachers knock on my door and ask if they may come in. They sit down in the armchairs (students and the younger teachers always sit on upright chairs) and ask how things are going. I realize that this is not going to be just a friendly visit, but also that we cannot start without the usual introductory manoeuvres.

'I hear you have cancelled your talk this morning,' says one of them with astonishment in his voice. We have completed the ritual and are now down to brass tacks.

'No,' I reply. 'I did not cancel it. It *has been* cancelled. I am using the passive form, but I do not know who cancelled it, or why.'

'What was the talk going to be about?' asked another.

'The Common Market seen from the European, but particularly the left-wing—or wings'—point of view.'

'Oh yes,' he says, with badly feigned sudden recollection. 'I had heard that you were going to talk about that and I wanted to hear it, but unfortunately I found I would not have time.'

It would have been rather aggressive on my part to have asked him how, if that were the case, he had time to come and gossip now, seeing that it was exactly at this time the talk should have been going on.

'Of course there are several views about the Common Market,' says a third, in an effort to keep the ball rolling.

'In principle only two,' I said, 'for and against.'

'You know China's attitude to it I am sure. We are of the opinion that in many ways the Common Market is a good thing. We are in favour of the European Community.'

I have difficulty in coping with this evasiveness. I don't know whether this is a delegation which has been sent with apologies and instructions to placate me—even though I have not expressed any annoyance—or to find out exactly what I was going to say. So I suggest we talk about it. I tell them that of course China's views on the Common Market are well known to me, that I don't happen to agree with them, but that is my own affair. I tell them that the reason I wanted to talk about opposition to the EEC in Europe was because I thought the students ought to be better informed about what was going on in the world—not because I wanted to enlarge on my personal point of view.

'Now I am going to ask you a direct question and I hope you will give me a straight answer. Is it because it is a controversial subject that you cancelled the talk? Because you knew that facts and opinions in conflict with China's official policy would inevitably have cropped up? Do you regard it as subversive? If that is the case of course I understand. I have not the slightest interest in subversive activities, and since I am working for you here, naturally it is on your terms. But I would like to know where I stand.'

This is where the lies begin to creep in. Up to this point it had been more or less straightforward, but now there is beating about the bush.

'There is no question of that,' says one of the trio. 'No question of our having censored you. It is only a question of a postponement.'

Apparently he now knows something about the circumstances he didn't know when he came in a few minutes ago. On the other hand, I suppose there is an infinitesimal chance that what he says is true and I feel it is only fair to give him the benefit of the doubt.

'It is a very important subject,' says a second. 'Why do you personally take such a negative view of it? It would be interesting to hear your reasons.'

I am quite willing to indulge them and begin explaining at great length. They listen intently, nodding from time to time and occasionally asking a question. None of them takes any notes. It would not be in order to do so since this is not an official meeting and my arguments are not exactly epoch-making for any of these extremely well-oriented veterans. They might, on the other hand, have seemed so to the less well-informed students, who have never had the chance of studying the political and economic background of the Common Market.

At one point I am told that my point of view is not in accordance with that of socialism. In China one never prefixes the word 'socialism' with 'Chinese', because here we all know there is only one kind of socialism.

'I am well aware,' I repeat, 'that the Chinese government and Party take a positive view of the EEC. But this view is not shared by all the fraternal Parties in Europe. There are some who strongly oppose it.'

'Which?' asks one, not unreasonably.

'The British Communist Party, Marxist and Leninist. They decided in the spring of 1975 to oppose it, and of the various British left organizations this is the one which China recognizes.'

'No longer,' says one of them. 'We broke off relations with them some time ago.'

I didn't know that.

'Was that because of their opposition to the Common Market?' I ask.

My guests laugh. 'I don't think so. I don't know the exact grounds, but it would be reasonable to believe that it had something to do with differing points of view between the parties on major political issues. Perhaps they have become revisionists.'

Later in the day Zhou comes in again. He still seems rather agitated and again begs me to forgive him for the inconvenience he has caused me. I feel sorry for him and also that it is a shame he should be in trouble over it, even if it really is his fault. I tell him again not to worry about it, and he seems relieved that I bear him no grudge. Perhaps he really did put his foot in it and failed to apply for approval in time, because all my other subjects had gone through so easily. Or maybe it was the 'relevant competent authority' which put off making a decision till the last minute. I cannot really believe he would have done anything off his own bat and not followed the usual procedure. That would not be at all typical of Chinese behaviour.

Anyway, he seems relieved and sits back and chats. We do not refer to the subject again until he suddenly appears to remember something.

'By the way,' he says, 'we would all appreciate it if you would prepare lecture number two for next Saturday. The students are very much looking forward to it.'

'What about number one, the one I should have given today?' I ask.

'Ah, yes. Well, we will postpone that for the time being. It would be better if you gave number two next week and we can talk about the other one later.'

And as he leaves hastily in order to avoid further discussion, I sit back and think of a quotation from Mao which seems to crop up constantly these days in connection with Jiang Qing and her crowd. The quotation runs: 'Be open and above board.' But perhaps that is applicable only to her.

It is a busy day in this corridor on the second floor. A bit later a veteran teacher comes in and asks if he may sit down. He is here on his own initiative. It is my general impression that he always is.

'I hear your talk has been cancelled,' he says, and his knowledge of the language is such that I know the use of the passive tense is not a slip. He looks at the floor and shakes his head. 'Too bad, too bad,' he says.

I agree with him to the point of saying that I find it damned annoying and that I would like to know a little more about the reasons.

'That is difficult,' he says, shaking his wise old head. 'That is very difficult to say. Sometimes things are cancelled. Too bad. If you don't mind telling me, I would like to know why you chose that particular subject.'

That I could easily do. Most of the teaching staff are agreed that the students' general knowledge is very limited and their picture of the world very restricted. The students who come to us have special need of a more comprehensive knowledge of the world. Most of them will become interpreters, work in foreign trade delegations, go into the diplomatic service, or in a few cases be assigned posts as customs officers at border stations or airports. They will all, unlike those students in the language schools who are training to be teachers, constantly be in contact with foreigners, either singly or in groups, on official and unofficial occasions. In my opinion they should learn that there are those who are against the Common Market—even businessmen. Otherwise they will be taken completely by surprise. Therefore, I say, we are equipping them badly for their jobs if we do not give them the opportunity to study the opposite point of view.

'That is true,' he says, shaking his head again.

'Incidentally,' I say, 'I have been told that after liberation there was a time when Chinese universities often invited foreign visiting professors, including economists with very bourgeois views. No one at that time was afraid that it would do the students any harm—on the contrary, it was regarded as good training for them. They had a chance to argue their socialist theories with an opponent, which could only serve to strengthen them.'

'I have heard of that being done in the past,' says my head-shaking friend. 'But I don't think it would work now. Too bad. I really would have enjoyed hearing what you had to say. Too bad.

What Colour China?

It has long been a regular habit in China to qualify with a descriptive word the concept one is talking about. And the language of official-dom has crept into daily speech so that nowadays we seldom refer to the Cultural Revolution, the Party, the Soviet government, capitalists or foreign people without adding to the words the approved rubrics: *Great Proletarian* Cultural Revolution, *Great, Glorious and Correct* Party, *Hegemonist* Soviet government, Capitalist *Oppressors*, and *Freedom-loving* foreign nations. My efforts to get my colleagues and students to refer to the 'masses' instead of the 'broad masses', on the grounds that the masses are broad anyway, has met with no success. 'It is an expression we use,' I am told. This practice leads in the end, from repetition after repetition, to the values of the qualifying word or words becoming synonymous with what they qualify—even if only superficially. In those cases in which any unconscious identifica-tion between concept and quality is not wanted, qualifying words are carefully avoided. For example, it is well known and often men-tioned in private conversation that the Chinese peasants—the real revolutionary masses—can be described as being very conservative. This alleged conservatism, which many Chinese claim to be deep-rooted in the social class which led the revolution to victory, in-evitably makes one wonder why one does not see more evidence of it among the peasants, what is it that is holding these undesirable tendencies down? How can those in power influence a people to act in a manner contrary to its way of thinking?

I have several times, in conversation with Chinese friends, put the hypothetical question: do you think that some time in the future China might change colour and become capitalist or even fascist?

Speculation and problems in the abstract, including guesswork about the future, seldom meet with much response in private con-versation. Most people would prefer not to hazard guesses about the future but refer to the Party and the people as being the guarantors that China will keep to the true course. In so doing they are ruling out the possibility of any internal splits or a coup within the party, and thus refusing to face the facts of the sequence of events which took place after Mao's death last year.

One of the things which strikes one forcibly about the new Chinese society, and which time after time is brought up as being one of the important underlying reasons for the success of the revolution, is that Chinese people are remarkably organizable. During the last several years this has shown itself in many different ways—in the huge campaigns in the years after liberation, in a mighty and dynamic work effort, which clearly follows a quite definite objective, in the revolution itself, and many years later in the Cultural Revolution.

Racists and anti-socialists may read the word 'organizable' as meaning 'tyrannized' or 'of slave mentality', indicating a people blindly led and bullied. I do not mean to imply by this that China has fascist tendencies. But it is true that this talent, this ability to co-operate in letting oneself be organized, could in some situations be very dangerous.

At the time of the coup in the spring of 1976 I tried to imagine that the present leaders, about whom at that time we knew nothing, *were* a Chinese equivalent to Chile's fascist dictator. I made the assumption that they represented the extreme right, but that they realized that indicating this too early might jeopardize their chances of survival.

At this point I should perhaps point out that when I use the word 'coup' to describe what happened at the time of the fall of the 'Four', it is not an expression of any particular political position, and does not imply sympathy with either the winning or the losing side; it is a simple statement of fact. That is what it was—a coup in which power either changed hands or was strengthened in the one group by the use of military force. Supporters of Hua Guofeng describe it as the 'warding off' of a coup. But when has a coup-maker ever declared it to be one?

The 'Gang of Four' has had whole batteries of criticism levelled against it in what may well be the most ferocious campaign the country has ever known. If one believes the stories, all of which are said to have emanated from official sources, they have committed every possible moral, criminal and political offence one can think of. And the sum of their activities adds up to their being not only felons, traitors and counter-revolutionaries, but fascists. Among the many caricatures one sees about since their removal from power are some depicting them with all the insignia of Nazism—swastika, Hitler moustache and so on. The implications of this are disturbing. If these allegations are true it means that China under the 'Four', who governed the country for a period of roughly ten years, had, if not a fascist government, at least one with that end in view. And if such a group has been in power for such a long time, this brings the whole idea of a Pinochet-type coup nearer to reality.

The political consciousness of the Chinese people is legendary. Their ability to make a political analysis of day-to-day problems and find a solution is recognized and has been testified to by both themselves and countless foreign visitors. But what is the use of this high degree of consciousness if the people can silently accept fascist rule for more than ten years?

'We have for a long time hated Jiang Qing and the three others,' says one of my colleagues to me, 'but what could we do? They used violence and terrorism to keep us down. There were few who dared speak against them and those who did usually ended up in prison.'

But if one objects that violence, terrorism and imprisonment have never before been effective in halting the revolutionary activities of the Chinese people, one gets a disheartening answer.

'That was when we were fighting against a corrupt and fascist government, one which had separated itself from and placed itself above the people. It is more difficult to fight internal enemies. It is more difficult to identify them because they put up a front of being united with the people. And there are very few people who want to risk getting into trouble by criticizing the Party or its officers.'

But what is the use of this high degree of consciousness, which enables most Chinese to distinguish clearly between the progressive and the reactionary, if they cannot give voice to it in the form of open protest? Many colleagues have told me that they were sick and tired of the 'Four', that they are fed up with political work which was long ago killed by dogmatism—but that these were views one kept to oneself.

'For many years,' one of my colleagues told me, 'I have sat pretending to be deeply engaged in reading the editorials in the *People's Daily*. And I assume most of my colleagues were doing the same. But we couldn't discuss it. So it continued until Hua Guofeng liberated us from, among other things, this particular form of oppression.'

It is perfectly true that China's new leaders have gained, and well deserve, great popularity by throwing open certain doors, doors which had made many aspects of daily life rather claustrophobic.

The compulsory reading aloud of Mao's works, along with the parrot-like repetition of slogans, which by their very repetition rapidly became only empty phrases, has been abolished. Strongly expressed political mistrust of intellectual work has been replaced by a more tolerant attitude which accords better with the wishes of the people as a whole for creative activity. Such changes of policy are seen by most people I speak to as a great liberation and are certainly among the reasons for the popularity of the new leaders.

Having said that, one can either, according to one's knowledge, wishes or political colour, see this new freedom as a carrot, a sop which the new government is offering the people while it consolidates its position, or as a necessary and genuine liberalization of a way of life which, in many ways and for many people, had become intolerably puritanical.

There is a tendency in China to voice criticism only retrospectively. Thus in the case of the 'Four' and certain other incidents, the social and political reforms which take place are more in the nature of a clearing-up *after* the event rather than an attempt to forestall events. When Chinese friends and colleagues say that in the few months which have elapsed since the coup, they have had much greater freedom to express criticism than they ever had before, there is some truth in it. But on closer examination one finds that this freedom is largely limited to freedom to criticize what has been—in particular, of course, the 'Gang of Four' and its activities. Looked at from this angle freedom—like criticism—also becomes retrospective.

A woman student at one of the institutes of higher education in Peking was liable, according to those with whom she shared a dormitory, to scream and become very restless in her sleep, apparently as the result of a recurring nightmare. When her comrades wakened her, she refused to talk about it, though she was obviously shaken. After some time, however, she confided in one of her close friends. She told her that the nightmare was about an experience she had had some years back when she was a student at the university. She had gone to the clinic with severe stomach-ache and the doctor on duty had diagnosed appendicitis. She agreed to be operated on and allowed herself to be persuaded by the clinic staff to have the operation without any form of anaesthetic. The doctor's reason for suggesting this unusual procedure was that as she was a member of the Red Guard, the student's revolutionary elite, she must be above such feelings as fear. 'Pain', the doctor is supposed to have said, 'is not something which should worry a young revolutionary.'

According to the story the operation was proceeded with until she finally passed out.

This story is not intended to demonstrate that Chinese doctors are uncivilized and inhuman. I tell it because whether it is true (which I doubt) or false it is in any case interesting. If it is in fact true, the question arises as to whether the lack of freedom to express criticism really went so far as to prevent inhuman practices of this kind being brought to light. In this case it could be read as camouflaged criticism of Jiang Qing and praise for Hua Guofeng, because with his advent things which had to be kept quiet in Jiang Qing's time could be openly discussed. And if the story is a fabrication, as I myself believe it to be, it could still be a political allegory. The use of real events and people in a fictitious story is a common device in everyday life in China, and one could interpret the story as being an attack on Jiang Qing (the doctor) maltreating China (the student).

The correct interpretation of the story may be dependent on *when* it first came into circulation. But true or false and whatever the interpretation, it serves to illustrate the difficulty in Chinese society today of coming out with unreserved criticism—until one has been given the all-clear.

There is also a marked difference between the government's attitude to public utterances now and its attitude in the 1960s. At that time, during the Cultural Revolution, there was a hard and fast rule that a wall newspaper, whoever had put it up, whether an individual or a group, must not be defaced, taken down, painted over or otherwise suppressed. The only accepted way of showing one's disapproval was by putting one up oneself. But since the fall of the 'Four' last year considerable restrictions have been put on this traditional method of self-expression. Wall newspapers which anticipate the turn of events, even when they are in criticism of the current official enemy, or support an as yet not public party decision, are, in most cases, pulled down or painted over as fast as they are put up.

China's new leaders are not appointed or chosen by the Chinese people. It is, of course, perfectly possible that they have, as the propaganda about them declares, grown up among the people, are at one with the people and only want to serve the interests of the people. But I am referring to the principle of democracy. The crux of the matter is that China's millions, through a coup, get new leaders about whom they know very little and have very little possibility of finding out about. Time and their actions alone will show whether they are the best government for the country. As I said, I do *not* believe that there has really been a fascist coup, but if there had, it would be too late to do anything about it. The possibility of any control by the people now has a built-in delay mechanism.

On one of the big northern roads leading out of Peking there is a high red concrete wall. On it are painted in large white characters admonitions to 'Carry on criticism of'—and under this, not surprisingly, the 'Gang of Four'. But beneath the paint one can just discern that there was another name, 'Deng Xiaoping', who was ousted by the 'Four'. And before him there had been others. It is difficult to believe that a change of leader is accepted by the people with the same ease as one paints one name over another.

Departure

I go to see the Chilean family off at the airport, where Swissair's large Boeing is standing waiting—a chromium-plated anachronism among the irrigated fields surrounding it. They have been stateless since Pinochet's coup, and as a member of the Communist Party the man has been sentenced to death in absentia. Their statelessness made it difficult for them to find a permanent abode until a Chinese ambassador in one of the Latin American countries got them permission to live and work in China. They had been here for several years when the fall of the 'Four' occurred. He said what he thought and made no secret of the fact that in his opinion it was a revisionist coup, and the reaction from the government was immediate. He was visited by a formal delegation who told him that in future he would not be addressed as 'comrade', and he and his family were given a deadline by which they could decide to leave the country.

He had a couple of months in which to find himself asylum in one of the European countries—a process which was not made easier by the fact that the family was without papers, that they were stateless, that he was a Communist and that he and his family had been living in China. Their status was ambiguous, and had been all along. They had not been treated as persons seeking political asylum, but had entered China normally with temporary United Nations identity cards. One of the things which strengthened our feeling that China has a strange attitude to reactionary governments—like, for example, the Chilean—was that the Chinese had forbidden these refugees to write or send political material to the underground press in their country or to the Communist underground movement there.

The choice, which was scarcely a choice, between finding a country willing to take them and, if that was not successful, seeking to become 'forced receivers' of asylum, was luckily solved at the last minute by their being accepted by a European country. The alternative of forced asylum would have been a tragedy. It would have meant the family being given Chinese status, they would probably have been removed from the aliens' quarter and sent off to do unskilled labour on the same terms as Chinese citizens. But they would have been known as opponents of Hua Guofeng and with that would have been labelled supporters of the 'Four'. It is not difficult to see how this would have affected their future in the country, without any possibility of leaving it.

As the family are leaving in disgrace, there is no farewell delegation to see them off, only a group of foreigners from Youyi. But on the eve of their departure, an anonymous Chinese official came and gave them 5,000 American dollars, together with single tickets to Europe. We have been discussing the meaning of this money and particularly the spirit in which it might have been given.

Another foreigner is also leaving today, but under slightly different circumstances. His two-year contract has come to an end, and he is entitled to the usual going-away ritual of banquets and escorts. But his place of work is giving him more than the usual. This particular foreign expert has, since Deng Xiaoping's second fall, consistently refused to take part in the general smear campaigns against him, has consistently maintained that Deng was, and remains, one of China's most outstanding leaders. He also told his Chinese colleagues who took part in the anti-Deng campaigns that they were political turncoats with no consistent political opinions or morals. And now that Deng is back on the rostrum, and is obviously very popular, this foreigner is getting a farewell over and above the usual. His superiors make moving speeches about him; they praise his courage and consistency, maintain that they bitterly regret that for more than a year they have been giving this colleague the cold shoulder, and that everyone must take a lesson from this outstanding foreigner who has demonstrated the importance of having the courage of one's political convictions. And following this tear-jerking accolade he is accompanied to the station by the highest leaders in his unit.

There are several departures from Youyi just now, some according to plan, others not. Some people's contracts have come to an end, others are being sent home, and still others are breaking their contracts and leaving the country. The new political situation has knocked us in Youyi. There is, as at the beginning of the Cultural Revolution, a sudden growing tendency towards the formation of small hostile groups following an almost predictable pattern—in the canteen, on the landings and between the grey buildings in our foreign enclave.

And the way things are going now, my own departure seems inevitable and imminent. The same applies to me as to the rest of the foreigners here: our employers have never required us to take part in political propaganda. If they had it would, of course, have put many of us in a very awkward situation over the years, whether we had refused or whether we had taken part. In the latter case we would have been accepting responsibility for the spreading of a political line which, were it later reversed, would have made its supporters liable to 'political criminalization'.

But although our unit leaders have made the sensible decision not to involve us directly, it is impossible, whether one likes it or not, to avoid taking some part in the spreading of propaganda, which constantly changes with the course of events. It is this constant changing which makes for difficulties. It is impossible to ignore a change in course without isolating oneself, or rather, being isolated. The problem is not so great for the majority of foreigners working here; most are employed as proof-readers and polishers of language at the Foreign Languages Press or Radio Peking and their jobs are comparatively routine. It is immaterial whether their proof sheets of the *Peking Review*, *China Pictorial* and a host of books and pamphlets contain violent denunciations of this line or that person. Their job is only to make sure that the language is correct.

It is rather different for those of us who work in the educational field. We cannot avoid taking part in spreading the current political ideas, and at times being involved in actually launching broadsides of political fire. The problem is made worse by the fact that we are expected to leap into the opposite camp at a moment's notice and open fire from there—it happened in the past and in the course of last year, when we found ourselves contributing to a campaign condemning Deng and then in a campaign condemning those who had condemned him.

It puts a great strain on one's personal integrity to be constantly subjected to this dichotomy, although it is true that the political struggle just now is not as violent as it was during the Cultural Revolution when the consequences of taking a stance could be catastrophic. Indeed it is only recently that the last of those imprisoned at that time have been released, after more than ten years.

Many of us in Youyi stick to our right to be consistent in our political opinions, and it is irritating to be a witness to the 'with it' foreigners among us who go out with clenched fists raised in joy over Deng's return the day after they had taken part in a massive march against him. And now, when the new government is trying to establish itself internationally as well as at home, it is very odd to see on TV transmissions leaders of foreign Marxist-Leninist parties, whose papers have echoed China's anti-Deng slogans, coming to pay their respects to Hua Guofeng and that very same Deng. When such a Danish delegation was here recently, some of my students came to me and asked me if I did not feel pleased and proud that the honourable Chairman of Denmark's Great, Glorious, and Correct Communist Party was in Peking to affirm the friendship between the parties in our two countries.

Among many of these foreigners of great flexibility in their attitude, I have often noticed a special feature in their use of language. They constantly refer to the 'Chinese'. According to them, a decision or attitude is Chinese, rather than that of one or other political wing or social group. There seems to be a strong propensity to see the whole population as an homogeneous mass, without acknowledging the fact that this is still a class society, without distinguishing between leaders and led. By talking in this way about the 'Chinese' saying and doing this or that, or holding this or that point of view, one is ignoring the fact that Mao, Jiang Qing, Lin Biao, Zhou Enlai and Deng Xiaoping, all 'Chinese', did not always say the same thing or hold identical points of view.

But the 'Chinese', in this case the officials who immediately and at a higher level have to do with us foreign experts, have obviously decided lately that we are to be more or less sacrosanct, politically speaking. By and large we are allowed to have our own political sympathies and antipathies as long as, should our feelings run contrary to the current correct line, it does not affect our work. But my work must be affected if I am not prepared uncritically to change my political horse and teach from a text which today lauds a person who was yesterday reviled.

My own position as a foreigner is, it is true, a very privileged one. As a last resort I can tear up my contract and demand a ticket home. But what can my Chinese colleagues, of whom even greater political liability is required, who are expected at a moment's notice to turn 180 degrees without any fuss, what can they do? They haven't the choice I have. Their alternatives are: ostracism, being moved, downgraded and, in extreme cases, imprisoned.

On the whole foreigners' political attitudes are unimportant. We are imported goods, brought here at China's expense to do a job under precisely laid-down conditions. The standard contract, with which we are all presented shortly after our arrival, is not very different from the one which was in force up to the time of the Cultural Revolution. It refers, in glossy bureaucratic jargon and with some amazing contradictions, to the contract 'herewith entered into between the two parties hereinafter referred to as the first party and the second party in a spirit of mutual friendship' (however unusual it might be to introduce friendship into a contractual obligation). These contracts are usually closely written documents five pages long, a hotchpotch of concrete requirements and vague conditions. My own contract, which was signed by neither party on account of my objections, describes my area of work as follows:

1. To teach . . . classes, correct the students' written work, and advise on extra-curricular work and the carrying out of end-of-term examinations.
2. To teach . . . teachers and research students.
3. To write and collect . . . teaching material and to carry out other work in connection with teaching the language.

When I asked for the dotted lines to be filled in with rather more precise information, I was told that that could always be done later. It is true that a contract here is not the same thing as a contract in the West. It is not considered so binding, and in any case it would be difficult for me to find an unbiased authority here to settle any dispute. The only thing the contract says about possible later disagreement is: 'Should any questions not covered by this contract arise, they should be settled by mutual agreement.'

The work itself and the conditions under which I am to do it are so vaguely formulated as to make a contract quite pointless anyway. Paragraph three of the contract uses the following verbiage to tell me that I must do as I am told:

> Details concerning working hours and concrete tasks will be settled by mutual discussion. The second party [me] undertakes to observe the rules of the institute [which are not available to me], carry out all his work punctually and see that the results are of a high standard [who will judge them?]. The first party [institute] will welcome any suggestions put forward by the second party during the carrying out of his (her) work and will give them

favourable consideration in so far as circumstances permit. On the other hand the second party agrees that he (she) will carry out the work in accordance with the decisions of the first party.

The fact is that I have no influence at all and that the expression 'mutual agreement' has shown itself time and again to be a euphemism for a decision by the 'relevant competent authority'.

Readers may object that this is no real problem and it is captious of me to lay so much stress on the text of this unimportant contract and call for something conforming to the Western model. On the other hand I think it is important to give these details as an example of Chinese bureaucracy. The whole thing is a bluff, with its blarney about friendship, and it not only ought to be, but *is* unnecessary and is not in accordance with the spirit which, in spite of everything, still prevails in this country. In language and spirit it is a sham, intended to give an impression of legality, duty and right. But I was aware of the conditions before I came here—even if the political situation has unexpectedly changed—and I came of my own free will because I wanted to work here.

Stine has received a letter. The envelope is addressed to our house. But on some of the papers inside her occupation is given as a language student at the Language Institute of Peking, and it was to the Language Institute that the letter was first delivered. This is just one more thing which confirms our suspicions that our post is censored. The most uncompromising Marxist-Leninists among our neighbours deny categorically that this could be so and have even taken the trouble to make enquiries at the highest level in their unit where, sure enough, they were told that letters to foreign experts were not subject to censorship. If letters had been opened, or the contents of two envelopes been interchanged (which has often happened), this must be due to censors and intelligence agencies outside China. But Stine's letter had not come from abroad and yet it had been first delivered to an address which was actually inside the sealed envelope.

We think we have succeeded in guessing roughly where the censor's office is to be found. In most cases, where it is linguistically possible, it seems to be the unit of the foreigner concerned which goes through the letters, both those which are sent and those which are received. A foreign teacher was visited by a Chinese colleague who, without any preamble, sat down and asked him what *Weltanschauung* meant; he did not think he had met it before and could not find it in the dictionary. The foreigner in question had used it in a letter home the day before.

Articles are often cut out of the papers and magazines we receive, which clearly indicates censorship, and Chinese office glue has certain characteristic features when it is dry which distinguish it from the glue on current West European envelopes.

Some readers will no doubt object that I am attaching too much importance to trifles and thereby adding fuel to the 'anti-Chinese fire'. Of course the question of whether our post is censored or not is, in itself, unimportant—even legally, since the new constitution says nothing about the confidentiality of letters, only that one has the right to send and receive them. It is, nevertheless, irritating. The fact that it happens at all is irritating, but is doubly irritating that it is denied. And the irritation is compounded further by the fact that according to our contracts it is all done in a spirit of friendship. When one day I received a magazine from abroad, half of which had been cut into ribbons by the censors, I talked to one of my colleagues about the censorship. As far as I was concerned I said, they could come and look over my shoulder while I wrote or read letters from home but I found it, to say the least, peculiar that it was done deceitfully. Nor did I find it in conformity with traditional Chinese politeness to open the letters of one's friends.

'It is a regrettable practice,' he said, 'but I think you would do best to ignore it. It certainly won't do any good complaining to the authorities. Personally, I think it's wrong, but there is nothing to be done about it.'

'Why is our post censored? It's not very nice to know that possibly one is suspected of subversive activities.'

'I don't think the authorities suspect you of anything. It is just their practice.'

'Why?'

'I couldn't say. I can only regret it. But I will give you one piece of advice. It often happens that at times of political unrest, such as now, you will find political pamphlets in your letters. Propaganda against the current development. If you find anything like that, don't throw it away, take it to your unit. Then you will be quite safe.'

'Where do they come from? How do they get into the letters?'

'It is difficult to say. Some say it is Taiwanese or Soviet propaganda which is smuggled into foreign letters before they ever get to the Chinese post office. Others say the CIA puts the material in the letters in Paris or Zurich before they are flown here. And yet others say that it is propaganda from class enemies in China which is somehow smuggled into the letters when they are being censored. But, as I said, you will avoid trouble if you pass on anything you find. It might help the authorities to find out where they are coming from, too.'

'Are we regarded as class enemies then, since our post has to be scrutinized? Or should I say "honoured class enemies"—guests one doesn't quite trust?'

'I don't think so. As far as I know everyone is subject to it. And it is not against the constitution.'

'No, but it is against my idea of right and wrong.'

'Well I suppose it is against most people's,' my friend concluded. 'It is rather absurd to censor foreign newspapers anyway. One can understand them doing it to us Chinese, but you, of course, can read as much anti-Chinese propaganda as you like, when you get home.'

As always, when 'special news items' are announced, TV screens are put up in the meeting halls the day before, the chairs arranged in rows and everyone puts in an appearance at the correct time to witness yet another non-event on the flickering screen. I describe them as non-events because in fact nothing ever happens. There is a well-rehearsed presentation of bigwigs in which the camera goes from one face to another and confirms that everything is as it is said to be—the order of the prominent persons is carefully arranged, and if a face is missing, or a new one appears in the established order of precedence, there is uneasy shuffling of chair-legs and whispering among the audience. Missing faces can lead to misinterpretation, even though their absence is often only due to the fact that they are no longer young men.

Transmissions are endless, static tranquillizers, but of late there has been an interesting change in one of the principal characters. When Hua Guofeng came into power he had had a fairly recent crew-cut—short black hair which stood straight up from his head. (When one day I remarked to one of my students that he had his hair cut very short he laughed and said, with astonishing lack of respect, 'Yes, I have a new haircut—peasant boy Hua Guofeng style.') But in the months following the coup, a gradual change has been taking place in Hua's hairstyle as seen on the television screen.

Imperceptibly, and as if in confirmation of the claim made at the time of the coup that he is Mao's only true successor, he has begun to adopt the deceased chairman's characteristic hairstyle, the high forehead and dense waves of hair brushed back above the temples. Perhaps it was this, in itself an insignificant change, which was the cause of, or at least contributed to, a persistent rumour that Hua was really Mao's long-concealed illegitimate son. There can be no doubt that, given the strong feeling for outward appearances and for the formal which prevails in China, it would be very much easier for a new chairman to consolidate his position if he bore certain resemblances to his predecessor, than if he were a small bald sparrow of a man resembling, for instance, the hated Lin Biao.

Following the highly emotional national memorial day for Zhou Enlai, Hua added a new detail to his appearance on the television screen. From pictures, everyone is aware that Zhou Enlai, since the days of the Long March, had not been able to use his right arm. It was always at an angle, with his forearm across his chest. It was said to be the result of a badly united fracture following a fall from a horse, though Edgar Snow once got a ticking-off from a high-ranking Chinese for saying so and was told that it was a slander and anti-Chinese propaganda to suggest that one of China's leaders was in any way disabled. But to our complete amazement Hua began to appear on the screen with a 'Zhou arm'. He had, however, taken the practical step of disabling the left arm, so the right is free for greeting. There have been many cautious comments about this hitherto unknown man who has adopted physical characteristics of two beloved leaders.

Today we are sitting on the same upright chairs, in front of the same television screens as we have done all winter, to watch the opening of the Mao Memorial Hall, the mausoleum which over the last year has been growing up in the southern part of the gigantic square in Peking. Because of the official ceremony, the square has been closed for the last few days and access to the opening is by invitation only. The leaders are assembled in a reception room from which they can survey the square, which can accommodate about a million and a half people. The people, Peking's citizens, are also represented in the square; a relatively inconspicuous band is standing huddled together in a corner of the vast area. The camera shifts to the room with the deep armchairs in which Hua sits relaxed, drinking tea with Deng, and goes close enough for my Chinese neighbour and interpreter to catch Deng's words as he says, pointing to the square: 'We should have requisitioned another 30,000.'

Over the last few months I have been witness to several rather painful scenes, even if as a rule they were enacted with characteristic Chinese understatement. They were concerned with violation of—no, crimes against—the established pecking order: subordinate Chinese who, inadvertently or deliberately, exceeded their competence in approaching someone from a superior circle. Everyone has a precisely defined place within the system, appears to know the channels of command, their own place and the lines of demarcation.

One day I was asked by a young Chinese colleague, a junior teacher, to deliver a message to a superior whom he happened to know I was going to see. This seemed to me a perfectly natural request. I took the message and at our meeting I gave the greetings of the young teacher and his message. The reaction of the superior cadre was staggering.

'I am quite sure that he knows the rules of procedure, but in case he does not, please will you tell him that it is not within his competence to approach me directly. Nor indirectly through you. You may tell him that if in future he has anything he wishes to communicate to me he must see to it that he does so through the proper channels. And finally, I cannot acknowledge the receipt of his message since it has not been correctly conveyed.'

When I passed on his answer—albeit in a somewhat watered-down version—my young friend was very embarrassed. He said that of course he did know that his procedure had not been entirely correct, but since it had been only a trifling matter he had thought it would be all right. He begged me to forgive him for having been the cause of the scene which, he said, must have put me in a very awkward situation. The superior was a man we had both previously respected, but I felt my respect for him drop to zero at this pompous and reactionary behaviour. On the other hand I have to admit that he was only sticking strictly to the 'rules of the system'.

On another occasion, when I was going to a meeting in a municipal office, I was given an interpreter who was new to me. Waiting-rooms in China are neither more nor less boring than waiting-rooms anywhere else in the world and bureaucracy no less extravagant with time. My unknown interpreter and I had plenty of time to sit chatting about things like work, the future and so on, relaxed waiting-room small-talk, until, from a sudden tension in his body, I realized that something was about to happen. I followed his glance and saw a man coming towards us down the corridor. My interpreter half got up, and as the stranger, in his immaculate cadre uniform, came level with us, he sprang to his feet, clutching his cap with one hand. Painful incidents seem to breed extra seconds, the minutest details being prolonged in echoes of humiliation. My colleague leaned a little forward as if to shake hands with the strange cadre, changed his mind and instead bowed respectfully from the hips. He muttered a brief and hasty greeting in Chinese but the accompanying smile got only half-way to the corners of his mouth before it was checked. The stranger regarded him coldly, muttered a few words and walked on. My escort's body, which had, in that short long-drawn-out moment, not quite left the sitting position, now sank back into the uncomfortable chair where he sat, cheeks flushed and his forehead covered in beads of perspiration.

'Who was that?' I asked.

'An old college friend I have not seen for a long time. We used to work together, but now he has a high position in a ministry.'

He fell silent and I could see that the painfulness of the incident had been made worse by the fact that I had been a witness to it. I could also see how his immediate pleasure at seeing an old friend unexpectedly had made him forget that now there is a barrier between them; a barrier which it is not within his competence to cross.

I have a feeling that this system of rank and position is more an inheritance from the past than a creation of the present society. But it is cultivated, not fought against, and has in it the seeds of something much more far-reaching than the individual painful or humiliating episode—restrictions on freedom of speech, introduction of material privileges and the consolidation of old-fashioned and reactionary social structures. And, when pushed to extremes, misuse of economic resources and corruption.

In Youyi there is an elderly Western expert who has been there for years and years. In order to show her solidarity with China she finally took the ultimate step: she applied for, and was granted, Chinese citizenship. In everyday life this does not make a great deal of difference, except that she can refer to 'we Chinese' whereas we others must use the second or third person. Her standard of living, which is reasonable, remains the same, and in day-to-day affairs it makes no difference that she has a new identity card. But when she wanted to go and visit her family in the West she had to go on a waiting list to get a visa to enter her former home country. She was told that there was an annual quota and the quota for that year was already full, therefore she must go on the waiting-list in the same way as other Chinese applicants.

She was very annoyed about this, and indeed it was a great disappointment because she had been looking forward to the visit, the first for many years. Her annoyance, however, was at being put on a par with the Chinese. And when I gently pointed out that strictly speaking that was what she now was, her answer was, 'Yes, I know. But not *ethnically*.'

I shall not have to go on a waiting-list to go home. According to my (unsigned) contract, we should be here for a year more. Stine and Lulu went home on holiday a short time ago and expect to return soon. But my work has become impossible; the slow death of my pleasure in working here under the present circumstances has reduced my unit's wish to keep me here considerably. At a meeting which lasted all day, and where we were all friendly, smooth and superficial to the best of our ability, we agreed on a solution which does not involve loss of face or prestige for anyone concerned. My contract has expired according to plan, although a year ahead of time. There is no question of breach of contract on either side.

My departure, normally a long-drawn-out procedure, is given high priority. Stine and Lulu are on the point of returning and I cable them to stay where they are, but in an intercontinental call later, from my bakelite apparatus at Youyi 8733, I find it difficult to explain what has happened.

There are many good colleagues and students I will miss working with. Indeed, even while here I have for a long time missed the *possibility* of so doing.

Conversation with a Shadow

The last few days have gone quickly. Less than a week ago four men in overalls appeared in my flat. They were from the shipping department of the Friendship Shop and came to see how many packing cases would be required for my things. I had been told that one sometimes had to wait weeks for them to come, but somehow either the Experts Bureau or my unit succeeded in arranging for me to jump the queue. They are formidably efficient.

The whole flat was a shambles when they turned up, complete with tape measures, cardboard boxes, wood shavings, waterproof paper, cord and a big reel of tape. They asked what had to be packed and I pointed round the flat and said everything, except the small pile of clothes I had put on one side for the journey and the last few days. They got going with great efficiency and had obviously been told to act on behalf of the customs department. Every box was sealed before it was stacked and it was made clear to me that I must not open them again.

The temperature was in the eighties, and I left them to it—partly because I did not want to get in the way, partly in order to go over to the shop in Youyi to buy bottles of nice cold beer which, even if it is not the tradition here, could well be acceptable. On my return they had finished—a whole flat occupied by three people stripped bare, packed and stacked in less than an hour.

We drank our cool Tsingtao beer, smoked a couple of cigarettes and filled in the necessary customs forms and clearing documents, and then the four hyper-efficient packers left me with my worldly goods in sealed-up symmetry. They *had* packed everything. Including the clothes I had put on one side.

The following day they returned with a huge packing case which they had had made to measure in the meantime and into which everything fitted perfectly. I stood out in the caustic sun watching them nail on the lid with great long nails. Together we lifted first one end and then the other so that we could slide some bricks under it, in case it rained while it stood there waiting to be shipped. And finally, for the same reason, it was shrouded in a large tarpaulin.

Four of my friends from Youyi come with me to the station. Above the pretentious entrance hangs the portrait of Mao which first appeared at the beginning of the Cultural Revolution. It is a remarkable bit of portraiture, with many qualities. The eyes and mouth catch the eye and there is a harmony in the expression, but not constant, not definite. One can see arrogance in that smile which is not quite a smile, but the resignation—or is it aloofness?—which the eyes sometimes express, hovers now and then round the mouth. The composition is not quite right—one has the feeling that his forehead is a little too close to the frame—and sometimes there seems to be no expression in the face at all.

Perhaps the latter is what happens when one sees a picture so often. From the day the service comrades came to nail it above the door of my flat at the beginning of the Cultural Revolution, shoals of identical pictures have appeared over the following years in which nothing changes in the face, be it in black-and-white or in colour. And the weeks of it draped in crêpe, followed by the unusual sight of a companion portrait, composed with the same care and precision but without soul. This companion picture is everywhere too, empty and yet with expression at the same time, round and soft in its left-hand three-quarter profile.

Zou and Liu and Xiao Wang are standing, with their customary precision, exactly under the portrait waiting for me. I have to go to the police office to show my permit to leave Peking—and in this case, China also. For one reason or another the moving staircase in this big building is never in working order, and flocks of travellers with bundles, bulging nets, suitcases, boxes and carrying poles with impossible loads have to force their way up and down the 'manual' staircase.

Wang gets hold of a railway official who has a key to the lift, but I say we can perfectly well walk up as I have almost no luggage. Zou takes us to the VIP waiting-room where we stand and look at one another. Liu stands, as always, a little behind and regards us with the suggestion of a smile, looking slightly down his nose.

On the platform Xiao Wang, warm-hearted little Wang, tells me that he has one last piece of *good* news for me. The Ministry of Rail has decided that from now on foreign experts will pay the same price for food on the trains as the Chinese. The higher price which foreigners pay, not unreasonably, for tickets has hitherto also applied to the food, which is unreasonably expensive. This is the last of a series of bits of information with which Wang has surprised me during the year we have worked together. He is pleased about it and so am I because I have very little money left.

Zou suggests we had better tell the conductor of the sleeping cars, who is also in charge of the dining car, that I have my status as a foreign expert which entitles me to this privilege as far as the frontier. Together with Wang he goes to the man in charge of the sleeping cars for the privileged classes and has a brief conversation. They come back and say that he flatly refuses to give any reduction. He has not been told anything, he says. They told him that it was a printed instruction from the Ministry of Rail, but he still said he knew nothing about it. The Ministry is in Peking, he said, and his train comes from Canton.

I embrace my French and British friends, and Wang, Zou and Liu all draw back slightly, smiling uncomfortably in case I commit a *faux pas*. But I behave correctly and shake hands with them, remembering the fuss the Chinese made when a visiting head of an East European state embraced Hua Guofeng. It's just not done.

There are no long farewells, no speeches, only the usual shuffling of feet and wishing that the train would leave quickly. And it does so. Thanks to the green plastic netting which covers the windows in the summer it is not possible to wave long goodbyes to the end of the seemingly endless platform. We wave once, I leave.

I have been given a seat in a four-berth compartment which I am sharing with one other person whom I take to be a Korean diplomat. At any rate he has a little round badge with Kim Il Sung's profile on his lapel, and if he is not a diplomat then I don't know why he should be going to the Hong Kong border. We will be sitting opposite one another on our cool bass mats for the day and a half it takes to get to the frontier. I try speaking to him, but he does not understand English—or does not wish to.

Near the ceiling is a little green fan whose blades hum away at terrific speed, and which at the same time gyrates slowly on its axis. Every time it reaches a certain point on its trip it makes a little click and one quickly learns to register the click without looking up and knows that one must wait a moment before lighting a cigarette or turning a page. The Korean diplomat sits and inspects his faultless fingernails. He has hung his dark lounge suit on the hook and is sitting in his vest and pale blue underpants. He has kept on his socks and highly polished black shoes. Whether he is just a courier or a first secretary I would find it hard to imagine his Western opposite number travel in similar undress.

A cheerful Cantonese cook comes to take orders for the next day's meals. Not only must one decide what one would like for breakfast, lunch and supper—everything has to be ordered now, which taxes the imagination somewhat—but one is also expected to know how thirsty one will be in the next thirty-six hours and order drinks accordingly. The cook stands swaying in the doorway taking down the orders, which my Korean companion and I select by pointing to items on the trilingual menu, nods with a cheerful grin and closes the door behind him.

I am leaving China, near enough twelve years after my first arrival, and just as at that time I had an invisible and unwished-for companion, so today I am not alone in the compartment with the Korean.

In the clear early morning, when the train is about half-way between Peking and the Yangtze, I get up and look out of the window at the soft grey light which hangs like a film over the landscape, just before the sun rises bringing colour to everything. And the long green train with its strict divisions into soft sleeping cars, hard sleeping cars, and hard sitting carriages, moves in long serpentine curves over the flat open country which marks the beginning of the Yangtze Delta, glistening from the floods of the as yet far-off mighty river.

The villages, those villages which we can never get nearer to than the slow-moving train permits, lie scattered on the flat ground, the colour of the soil in their walls. Where it is chalky, the walls are lighter, and where the clay contains ochre, rusty tones predominate in the groups of houses which separate one field from the next. This subdued play of colours is punctuated by the vivid red of flags and slogans.

The Korean wakes up, too. He sits as he sat last evening, immobile and distant. He has a gold-plated lighter and cigarette case and chain-smokes. He does not look out of the window.

The sun is not yet up but the people out there are already going to work. During the course of this last journey across this long stretch of China, I have begun to wonder what effect the events of the last few years have had on these people who, barefoot and with their implements slung over their shoulders, are on their way to work in the fields in the early morning mist—if and how their daily life has been affected by Mao's death, by the fall of the 'Gang of Four', by Deng Xiaoping's return. Decisions have been made which, naturally, in the long run will affect them closely. The new efficiency drive has as one of its goals that they should all have tractors, electric pumps, threshing machines, reaping machines, excavators and chemical fertilizers. They are to be mechanized. Work is to be made less arduous, output greater. The whole thing is to be of immediate benefit to all those now walking in long columns out over the plains. Of immediate benefit to the whole of China.

And then I think of the bureaucrats in Peking, Shanghai, Wuhan, and other cities large and small who are to administer this mechanization. And of that administrative organization which from time to time has been crippled by corruption, political uncertainty, or plain perversity. And a travelling companion, who constantly, over the years, has popped up beside me, says coldly, 'If you have not confidence in the cadres then you have not confidence in the people. The people created their leaders and the leaders are one with the people. You know that.'

'I know that is what they say, but I think in practice it does not always seem to be the case.'

'The "Gang of Four" grew away from the people, if it is them you are thinking of. In fact they were never really one with the people.'

'How did they get to be leaders then?'

'By swindling and cheating and exploiting their positions of power. By terrorism and throwing dust in the eyes of the people. It is only through the strength of society, of the people, that they have been exposed, convicted and cast on the "dunghill of history", as the saying goes.'

'And what about the next leaders? The present ones for that matter? Is there not a possibility that they, at some point, may find themselves in the same situation?'

'Don't tell me that power corrupts. It is only dictatorial power that does. And power is now really in the hands of the people.'

'On the contrary,' I say, 'the people have seldom had less power in modern China than they have today. There was a time when the peasants had direct responsibility for their commune, when the workers were really responsible for the running of their factory. They have never had less influence than they have now. If they had any influence how would it have been possible for the "Four" to have installed all their own people in the highest posts? And *if*, as we are constantly being told, that was what they did, why are they not still in power? Why was it not they who succeeded with the coup?'

'They tried, as you know, but they were not strong enough. They lacked the support of the people. Do you think the "Four" would have been good for China if they had remained in power? Do you think the people would have been better off under their rule?'

'Now and then I have a feeling that the dictatorship of the proletariat is turning into dictatorship *to* the proletariat. I see careerists, pecking order, alms doled out by the state and arrogance in the upper strata of society. I see lies and dissimulation by the leaders at all levels. It was not like that before the Cultural Revolution or, more correctly, it was significantly less. It is now, at this moment, that this is happening.'

'You are no friend of the Chinese people,' my shadow continues.

'Yes I am. I have gone full circle. From those times when people were lulled into a sense of false security thinking the goal was just round the corner, socialism was just about to take shape. There was promise at that time, there was even promise in the apparent chaos which appeared with the Cultural Revolution. Maybe there was some violence and injustice, but at least it was the injustice of the people towards the people. What has come out of the promise of those days manifests itself now as injustices of the leaders towards the people. And in my opinion it is not a passive people without courage but one which has had its weapons worn down—its weapons and its strength.'

'I do not share the view expressed by many people after the coup in which the leaders are accused of buttering up the people with material goods and a controlled rise in the standard of living. It seems to me reactionary puritanism to maintain that prosperity destroys the awareness which leads to socialism. If socialism is not concerned with raising everyone's standard of living, what is it concerned with?'

In Wuhan, the station at the end of the long iron bridge which spans the Yangtze, our half-empty carriage fills up. For the most part it is older military men, with four pockets on their jackets, their luggage carried in by orderlies with two. Military people get onto the platform from a special waiting-room so that they avoid the huge crowds of baggage-laden civilian passengers who storm the whole length of the train as soon as the doors of the overcrowded waiting-room are opened.

'Why should high-ranking military people have that privilege?' I ask my invisible companion.

'Why not? They are the guardians of the state and the people, and if they could not travel in comfort they might not get sufficient rest to be able to carry out their duties properly.'

'And what about their children being driven to school in a Red Flag limousine?'

'It is always better that things should be used rather than stand idle. At present the service vehicles are being used to capacity. It is important to use things to the full. Also people's gifts.'

'There were three young people from Peking who had just finished their studies. They had all done well in their respective subjects and looked forward to doing just that, using their gifts. The jobs they were assigned were a great disappointment. They were given jobs as general handymen at the crematorium in Babaoshan, the cemetery where the heroes are buried.'

'You know that it is a usual and not unreasonable practice to make academics do manual labour from time to time.'

'This was a permanent job. They complained to the central labour exchange in Peking and were told that if they were not satisfied they could consider themselves released from work. But no other work was offered them and to be without work would have involved great difficulties with residence permits, accommodation, ration cards and so on. And it would not have been long before they were branded as being work-shy and anti-social—with all the consequences which *that* implies. They pointed this out to the authority and were told that they could go and find another job for themselves. The last I heard was that they had written pointing out that China is a socialist country and this was not correct procedure. It was the duty of society to find jobs for people relevant not only to the needs of society, but also to their own needs and abilities. The "free labour market" where one has to find work for oneself did not belong here, they said.'

'There you are, a concrete example of the evil influence of the "Four". They wanted a capitalist China.'

'This happened after the fall of the "Four".'

'That just goes to show how powerful they were. But the new leaders will change all that. It can and will be changed.'

'For them too?' I ask, looking out of the window at columns of brigade members walking along the narrow paths which stretch like ramparts between the flat fields. We are winding our way south and the further we get from Peking the more labour-intensive the work becomes. In the north one sees it seldom, but here irrigation is often done by means of a two-man treadmill and it is water buffaloes which haul the ploughs through the heavy soil.

'Yes, their conditions will be improved too. Mechanization will be introduced. The leaders give their welfare and conditions the highest priority.'

'I know they often refer to their local leaders as the "landlords".'

In the thirty-six hours straight down the mighty continent, my shadow and I scrap with one another, trying to come to some sort of agreement. My Korean companion sits silently opposite, and in the corridor outside our little box, passengers who have not been able to find a seat are squatting. I have tried several times by means of signs to persuade them to come into our sanctuary, but the invitation cannot be accepted. At mealtimes the other passengers file past us in gangs on their way to the dining car. When the last party has finished, it is cleaned up before we, that is the Korean and I, the only foreigners on the train, are ushered into the empty dining car with the expensive food. We sit at two separate tables at one end of the carriage, while the cooks, mechanics, the armed train guards and conductors all sit at the other, picking their teeth.

After the second night the long run into Canton appears in the early morning mist. I applied for permission to spend a few days there to revisit my first Chinese town of twelve years ago and say goodbye to old friends and colleagues. My letter to Canton remained unanswered and my request to the 'relevant competent authority' in Peking produced a curt note saying that it was not practical for me to break my journey in Canton.

I look round the platform in the big new station, but I see no familiar faces during the half-hour wait I have before the blue air-conditioned train carries me on to Hong Kong.

In the big hall close to the iron bridge leading to the Hong Kong frontier, a young customs officer comes over to inspect my papers. I had taught one of his colleagues in Peking.

'I have heard about you from my comrade in Peking. Open your bag please.'

He glances into it, stamps my customs declaration, and asks if I have any more luggage.

'Will you be coming back?' he asks.

I reply that I don't think so.

He points to the bridge. 'You can go. The formalities have been completed.'

The Author

Jan Bredsdorff was born in Denmark and has lived in England for a total of sixteen years. He attended schools in both England and Denmark until the age of fourteen, when he began a series of part-time jobs in a number of different fields. He traveled through Europe and, after 1965, through Asia. The time that he spent living and working in China is the subject of this book.

Mr. Bredsdorff has written three works of fiction and two of nonfiction in Danish, as well as one work of fiction in English. At present he is working on a novel. He lives in Copenhagen with his wife and their young daughter.